POSTMILLENNIAL POP

*General Editors: Karen Tongson and Henry Jenkins*

*Puro Arte: Filipinos on the Stages of Empire*
Lucy Mae San Pablo Burns

*Spreadable Media: Creating Value and
Meaning in a Networked Culture*
Henry Jenkins, Sam Ford,
and Joshua Green

*Franchising Culture: Creative License,
Collaboration, and the Media Industries*
Derek Johnson

*Your Ad Here: The Cool Sell
of Guerrilla Marketing*
Michael Serazio

# Your Ad Here

*The Cool Sell of Guerrilla Marketing*

*Michael Serazio*

NEW YORK UNIVERSITY PRESS
*New York and London*

NEW YORK UNIVERSITY PRESS
New York and London
www.nyupress.org

References to Internet Websites (URLs) were accurate at the time of writing. Neither the author nor New York University Press is responsible for URLs that may have expired or changed since the manuscript was prepared.

LIBRARY OF CONGRESS CATALOGING-IN-PUBLICATION DATA
Serazio, Michael.
Your ad here : the cool sell of guerrilla marketing / Michael Serazio.
pages cm. — (Postmillenial pop)
Includes bibliographical references and index.
ISBN 978-0-8147-4547-2 (cl : alk. paper)
ISBN 978-0-8147-8590-4 (pb : alk. paper)
ISBN 978-0-8147-6494-7 (e-book) (print)
ISBN 978-0-8147-2459-0 (e-book) (print)
1. Marketing. 2. Marketing—Technological innovations. I. Title.
HF5415.S373 2013
658.8—dc23

2012042108

New York University Press books are printed on acid-free paper, and their binding materials are chosen for strength and durability. We strive to use environmentally responsible suppliers and materials to the greatest extent possible in publishing our books.

Manufactured in the United States of America
c 10 9 8 7 6 5 4 3 2 1
p 10 9 8 7 6 5 4 3 2 1

*For Mom, Dad, and Jules—those who made me and she who sustains me*

CONTENTS

ACKNOWLEDGMENTS

I've been hoping to be able to write a book since I was a little kid, so there's no shortage of wonderful people to whom I'm indebted—indeed, far more than space allows for here. Know that I count myself as immeasurably blessed and that you remain deeply ensconced in my heart. Let me begin by offering my gratitude to the University of Pennsylvania's Annenberg School for Communication and its staff and administration for the generous support that made this work possible. Thanks to Eric Zinner, Ciara McLaughlin, Karen Tongson, Henry Jenkins, Despina Papazoglou Gimbel, Mary Sutherland, New York University Press, David Amrani, and the anonymous readers of this manuscript for their thorough and insightful feedback. Thanks to all my teachers, mentors, and institutions whose formative wisdom and selfless dedication shaped my writing, curiosity, and character over the years, including: Joseph Jones, Amy Schuff, and C.F.H.S.; Bryan Whaley, Bernadette Barker-Plummer, Michael Robertson, Rick Roberts, and the University of San Francisco; Thierry Robouam and Sophia University; Stephen Isaacs and Columbia University's Graduate School of Journalism; and Margaret Downing and the *Houston Press*.

Thanks to the influential faculty at Annenberg, including: Paul Messaris, Elihu Katz, Monroe Price, and Carolyn Marvin. Thanks to my warm-hearted, inspiring colleagues and students at Fairfield University and, in particular, in the Department of Communication: Colleen Arendt, Robbin Crabtree, Gisela Gil-Egui, David Gudelunas, Michael Pagano, Sallyanne Ryan, Maggie Wills, and Qin Zhang. Thanks to my PhD committee: to Joseph Turow for putting advertising and cultural production at the forefront of my research agenda; to Katherine Sender for coaching me through qualitative methods and modeling a diverse and creative scholarly output that I aspire toward; and, most of all, to Barbie Zelizer. I couldn't ask for a more dedicated, thoughtful, and encouraging advisor—you've made this career possible and, for that, I am forever indebted.

Thanks to all my classmates and friends, the good Company I've been fortunate to keep from first to twenty-second-grade (if calculations are correct): Your charms and sense of humor have made the challenges tolerable, and your capacity for brilliance and zest for life have made the experiences memorable. To my mother and father, and all my family: Because of your love and sacrifice, it's possible to fulfill this childhood ambition. There aren't words to express what you mean to me, but that's OK, because I think you know how I feel.

And, finally, to my beautiful and brilliant, fun and funny wife, Julia—I thank you letting me go on this journey together with you and for supporting me throughout it. Thanks to God for putting all of these people in my life and for giving me these opportunities. Make the most of your work and allow it to make the most of you.

# 1

## Buying into the Cool Sell

Cool is the opiate of our time.
—Kalle Lasn[1]

For much of the 20th century, marketers relied upon the conventional weaponry of the mass media to deliver their commercial payload: newspapers, magazines, radio, television, and billboards structured the information environment and furnished the primary venues for the placement of paid advertising. Within that environment, advertisers jockeyed for attention in predictable, delimited contexts through persuasive campaigns that could be clearly and openly identified as such. By and large, we knew what advertising looked like and we knew where to find it: during the programming break on TV, surrounding the editorial content in a newspaper, or across banners atop a webpage.

At the dawn of a new millennium, however, thanks to profound upheavals in technology, markets, commercial clutter, and audience expectations, that traditional model seems to be crumbling in slow motion. Given those challenges, marketers are exploring new and reimagining old techniques of communicating messages in the hopes of somehow managing consumer audiences and bleeding out promotion from previously confined, more readily apparent media spaces. These innovations and reinventions—many reflecting an ethos of public relations as much as advertising—proffer a solution to an industry ever-evolving by deploying commercial appeals more intended to slide "under the radar" of audiences rather than announcing themselves forthrightly. They represent, in a sense, an effort at a new breed of "hidden persuaders" optimized for 21st-century media content, social patterns, and digital platforms.

*Your Ad Here* takes these techniques of commercial self-effacement seriously—examining them to uncover and map the institutional discourse, cultural logic, and technological context underpinning such "invisible" consumer governance: that is, the *subtle* way in which desire might be orchestrated and the agency of imagined subjects might be positioned in order to get them to shop. By exploring the practice of "guerrilla marketing"—the umbrella term here for a wide assortment of product placement, alternative outdoor, word-of-mouth, and consumer-generated approaches—we might better understand a new media environment where cultural producers like advertisers strategize and experiment with persuasion through increasingly covert and outsourced flows. By looking at a diverse set of campaign examples—from the *America's Army* video game and Pabst Blue Ribbon's hipster "hijack" to buzz agent bloggers and tweeters and Burger King's "Subservient Chicken" micro-site—we can appreciate how Madison Avenue is now thinking through technology, subculture, and audiences.

A caveat of emphasis is warranted right from the start: This is not a book about audiences directly, yet the discussion of audiences (and, most especially, millennial audiences) will figure prominently throughout. This is, in a sense, a second-order study of audiences—of how marketers and the producers of cultural content at the beginning of a new media era think about them and attempt to exercise power in today's consumer society. That governance will sometimes succeed and will sometimes fail, but here, too, I elide inquisitions into and declarations of actual *effect* in favor of an intense focus on "encoding" *effort*—that first stage in the commercial process that is, at once, essential to understand and yet critically understudied.

As befitting a public relations mind-set, the guerrilla message these marketers seek to seed travels "bottom-up," through invisible relay and from decentralized corners in order to engage audiences in seemingly serendipitous ways. The consumer engagement and commercial discovery meant to be orchestrated through such strategies reflects an "exercise of power [that] is a 'conduct of conducts' and a management of possibilities" without any semblance of force, intervention, or determination in managing that conduct.[2] Thus emerges a regime of governance that accommodates yet structures participatory agency; self-effaces its own authority and intent through disinterested spaces and anti-establishment formats; opens the brand up as a more flexible textual form; and democratizes and decentralizes in favor of populist collaboration. It is, in short, advertising not meant to seem like advertising.

Audiences, these strategies suggest, might be governed differently in a 21st-century networked media world: Their agency can be presupposed and coordinated as part of the formula for cultural production. The exercise of "push" media addressed audiences comparatively imperiously, while "pull" media, by contrast, deliberately accords liberty and complies with the interactive (and autonomous) choice that ensues. Advertising based on that invitation (i.e., pull) rather than interruption (push) presumes to flatter the capacities of a free subject more conspicuously and then utilizes subsequent contributions to more effectively and individually tailor a message to that subject. In so doing, this further separates the "mass" in "mass media"—usefully so, for cultural reasons, because whatever remains of that mass audience carries with it an indelibly "mainstream" connotation that the guerrilla advertiser tries to avoid by opting for channels that exude a more underground ethos (a valuable pose to strike when catering to millennials, who are routinely conceptualized as jaded, resistant consumer targets).[3]

To be certain, guerrilla marketing has a relatively narrow designation and comparatively exclusive usage within the industry; it is clearly not the dominant form of advertising media outlay when it comes to budgets and, by and large, courts youth niches more than any other demographic. Practitioners would probably most commonly recognize it as the label for only the variety of out-of-home stunts examined here in chapter 3. The term itself appears to have originated in the mid-1980s in the title of advertising executive Jay Conrad Levinson's best-selling book, *Guerrilla Marketing*.[4] Nonetheless, by expanding the scope of this label to encompass a range of marketing phenomena not typically termed "guerrilla," we can better appreciate the philosophy of governance that accompanies diverse promotional tactics. For product placement, word-of-mouth, and crowd-sourced campaigns equally merit conceptual claim to the "guerrilla" label, and by studying the inspirations, machinations, and deliberations behind them, we can identify and analyze common themes of power and practice that seem to animate otherwise disparate advertising executions.

Guerrilla marketing therefore serves as a label for nontraditional communications between advertisers and audiences, which rely on an element of creativity or surprise in the intermediary itself. It is advertising through unexpected, often online, interpersonal, and outdoor avenues—unconventional, literally, in its choice of media platforms (i.e., engaging a medium beyond the traditional television commercial or newspaper advertisement). Guerrilla marketing's resourceful license is remarkable not only in terms of content but equally that of context: expansively reconfiguring the space typically partitioned for commercial petition. Yet guerrilla marketing, as heir to an extensive proto-history, is not necessarily strictly "new" either but rather the latest outgrowth in an ongoing cycle of advertiser innovation.

A wide-ranging terminology has sprung up to characterize these techniques: ambient, astroturfing, branded content, buzz, graffadi, interactive, stealth, and viral, among others. They share a common allegiance to this organizing principle—the deployment of a space or channel that seeks to engineer engagement through a "cool sell" strategy. Guerrilla marketing is, therefore, a project of persuasion that cloaks itself casually and even invisibly to the consumer targets it courts in an attempt to orchestrate "discovery" of the commercial message as the constitutive experience; stated more abstractly, in Foucauldian terms, it is a mode of governance set upon an *active* subject, not a form of *domination* that has stereotypically defined the exercise of power.

To date, little research has analyzed how and why this form of marketing has grown as a means of reaching consumers, yet these tactics fit within a trajectory stretching back nearly a century, and this inquiry can be situated within and build upon related scholarly discussions at the intersection of advertising, audiences, governmentality, hegemony, public relations, new media, and the creative industries. Through a close examination of emblematic campaign examples, an archival analysis of trade discourse, and in-depth interviews with dozens of prominent practitioners, *Your Ad Here* peels back the curtain on a form of cultural production that reworks the conventional archetype of mass communication. It re-conceptualizes consumer governance through themes and practices of participation, populism, heterarchicality, decentralization, and freedom. At stake is no less than the structure by which the media environment is underwritten, the waning spaces in which one might avoid commercial entreaty, and the potential for devaluing, contaminating, or even burning out the "original institution[s]" hosting the new promotional forms.[5]

What these guerrilla strategies also suggest is that advertising might be evolving beyond certain basic organizing principles of the mass communication process, which have long defined it. Take, as one example, this classic definition: "Mass communications comprise the institutions and techniques by which specialized groups employ technological devices (press, radio, films, etc.) to disseminate symbolic content to large, heterogeneous and widely dispersed audiences."[6] Such a characterization tends to assume that the content is standardized, the context is delimited, and that messages start from a structural center and work their way to a social periphery. Above all, it seems to imply an *obviousness*—an intrinsic visibility—about the mass communication process, whether it be transmitting news, entertainment, or, indeed, advertising. *Broad*-casting long meant just that: a patent, top-down, one-to-many, centrifugal model of messaging.

If traditional advertising fit snugly within such a rubric, the challenges posed and opportunities raised by networked interactivity illuminate a different philosophy of consumer governance. In response, these guerrilla tactics demonstrate a decidedly more flexible, niche-seeking, and ambiguous bent, one more reflective of the aims and designs of public relations. Media and cultural studies—notably Stuart Hall's theory of "decoding" reception and James Carey's alternate emphasis on "ritual"—have long since challenged the primacy and simplicity of this transmission model, yet "the linear casual approach was what many wanted, and still do want, from communication research."[7] Advertisers might certainly be counted among this group, for much of their work has traditionally reflected an unspoken faith in linear causality, centralized dissemination, and unchanging content. Thanks to technology, at a juncture when once-firmly ascribed roles like sender and receiver are blurring and that content meaning is less stable and more spreadable than ever before—developments that media and cultural studies have long posited—advertisers might now more adeptly insinuate themselves into such dynamic processes.[8]

This flexibility points to an ongoing redefinition and reinvention of the industry overall. As but one outgrowth of this, awards shows have started crafting new categories to accommodate such originality with the medium itself. In 2004, the Clio Awards launched a new category called "Content and Contact" to honor "campaigns that are innovative in terms of the way they communicate . . . [and] because the most exciting leading agencies were focusing their efforts on projects that included creatives and also media strategists at the same time."[9] A year earlier, the Cannes Lions International Advertising Festival had inaugurated its "Titanium Lion" to honor work that "causes the industry to [stop in its tracks and] reconsider the way forward."[10] Two campaigns that have taken home this prize are analyzed in chapters 2 and 5: BMW's *The Hire* and Burger King's "Subservient Chicken." On a smaller scale, the Lisbon Ad School inaugurated its Croquette Awards, the "first international guerrilla marketing festival," in the summer of 2009.

More broadly, this media evolution comports with a larger post-Fordist shift in advanced capitalism. In recent decades, the Fordist assembly line—emblematic of large-scale, standardized mass production in the 20th century—has given way to more agile, unique, cost-effective industrial output: "The rigorously hierarchical chain of command of the Fordist system is rendered unnecessary by distributed information networks, while smaller, more autonomous work units compromising flexibly trained workers rather than Taylorized machine-tenders respond quickly and creatively and more in keeping with the new technologies themselves."[11]

Much in the same way, guerrilla advertising like BzzAgent's word-of-mouth seeding and MadMenYourself.com's viral fodder represents a break from Madison Avenue's classic, one-size-fits-all content, mass-produced and disseminated by centralized broadcasters in favor of smaller-scale flexibility more beholden to heterarchical patterns of information flow. That textual fluidity, being negotiable and improvised, bespeaks a recalculated approach to the exercise of producer power: working with the agency (and, as needed, the contested exchange) of autonomous networks, spaces, outputs, and "receivers."

It is not broadcasting so much as the network that perhaps best represents "the core organizing principle of this [new] communicative environment;" the network being a model where agency is, fittingly, coded into structure.[12] Guerrilla advertising strives to accommodate that evolving media ecology, coordinating and capitalizing on a more latent, many-to-many, centripetal model of participatory, contingent content distributed through social networks, be they online or off. If mass marketing was born of the need, meaning post–Industrial Revolution, to sell mass-produced goods, then the revolutionary forces calibrating this shift from push to pull media perhaps now require adaptively tailored interactions rather than monolithically Taylorized messages.

Thus, guerrilla marketing like that of word-of-mouth and its Web 2.0 equivalence depends upon a kind of promotional crowd-sourcing—one that is both enabled technologically (networked infrastructure makes it now more possible than ever) and advantageous culturally (for youth especially, because trickling up from the underground semiotically trumps fanning out through the mainstream). This collaboration burnishes an egalitarian image of "brand democratization," a buzzword myth thought to be capable of equivocating any appearance of marketer power. Such a project, in turn, foregrounds "conviviality" rather than "transmission" as the "prevailing model of communication"—a move that suggests a different form and logic in how it seeks to manage consumers.[13] Even product placement, one form of guerrilla advertising that still occurs within the confines of mass broadcasting, represents a blurring of that division between editorial and advertising content to which audiences have grown accustomed: leaking a promotional message into hitherto more commercially dormant zones.

For at its core, guerrilla marketing—much like the warfare it models itself after, not to mention the heritage of public relations—is about trying to catch the target off-guard: governing the consumer subject without that subject ever sensing the weight of such disciplinary measures; "acting upon actions," in Michel Foucault's terminology, without being seen as involved in an exercise of power.[14] Thus, Jonathan Bond and Richard Kirshenbaum, creative executives who quite literally wrote the book on *Under the Radar* advertising, emblematically advocate that the best "marketing should be invisible, with the consumer *feeling* the benefit rather than having to uncomfortably digest its overt message."[15] Increasingly, this means embedding commercial appeals outside the boundaries of mass communication institutions where, traditionally, that governance has manifestly taken place, whether deserting the programming breaks partitioned for sponsorship and worming into the content itself (as in product placement) or vacating the television medium as a whole (as in, say, word-of-mouth).

Investigating these developments provides an opportunity to take into account emergent communication patterns whereby the channel itself—the medium for delivery—is less explicit, visible, centralized, or circumscribed than ever before. It suggests a porousness of advertising across former borders and points to a horizon where sponsorship may be increasingly inescapable: both in the wheezing vestiges of "old media" as well as the outdoor, interpersonal, and online locations I collate broadly under the banner of "new media." By studying guerrilla marketing, we can better understand "new media" in the widest sense: channels, forms, surfaces, and spaces invented or annexed for promotional experience. For advertisers who turn to these methods, the guerrilla ideal is, paradoxically, to be everywhere and nowhere at once: to achieve what advertisers have always wanted—the ubiquity that commands the attention of a desired (here youth) consumer set—but to do so in a way that remains less obvious and more serendipitous in its mode of engagement.

The term "guerrilla" is, in fact, an apt turn of phrase for what increasingly resembles an insurrectionary war for the attention of consumers thought to be capable of resisting conventional advertising assaults. By featuring unidentified combatants skirmishing outside clearly demarcated battle zones, guerrilla warfare breaks from the customs of conventional warfare. Similarly, by featuring subtle appeals engaging consumers outside clearly circumscribed commercial contexts, guerrilla marketing breaks from mass media conventions and embraces more of a PR mentality. The stealth movements and ambush tactics often emblematic of guerrilla marketing point to a militarized metaphor that is significant and revealing.[16]

Like the low-intensity, decentralized, surreptitious combat of its name-sake—*guerrilla* literally translates to "little war"—guerrilla marketing pro-vides an alternative "little war" commercial communication strategy in con-trast to the "big war" waged through 20th century weaponry (i.e., mass media channels). In that so-called big war, the 30-second Super Bowl spot per-haps functions as the "[atomic] bomb" of attention seeking (that is, crudely obvious, uniformly ubiquitous, and largely undifferentiated in its mode of address) whereas guerrilla methods like buzz agents' brand evangelism take a sniper's aim of the audience, flexibly improvising as needed.[17] Just as over-matched guerrilla rebels would typically lose if they were to amass for com-bat against official state armies in a conventional sense (donning uniforms, assembling on restricted battlefields), so, too, do guerrilla marketers often rationalize and justify their approach as the necessary recourse in an asym-metrical battle against what they characterize as cynical, ad-zapping, "all-powerful" audiences. Just as guerrilla warfare redefined the meaning of war, so might guerrilla marketing redefine the rules of commercial engagement.

A browse through Che Guevara's *Guerrilla Warfare* textbook holds some instructive parallels: "Guerrilla fighters must have a degree of adaptability that allows them to identify themselves with the environment in which they live, to become a part of it, and to take advantage of it."[18] Translated here, the guerrilla advertisement, much like the guerrilla insurgent, seeks to "blend" in order to achieve any hope of success. If, for most of a century, advertisers were content to wage this war in such predictable contexts as the designated commercial zones in newspapers, over radio, and on billboards, that famil-iar structure is now undergoing seismic transformation. One recent book on nontraditional advertising embraces this metaphor in a passage worth quot-ing in full for the logic of media and culture it divulges:

> In guerrilla warfare, invisibility is a mighty weapon. . . . Conventional advertising . . . is so visible, so explicit, so identifiable as advertising that consumers can easily spot it and tune it out. . . . It is precisely this undis-guised visibility, this clear line between content and commerce that makes the traditional television commercial so vulnerable to ad-skipping tech-nology. . . . Advertising that gets away with it is advertising that does not look or feel like advertising. *It is advertising that blends in seamlessly with real entertainment, real events or real life to the extent that it is not possible to tell what is advertising and what is not.* What smart product placement, cleverly disguised guerrilla tactics, branded content and word of mouth all have in common is that they are harder to trace and label than advertis-ing. And something that is harder to trace is harder to ignore . . . . In other

words, while visibility is the mantra in conventional advertising, in an ad-cynic era it proves more effective to be invisible, as small and as humble as possible. The less pushy and the less dominant the commercial nature of the message, the more chance it has of being digested. Brands cannot simply force their way into the lives of consumers; they need to act like chameleons and subtly blend in.[19]

What we seem to be witnessing, then, is not merely "not advertising" in the sense of PR- and branding-informed methods outside the scope of traditional marketing space, but rather "not advertising" literally at the core of the guerrilla performance (i.e., a fundamental act of self-effacement): advertising that seems to deny itself as advertising by avoiding contexts where it might be easily identified as such (and tuned out)—obscuring its aims, obfuscating its source, and blurring "the line between branding channels and everyday life" so as to abdicate an appearance of authority while seeking to exercise a program of governance.[20] Guerrilla marketing thus functions as camouflage on two levels: (1) It shrouds the advertising message in unexpected media spaces, and (2) it also shrouds the fundamental project of consumer management that is, ultimately, the eventual purview of and necessary imperative for advertising. In so doing, *agency* emerges at the complex theoretical forefront of this project of discipline.

## Theorizing Power and Agency in Advertising's Struggle

Central to the logic of governance here is a contest over the primacy and locus of agency within the project of power. The tension between and debates over structure and agency color one of the long-standing struggles in both social theory at large as well as media studies more particularly.[21] Major thinkers across the ideological spectrum have wrestled with how to reconcile the potential for autonomous individual choice against broader exigencies and machinations. The fulcrum for this complex negotiation rests upon the theorization of the agent who, at once, seems to act as well as be acted upon in equal measure.

Advertising represents a fruitful site in which to situate these tensions because, in a free market, advertising has to pragmatically reconcile much the same challenge: to attempt to determine the participation of what is, ultimately, a self-determining subject. This renders agency central to the logic of that management, yet after years' worth of commercial incantations—and in the midst of monumental transformations in technology and media ecology—consumers seem ever restive to governance in the usual manner.

Guerrilla marketing, as an abstracted philosophy and in concrete practice, pursues a framework of engagement that projects influence by self-effacing any appearance of it. Such a project therefore represents a sophisticated instrumentalization of governance.

Antonio Gramsci and Michel Foucault largely inform this conceptualization of power and agency. Pivoting from the economic reductionism of orthodox Marxism, Gramsci charts those fluid accommodations by authority that forestall outright revolution and, by according the theoretical space for subordinate agency, thereby softens, even "naturalizes," the application of power to lesser groups in what is an "active consent, not a passive submission. It is not imposed, rather it is 'negotiated' by unequal forces in a complex process."[22] Though more expressly oriented to politics than consumption, his formula for "hegemony" helps to distinguish this subtle exercise of suggestion by leadership rather than forcible coercion in ways that advertisers might well recognize; they, too, are ultimately faced with the task of engineering consent (to buy).

Foucault also leavens (and diffuses) the exercise of power in his explication of "conduct": "To 'conduct' is at the same time to 'lead' others (according to mechanisms of coercion that are, to varying degrees, strict). . . . Power is less a confrontation between two adversaries . . . than a question of 'government.'"[23] "Government" is the central question here as well, not just as a viable and constructive theoretical frame and metaphor for the analysis of advertising but for the nuance it introduces into that continuum of power and agency. For governance, as illuminated in the later work of Foucault, functions as an enterprise by which the "[disposition]" of a subject or subjects might be patterned, molded, or impressed; a means of economy of discipline that could apply to the self, community, institution, or nation.[24] It represents the application of power to "the conduct of others' conduct" in circumstances large and small: a parent's governance of a child's manners; a boss's governance of an employee's labor; a ruler's governance of a citizen's dealings.[25] In each of these scenarios, the subject simultaneously acts and is acted upon—a subject conceived as fundamentally sovereign, yet also operating within larger, sometimes less visible machinations that pursue that "management of possibilities" (in this case, guerrilla marketing).[26] And this lends itself to a soft, subtle, and sophisticated rendering of "power," which will be useful for these purposes; it is a conceptualization of power that has to be constantly negotiated and revised, and necessitates rather than obviates the agency of the subject. Power is not simply a repressive and totalizing apparatus, but as Foucault showed it can be productive and mobilizing from the "bottom-up"—the self administering to the self—by inducing "particular types of behaviors, by regulating people's everyday activities, right down to the way school children hold a pen or sit a desk."[27] In other words:

> What defines a relationship of power is that it is a mode of action that does not act directly and immediately upon others. Instead, it acts upon their actions: an action upon an action, on possible or actual future or present actions. . . . The exercise of power . . . operates on the field of possibilities in which the behavior of active subjects is able to inscribe itself. . . . It is always a way of acting upon one or more acting subjects by virtue of their acting or being capable of action. . . . [Government] covered not only the legitimately constituted forms of political or economic subjection but also modes of action, more or less considered and calculated, that were destined to act upon the possibilities of action of other people. *To govern, in this sense, is to structure the possible field of action of others.*[28]

Resistance, on the other hand, represents the often unanticipated means by which the agent asserts herself as an unmistakably autonomous and, if necessary, antithetical participant within or against the project of discipline. Foucault, cycling through various terms to use for this mode of opposition (including "revolt" and "dissidence"), settles on "counter-conducts" as an expression of "the sense of struggle against the processes implemented for conducting others"; elsewhere, he acknowledges, "in power relations, there is necessarily the possibility of resistance because if there were no possibility of resistance . . . there would be no power relations at all."[29] Resistance therefore represents the key corollary in such a diagram of power and registers, vis-à-vis marketing and consumption, at varying degrees of obstinacy: from the consumer subject who fails to be persuaded by a marketer's entreaty to the consumer subject who actively avoids that appeal (e.g., by way of TiVo) to the consumer subject who openly challenges the structure or grammar of governance enacted through advertising (e.g., by way of culture jamming).

Gramsci also made space for a provocative (in the sense of "provoking" power) "recalcitrance of the will" and "intransigence of freedom" that Foucault identified in his subject, albeit each conceptualized that resistance somewhat differently.[30] As interpreted and applied by a generation of cultural studies theorists and revived as a model for "critical media industry studies" work, his notion of hegemony came to serve as the template for how pop culture might function as a site of contestation—a "compromise equilibrium" that, by definition, accommodates that expression of agency.[31] Marketing, too, represents just such a compromise equilibrium in concurrently governing consumers and adapting to them, in seeking to conduct *and* responding to their conduct as needed. I highlight throughout how guerrilla marketing—as a Gramscian terrain of "exchange and negotiation," "a 'negotiated' mix of intentions and counter-intentions; both from 'above' and from 'below', both 'commercial' and 'authentic'"—flexibly incorporates both that outright resistance to advertising as well as alternate, improvised textual articulations of the brand.[32] In fact, many of the strategies and their attendant logics of governance illuminated here embody a fundamental, even systematic, fluidity on the part of power (one equally true of public relations); for any project steeped in participation, populism, heterarchicality, decentralization, and freedom as operational ideals must be lithe at heart.

It was, in fact, Foucault's insistence upon differentiating power from domination—retrieving the former as "power relations . . . thus mobile, reversible and unstable . . . [and] possible only insofar as the subjects are free" and extraditing the latter as "power relations, instead of being mobile, allowing the various participants to adopt strategies modifying them, remain blocked, frozen [such that . . . ] the practices of freedom do not exist or exist only unilaterally or are extremely constrained or limited"—that marks a revised focus on agency from his earlier thinking.[33] Governmentality, in short, regards "the forces and capacities of living individuals . . . as resources to be fostered, to be used, and to be optimized," and, yet, as some scholars have complained, studies of governmentality often seem to pay mere lip service to the "free and creative ways" that "resistance and agency" is expressed, almost as an "afterthought."[34] Once again, this project, though preoccupied with the machinations of those seeking to wield power over consumers (in other words, I have spoken *only* with advertisers, not the audiences *they* constantly speak of), intends to be equally cautious to not "assume that the subject-effects implied or aimed for by programmes of rule actually come off in practice."[35] This is a study, rather, of attempted effort based on social constructions, not actual effect derived from empirical conclusions. To that end, as a useful contribution to these questions of power and agency, Mark Bevir and Frank Trentmann offer "situated agency" as a way of framing how "if people cannot embody an illusory vision of perfect autonomy, neither are they stuck in fixed locations that leave them no freedom to change and room to manoeuvre."[36] Situated agency aptly articulates the push-and-pull between the conduct of marketers and the conduct of consumers.

This push-and-pull of power registers in the narrative arc cast by Ronald Rust and Richard Oliver in an emblematic *Journal of Advertising* piece from the 1990s announcing the "death of advertising:"

In advertising's prime, producers held virtually all of the power in the marketplace. This was true in part because their agents, the advertising agencies, controlled the then very powerful mass media. Producers controlled
the products, terms, and conditions of sale, and the communications environment. Power has been steadily shifting toward the consumer.[37]

This myth is heard throughout the advertising literature and the perception—or, more accurately, construction—of an empowered audience gives
marketers license to react defensively given their self-ascribed, comparatively
"feeble" position of influence. One frequent refrain, for example, was to hear
interviewees describe their target populations as increasingly "in control" of
their "communications environment," as Rust and Oliver summarize it, and
therefore well capable of resisting marketer discipline through conventional
channels, a characterization most acute when that target is youth and young
adults. A "regime of governance" that produces knowledge about such audiences in this way (i.e., as empowered, even indomitable) thereby rationalizes reactionary programs, which can address subjects so as to "conduct their
conduct" adequately in light of that presumed empowerment.

Almost since the birth of their modern industry in the late 1800s, advertisers have fretted about their impotence in influencing consumers, just
as audiences have long been capable of ad-avoidance even without today's
sophisticated technological augmentation. Take, for instance, the amusing
anecdote from the 1950s of water pressure in one midwestern city dropping
precipitously when viewers simultaneously flushed toilets during Milton
Berle's commercial break.[38] In more recent decades, however, marketers have
faced one ad-zapping defense mechanism after another, from the VCR and
the remote control to newer digital apparatus like TiVo (60 percent of which
were used to avoid advertising by 2006), pop-up blockers, and spam filters
(employed by 81 percent of broadband subscribers).[39]

Today, at a time when one survey finds that almost three-quarters of
Americans are eager to opt out, skip, or block advertising, "The verities of
twentieth century advertising seemed to be crumbling."[40] As advertisers take
steps to restore the balance of power, and "as new media raise the ghost of
large-scale audience unpredictability and unresponsiveness," guerrilla marketing represents one possible recourse to cope with continuing volatility
and indifference.[41] One marketing consultant, Joseph Jaffe, boldly frames this
challenge and opportunity:

> Google, TiVo, and iPod empower the end user to retrieve, navigate, and
> manipulate content, and to do so in ways that are aligned with his or her

passions and interests. In this new relationship, the consumer chooses if, when, and how to interact with the content. The manufacturers, distributors, advertisers, and publishers can no longer dictate these experiences. They can only search for new ways to give the end user *"godlike power"* over his or her environment.[42]

Such a prescription represents a notable turnabout. Matthew McAllister argues that because a sense of "control" sits at the heart of advertiser worry, these empowered audiences necessitate inventive avenues for communication: "either exploring new social locations for [promotion], or tightening control over established, already exploited, advertising locations."[43] A consumer subject that marketers had traditionally attempted to govern through a particularly interruptive force (that is, conventional advertising) is now hyperbolically said to hold such "godlike" digital power, and necessarily portends a certain response from marketers who, in turn, cozy up to that assertion of agency rather than seeking to confront "resistance, refusal, or revolt" head-on.[44] This, then, is the basic logic of guerrilla advertising power: It fluidly accommodates rather than dominates; rather than try to "dictate" experiences, as Jaffe puts it, and risk being turned aside, it arranges the conditions so that commercial engagement might somehow be solicited. It attempts, in short, to "situate" agency, given that agency is, by definition, always situated.[45]

The Cool Sell and the Regime of Engagement

Guerrilla marketing might further be considered the ascent of the cool sell over the hot sell. These terms tweak, somewhat coyly, Marshall McLuhan's "hot" to "cold" media continuum.[46] McLuhan defines "cool" media as those that are low in resolution and high in audience participation (and therefore seek to conduct audiences through ambiguity and agency); "hot" media, by contrast, are high definition, low engagement (and therefore seek to conduct audiences through lucidity and submission).[47] As usual, an intellectual descendent better elucidated McLuhan's thinking here:

> The crux of hot and cool is that media which are loud, bright, clear, fixed ("hot" or high-definition) evoke less involvement from perceivers than media whose presentations are soft, shadowy, blurred and changeable. The psychological logic of this distinction is that we are obliged and seduced to work harder—get more involved—to fill in the gaps with the lower profile, less complete media.[48]

I appropriate McLuhan's taxonomy here more metaphorically: That is, relative to the "hot," "top-down" explicit advertisements through the conventional means of the mass media (think, at one extreme, Billy Mays's direct-response TV commercials), the "bottom-up," "cool" sell of guerrilla marketing generates enigma toward ensnaring engagement, necessitating, as McLuhan observes, "completion by the audience."[49] Such a recourse to collaboration tacitly acknowledges that marketers lack the full control over brand "meaning"—a long-standing concession and point of departure for public relations as well as a staple of cultural studies theory for many years— and models the *re*-modeling of not just the advertising industry but perhaps other creative industries as well.

If the hot sell is about the assured delivery of a commercial message through obvious channels, the cool sell is about the (seemingly) accidental discovery of it through less visible ones. If the hot sell prefers proclamation to reach audiences, the cool sell stages surprise and serendipity. If the hot sell is overt and mass mediated, the cool sell is covert and niche-oriented and involves engaging the consumer in ways ranging from pleasantly interactive to downright deceptive. If the hot sell is about "aggressively shouting to everybody at the same time," the cool sell "tends to whisper occasionally to a few individuals."[50] If the hot sell tells you what to buy, the cool sell "lets" you figure it out for yourself. If the hot sell betrays a presumption of marketer determinism, the cool sell outwardly embraces consumer agency.

Thus, the cool sell also signals a shift in advertising industry metrics and values. Advertisers have long used "impressions" (the number of people who simply saw a campaign) as the crucible for determining success. In the past decade, the industry has become more and more obsessed with "engagement" (and, specifically, user interactivity) as a better measure of efficacy; indeed, one recent report from Cannes calls it "the new holy grail of advertising."[51] This shift corresponds, not coincidentally, to the period in which the Internet has radically altered the traditional information environment and lends itself to what I call a regime of engagement when it comes to consumer governance.

At one level, this so-called regime speaks to the increasing value that clients and agencies seem to place upon robust engagement rather than mere impressions as an index of the depth of participation with and subsequent ROI (Return-on-Investment) value attributed to a particular advertising program. But the concept is also meant to signify the ways marketers are incorporating interactive communication ecology and the paradigm shift from push to pull media that such technologies capacitate. And, more abstractly still, it also speaks to a particular approach to governance whereby brands seek to establish themselves in more flexible, open, and ambiguous ways in order to anticipate the productive labor and collaborative agency of promotional interlocutors and consumer subjects. By utilizing a cool sell approach, brand management seeks to stage a process of commercial discovery, engineer participation, and achieve persuasion that unfolds in a naturalized, even invisible way to that subject because the advertiser is avoiding a position of didactic disciplinary authority that might otherwise be typical of much traditional display advertising. In other words, it's not interrupting and lecturing you, the consumer, to buy what it's selling.

Such strategies are taking shape, in part, as a response to seemingly unabated commercial clutter:

> What distinguishes modern advertising is that it has jumped from the human voice and printed posters to anything that can carry it. Almost every physical object now carries advertising, almost every human environment is suffused with advertising, almost every moment of time is calibrated by advertising.[52]

It is estimated that the average person is exposed to thousands of advertisements daily, and all signs seem to indicate that this amount will only grow with the adoption of each new screen in the consumer's life. That fierce struggle has littered the conventional battlefield of old (i.e., media and information environment) with the carcasses of advertising campaigns past; because semiotic clutter has so choked the contemporary landscape, guerrilla marketers hype their capacity to stage campaigns in unconventional spaces that might better capture audience attention. Thus, in turn, one of the most frequent complaints from agencies, clients, and consumers is that commercial clutter continues to pile up relentlessly in these new zones.[53]

Given such a crushing onslaught of clutter, some argue for the existence of an "advertising schema."[54] This represents the so-called mental shortcuts that audiences employ to process the ubiquity of commercial appeals surrounding them such as the automated skepticism activated in the presence of communication perceived as advertising.[55] Because coping with this exhausting abundance of advertising seems to be one of our main chores as consumers, we construct this schema to "identify how, when and why marketers try to influence us."[56] The more obvious their efforts to influence, the more resistant we screen out their messages: One researcher found, for example, that the stronger a person perceived this hot sell—that is, an explicit indication of persuasive objectives—the less he or she was likely to pay attention to the advertisement, unconsciously filtering out the overture.[57] And because "each passing round of advertisements contributes to creating audiences who are increasingly media-literate, cynical, and alienated," a main factor in the cultural production of advertising today seems to be "the advertiser's perception of the alienated spectator."[58] Certainly this seems to hold true in the case of guerrilla marketing; audience cynicism, particularly among young consumers, is frequently cited as a major factor in choosing to deploy unconventional methods.

Experimental research has begun to probe nontraditional alternatives as a solution to such this crisis of credibility. One study, for example, discovered that the same advertisements for an insurance company and an energy drink placed in creative and unexpected (i.e., guerrilla) locations (respectively, on an egg's shell inside its grocery store carton and on an elevator panel of buttons) were rated more highly than the same advertisements that showed up in traditional media.[59] Subsequent investigation showed how placing advertisements in these nontraditional settings, moreover, makes it difficult to even identify the appeal as advertising, thus disabling that advertising schema and cultivating favorability.[60]

Traditional media provide "an easily recognizable topography" and trigger an apparently instant allergy toward and mistrust of commercial appeals located there.[61] On the other hand, reducing that immediate contrast with the non-advertising content and blending into the surroundings—recall Che Guevara's admonition for guerrilla warriors—seems to hold potential for the guerrilla marketer bold enough to chart unusual topography (an eggshell, a pop song, a street performance, someone's Twitter stream). Some who have studied word-of-mouth marketing's "corporate colonization of the life world" see this as a sign of efforts to reach consumer audiences where they can't "'tune out' or 'turn off'" the promotional appeal.[62]

To be certain, though, some of these guerrilla tactics can still be situated within traditional mass media while trying to overcome the cynicism attendant to conventional advertising there, and McAllister tracks this in detail through history.[63] Like the product placement and branded entertainment detailed in chapter 2, advertorials and infomercials are a clear example of this "camouflaging" of commercialization as part of the editorial and programming content they are adjacent to and embedded within.[64] And public relations is, of course, similarly predicated upon insinuating a corporate or political message into news coverage so as to gain legitimacy.[65] These pursuits, though still executed over the broadcast airwaves or in daily newsprint, bespeak a guerrilla ethos of sneaking under the radar or self-effacing true intentions without necessarily exploiting "new" media as such. McAllister thus concludes: "Advertising is . . . geographically imperialistic, looking for new territories it has not yet conquered. When it finds such a territory, it fills it with ads—at least until this new place, like traditional media, has so many ads that it becomes cluttered and is no longer effective as an ad medium."[66]

Guerrilla marketing offers two creative approaches to solve such cultural and institutional exhaustion. On one hand, it can be dexterously intertextual, absorbing and appropriating from the cluttered existing symbolic economy as needed (witness the "graffadi" exhibited on behalf of *House, M.D.* and Le Tigre clothing presented in chapter 3). On the other hand, in its capacity for seeking "unoccupied cultural spaces," it runs an end route around that "junk heap" pile-up, positioning itself in unexpected contexts that clutter has yet to despoil, as for example related in a conversation between friends, revealed in chapter 4's discussion of word-of-mouth.

To appreciate how this philosophy of governance through subtle engagement registers discursively, I offer one brief, initial example drawn from the trade pages. A decade ago, Jonathan Ressler, a guerrilla marketing CEO whose work is covered in detail in chapter 4, encapsulated for *Promo* magazine the ideology of his operation: "As marketers, you can't choose the target. The target has to choose you. We have to find a way to put a brand in front of the target *in a way that will make them choose.*"[67] This excerpt hints at how marketers structure influence and govern the freedom of the consumer subject, while underscoring the obviously contradictory tensions of passivity and activity inherent to such an approach: the "choice" has to feel genuine even as Ressler attempts to "make" it.

Through this lens, consumers are no longer conceived as the stereotypical "couch potatoes" of old, but neither are they fully autonomous agents of new; rather, that positioning of their agency is "gamed," for lack of a better word, along a continuum, within commercial programs intent on persuading without appearing to persuade. As *Adweek* paradoxically summarizes these scenarios: "[They] are designed to *make consumers willing participants* of marketing rather than passive observers."[68]

Herbert Simon once famously noted that "a wealth of information creates a poverty of attention," and this appears to be precisely the guerrilla logic governing the cool sell turn; amid a noisy, busy media landscape full of *obvious* appeals, less might actually mean more.[69] Conversely, it is presumed that prattling off a laundry list of interruptive ad messages—located in an environment already overloaded with information—probably renders few effective. But by baiting millennials who are thought to be otherwise ad-weary and media literate with more collaborative, indirect, and even clandestine campaigns, guerrilla marketers can claim to be responding to contemporary technological developments as well as cultural conditions.

To that end, guerrilla marketing's cool sell can be understood in a second, more substantive sense: It seeks to bestow "subcultural capital" upon the product being pitched.[70] Sarah Thornton, here updating Pierre Bourdieu's terminology, proposes that the taste hierarchies of youth cultures so coveted by corporations, which employ guerrilla tactics to impress them, can be evaluated across three distinctions: "the authentic versus the phoney, the 'hip' versus the 'mainstream', and the 'underground' versus 'the media.'"[71] Guerrilla advertising fancies itself similarly in contrast to traditional advertising. While the latter is thought to be phony and mainstream in its ham-handed, "lowest-common-denominator" pursuit of "the masses," the former seeks to simulate something more flexible, hip, and authentic.

Authenticity may seem a hypocritical ideal to include here, given guerrilla marketing's propensity to falsify its own pretenses—chief among them that there is even a marketing effort taking place. And yet authenticity is essential to a subculture's positioning as underground and not "mass mediated" in an explicit way, and authenticity represents the ever-elusive ideal in a field of practice (that is, advertising) intrinsically marked by contrivance. Moreover, authentication is part of the project of outsourcing the promotional message to creatively disinterested (i.e., characteristic of branded content), anti-establishment (alternative outdoor), flexibly vernacular (word-of-mouth), or democratically viral (consumer-generated) conversations.

In some ways, then, Thornton's theorization extends the Gramscian schematic mentioned earlier: Resistance is a *source of* as much as a *response to* power here. For as Thornton demonstrates, countercultures are lucrative market segments in their own right—valuable because they operate, semantically and spatially, among the "underground," farthest from the appearance of top-down power, and thus showcase, exhibitionistically, agency as an autonomous force.

It is in this youth media "field" that inaccessibility is a subcultural badge of honor, a mark of power, fortified against the impurities of commercialization and incorporation. Naturally, then, it is to this leading edge of the underground that marketers would proceed; it is the site at which agency is articulated through individual expression rather than mediated modeling and the productivity of the bottom-up is most fertile and apparent. For those who have wrestled with how to situate and track agency against the project of power, the invisibility of the guerrilla-marketing ethos affords a means of compromise: to the consumer subject, agency still *feels* within reach, because the disciplinary force historically endemic to marketing is located in spaces and flows atypical of its techniques of power.

## Guerrilla Marketing's "Unseen" Predecessor

Though innovative, the advertising techniques under examination are not without philosophical and empirical precedence; in order to understand the logic of consumer governance when it comes to guerrilla marketing, the practice of public relations over the past century looms large as a tactical antecedent. Moreover, given guerrilla marketing's management ethos of "governance without feeling like governance," Edward Bernays, considered by many to be the founding father of PR, might well be its intellectual precursor considering his emphasis on the "invisibility with which public relations experts must, ideally, perform their handiwork."[72]

At a turn-of-the-century juncture when subaltern classes were emboldened and making new demands on the powerful, "compliance professionals" like Bernays emerged to help align "popular aspirations and the exigencies of elite power" by "manufactur[ing] a commonality of interests between [businessmen] and an often censorious public," seeking to "organize consent," as Gramsci might have termed it.[73] Public relations is, then, essentially a "management function"; yet it is a management function much like guerrilla marketing, with subtlety, even invisible governance, as its imprimatur.[74] Fundamentally, the two practices seem to share a similar disposition of power and regard for their subjects of influence:

> The old-fashioned propagandist, using almost exclusively the appeal of the printed word, tried to persuade the individual reader to buy a definite article, immediately. This approach is exemplified in a type of advertisement which used to be considered ideal from the point of view of effectiveness and directness: "YOU (perhaps with a finger pointing at the reader) *buy O'Leary's rubber heels—NOW."* . . . Instead of assaulting sales resistance by direct attack, [the new salesman] is interested in removing sales resistance. . . . Under the old salesmanship the manufacturer said to the prospective purchaser, "Please buy a piano." The new salesmanship has reversed the process and caused the prospective purchaser to say to the manufacturer, "Please sell me a piano."[75]

Bernays's now-eighty-year-old distinction between "old-fashioned" approaches to persuasion and his "new salesmanship" breakthrough presages contrasts almost identical to the "let them say yes" framing discussed in chapter 2. And that logic of governance and channeling of agency that Bernays evokes is equally in line with a dynamic mode of consumer management: It is oblique rather than unswerving; subtle rather than imposing; and it reverses the flow of power in a way that "does not act directly and immediately upon others" but instead seeks to "structure the possible field of action" such that the desired behavior unfolds rather than acquiesces.[76]

Today, organizationally, nearly every major ad agency either holds or is conjoined to a public relations firm (under a conglomerate banner) and various trends are "hastening the crumbling of walls that supposedly separate . . . advertising and PR."[77] Early in the last decade, the Madison Avenue veteran Al Ries co-authored a bestselling trade text, *The Fall of Advertising and the Rise of PR*, in which he and his daughter Laura proclaimed that because of advertising's credibility gap, "Wherever we look, we see a dramatic shift from advertising-oriented marketing to public-relations-oriented marketing."[78] In 2009, the Cannes Advertising Festival added a public relations category to recognize this increasing blur. And an influential *Journal of Advertising* piece traces the growing genre of "hybrid messages"—that is, "all paid attempts to influence audiences for commercial benefit that project a non-commercial character" by "covertly or overtly [disguising] their commercial origins"—a genre that very clearly draws lessons and techniques from both advertising and public relations.[79]

Guerrilla marketing might therefore be understood as easing public relations beyond the borders of its usual bailiwick of writing press releases, issuing media kits, staging photo opportunities, and handling crisis management so as to take on responsibilities where marketers have grown frustrated with the form and "disposition" of traditional consumer governance (i.e., interruptive mass media advertising). PR represents a strategic forbearer to draw upon in re-envisioning the field of practice, particularly given the long-standing frustrations of the advertising industry (ad-zapping technologies, cluttered semiotic environments, incredulous audiences) and those perennial tensions between structure and agency. In short, "a rough composite emerges of a wary, jaded, and recalcitrant postmodern consumer who has been variously described as unmanageable . . . vigilant . . . and reflexively defiant."[80] Nowhere is this composite in sharper focus than when it came to Generation X and now millennial youth demographics.

It seems important, however, to again contextualize this current unease against the backdrop of a long history of advertiser anxiety. As far back as the 1920s, marketers have been distressed about commercial clutter and consumer cynicism.[81] In 1966 Mary Wells, a partner at Wells, Rich, Greene, an influential creative agency, presciently complained, "People have seen so many promotions and big ideas and new products and new advertising campaigns and new packaging gimmicks, and they've heard so many lies and so many meaningless slogans and so many commercialized holy truths that it's getting harder to get their attention, let alone their trust."[82] And "unease" was the focal point and subtitle of Michael Schudson's landmark inquiry into advertising's dubious claims to efficacy.[83] Today's apprehension among marketers is not, therefore, an entirely new phenomenon, nor are the guerrilla tactics deconstructed here necessarily without precedent. Rather, these represent the latest iteration in an ongoing redevelopment of strategy, one that nonetheless shows marked growth at a time of widespread institutional disquiet.

Various figures bear this out: A 2003 survey of marketers found that 90 percent believed that advertising's influence on consumers had declined in recent years and the same vast majority thought it would continue to do so (even as this group thought guerrilla, PR, sponsorship, and other alternatives would become more important).[84] A 2006 survey of consumers found that 63 percent of respondents felt there were too many ads in mass media; 47 percent said that ads "spoil" the pleasure of watching or reading content; and 48 percent believed it's their "right to decide whether or not to receive" those ad messages.[85] The proportion of the average media plan devoted to TV buys was forecast to drop from two-thirds to one-half, as revenues from newspaper advertising plummeted from a peak of $49 billion to a nadir of $28 billion in the second half of the last decade.[86] Online, a mere 2 percent of consumers actually trust banner ads, giving way to pitiful click-through rates.[87]

In that context, huge multinationals like General Motors and Proctor & Gamble are shifting ad dollars toward new media experiments and branded entertainment. PQ Media, an analytics firm, finds that "alternative media spending"—which includes eighteen digital and nontraditional segments like consumer-generated, videogame advertising, word-of-mouth, and product placement, among others—grew 22 percent annually between 2002 and 2007 to reach sums of $73 billion and was forecast to represent 26 percent of total U.S. advertising and marketing spending by 2012.[88] Veronis Suhler Stevenson, which publishes the "Communication Industry Forecast," projects a similar category of "alternative advertising" to grow to 32 percent of all ad spending by 2013, a leap from its 6 percent market share just a decade earlier.[89] That said, guerrilla marketing is far from the dominant outlay at this point (indeed, it is still largely exclusive to millennial consumers), as more traditional outlets continue to garner the bulk of U.S. measured-media spending: for example, still $43 billion for newspapers and magazines and $66 billion for television, as of 2011.[90]

Nonetheless, the *definition* of advertising itself seems up for debate as an industry sets out to rethink itself through the strategies and practices explored in the chapters that follow. The earliest textbook definition from

1923 ("selling in print") reflects the way advertising has always articulated itself in relation to the ascendant medium, which at that time was newspapers. Others point out:

> What was most affected by the emergence of new means of communication was the "shape" of advertising or the design strategy rather than the volume. As new media brought new styles and approaches to the tasks of mass communication, advertisers adapted them to the special requirements of persuasion. *The selling message was altered by the communications environment.*[91]

In the following section I take a closer look at the features of that ecology to begin to appraise what it might signal for an industry that has, historically, always had to adapt to changes in the information environment—foregrounding the technological potential for governance that comes with incorporating audience agency into the exercise of marketer power.

A Changing Media Ecosystem

In 2006 the *Economist* issued what it termed "the gazillion-dollar question": "What is a media company?" The answer is key to understanding how new forms of alternative marketing navigate a fluid, participatory, networked media world where, more and more, popular communication often seems to follow "guerrilla" paths when trends rise to cultural prominence. The overall information environment (and attendant social patterns of two-way media ecology) can be mapped from the perspective of cultural producers trying to redefine their power and relevance, given those changing conditions. In order to understand advertising at any given moment in history, one must first make sense of that media landscape through which consumers are engaged; as Mark Deuze notes, "Technology is the skeleton around which advertising has formed."[92] Today, the overlapping buzzwords of social networking, self-publishing, and crowd-sourcing herald an ecology of memes more so than mass, creating a bottom-up tectonic shift, which advertisers are, quite naturally, attempting to comprehend and capitalize on from the top down.

In the past decade, a host of scholarship started to grapple with these contemporary patterns of information flow.[93] Manuel Castells's work on the "network society" —his term for the "new social morphology" of our era in which information technology networks become the basis for and logic of social structures, activities, and "the processes of production, experience, power, and culture"—is an essential backdrop here.[94] When it comes to information and media, corporations find themselves engaged with more publicly "active" audiences than ever before: audiences whose co-creative and collaborative agency can be counted on and factored into production in the form of amateur participants creating and populating cyberspace with massive amounts of personal and remixed material. This propels what Deuze terms a "supercharged" blur in terms of the boundaries between those who make and those who consume media.[95] Because the network now represents the "core organizing principle of this communicative environment" as much as broadcasting, and, as such, complicates what had been a comparatively hierarchical, more predictable flow of media and culture, advertisers are scrambling to figure out which commercial appeals to employ through which channels and how to situate audiences in their schematics such that marketer power might be more coyly embedded in consumer freedoms.

Castells recently revisited the question of structure and agency in the context of individuals navigating the network society.[96] Sizing up the networked patterns of new media, Castells is sanguine on the potential for resistance to exert itself: "The capacity of social actors to set up autonomously their political agenda is greater in the networks of mass self-communication than in the corporate world of the mass media" because the space itself is "bias[ed]" away from those "powers that be."[97] Yet he petitions scholars to "observe the attempt by the holders of power to reassert their domination into the communication realm, once they acknowledged the decreasing capacity of institutions to channel the projects and demands from people around the world."[98] This research answers that call to examine how marketing companies and their affiliates are responding to what Castells terms the "mass self-communication" of the early 21st century.

Christina Spurgeon similarly frames this shift as a transition from "mass media to the new media of mass conversation," where the process of "co-adaptation" to that "mass conversation" by the culture industries shows up in many of the integrated marketing communication (IMC) strategies of the past two decades.[99] In this book, I illustrate how guerrilla marketing emerges from such a "flattening of . . . hierarchies," which could spell the end of the monopoly of "'show-and-tell' advertising" in favor of options more flexible, participatory, and decentralized.[100] Thus, the one-size-fits-all, "interruptive" advertising model (prescribed by vertically oriented institutions of expertise) seems to be evolving; buzz agency and crowd-sourced marketing (driven by horizontally integrated networks of expertise) can be more understated and elastic than that which media structure necessitated in that "lowest common denominator" mass media era.[101] Online, especially, brands can represent themselves in more flexible capacities, as interactivity is programmed and meaning is outsourced in an effort to foment digital engagement. This fluidity is, moreover, diagrammed to be read by consumer audiences as an egalitarian gesture.

Media theorists have taken stock of these trends often classified under the catchphrase Web 2.0—the umbrella term for user-generated content and collaboration online—where "firms are built on, and make use of, network and information economics, conversational interaction and intercreative innovation."[102] As Axel Bruns extrapolates from his study of blog authors, Wikipedia entries, and Second Life avatars: "Such modes of content creation—involving large communities of users ['produsers'], who act without an all-controlling, coordinating hierarchy—operate along lines which are fluid, flexible, heterarchical, and organized ad hoc as required by the ongoing process of development."[103] Many of the nontraditional marketing campaigns documented here can be read as both a consequence of and response to that incipient environment: It is an attempt to engage, initiate, or co-opt the ideals of these heterarchical guerrilla media flows (at the other end of a continuum from hierarchical "mass"). In that environment, content producers like advertisers are being urged to be ever more comfortable with textual plasticity (whereby the consumer supposedly "owns" and "controls" the brand) and serendipitous and unbounded rather than deliberate and restricted engagement of audiences. Within such a framework, goes the mythology, those who would purport to govern consumption have to figure out how to "democratically" woo that peripatetic "produser" rather than "autocratically" targeting a fixed consumer.

Henry Jenkins's work on "convergence culture" helps illuminate what is "both a top-down corporate driven process and a bottom-up consumer driven process" in this regard.[104] Many of the examples of guerrilla marketing on display here will illustrate the complex interplay of such polarities of corporate power and consumer agency:

> Convergence requires media companies to rethink old assumptions about what it means to consume media, assumptions that shape both programming and marketing decisions. If old consumers were assumed to be passive, the new consumers are active. If old consumers were predictable and stayed where you told them to stay, then new consumers are migratory, showing a declining loyalty to networks or media. If old consumers were isolated individuals, the new consumers are more socially connected. If the work of media consumers was once silent and invisible, the new consumers are now noisy and public.[105]

To that end, as economies increasingly center themselves on culture and information, Deuze reports on how companies in the media and cultural industries are "incorporat[ing] the productive activities of consumers in their business strategies."[106] For example, Deuze examines the work of the guerrilla powerhouse Crispin Porter + Bogusky and finds that amateur collaboration in cultural production has reshaped expectations and executions there. He quotes one agency executive who claims, "The more stuff people can do with these ads, the better. . . . It's more fun, but they also feel like they own it. *They feel more empowered as consumers.*"[107] Thus, a framework of engagement-oriented governance emerges, a framework that embraces disinterested spaces and participatory flows, because this is where that agency might optimally be situated. Decentralized participation in a networked communicative environment shows subjects to be, at once, resourceful as autonomous agents and resources for power.

Larry Light, the global chief marketing officer for McDonald's, declared in a *BusinessWeek* interview: "We're not a mass marketer. . . . Technology has facilitated our ability to reach people on a more customized, more personalized basis. That's a revolution."[108] The terms "interactivity" and "customization" (words inherently antithetical to the notion and operationalization of "mass-ness") are much touted as technological panacea for the challenges that, in a sense, technology hath wrought in the first place. The *Journal of Interactive Advertising* launched its inaugural issue in 2000 with auspicious edicts from various CEOs that interactivity could resuscitate an industry had been pronounced dead (alongside "mass" media) six years earlier in the *Journal of Advertising*.[109] The advent of two-way channels made possible by the Internet would produce "a stark contrast to the mass-communication model wherein marketers conduct 'monologues' with nameless, faceless individuals."[110] Deuze thus sums up, "As more and more people immerse themselves in all kinds of networked, portable and personalized media, the consensus in the advertising industry is that the age of mass advertising is over."[111]

The gradual transformation of the traditional information environment can be understood through these efforts to generate new and reinvigorate old alternatives for the advertising industry. It is probably not coincidence that the same year *Time* magazine broke with decades of tradition to name "You"—the "amateur-revolutionary" at the heart of Web 2.0—as its "Person of the Year," *Advertising Age* also named the consumer its "Advertising Agency of the Year."[112] This book then is an exploration of guerrilla marketing as a means of processing the profound changes that resulted in those sorts of accolades. Much like Deuze, I set out to chart guerrilla marketing's "media logic": "[This] points to specific forms and processes which organize the work done within a particular medium. Yet, media logic also indicates the cultural competence frames of perception of audiences/users, which in turn reinforces how production within the medium takes place."[113] By going "behind the scenes" and looking at the "strategies, tactics, and processes of meaning-making" of guerrilla creatives, we can perhaps "catch a glimpse of the future that many assume lies ahead in the knowledge economy of the information age."[114]

## Studies of Cultural Production

As a study of the creation of guerrilla advertising, this book contributes to a tradition of communication scholarship on cultural *production,* a tradition that, while valuable, seems to have received comparatively scant attention relative to the moment of cultural *reception.*[115] Cultural production research, as David Hesmondhalgh observes in *The Cultural Industries,* has historically fallen in the gap between two competing schools of inquiry.[116] On one hand, political economy approaches tend to lack "the empirical attention to what happens in cultural industry *organizations"* and "often choose to ignore the issue of textual meaning."[117] These efforts have tended to take a high-altitude view of how media content is regulated, supervised, manufactured, and circulated, without the nuanced, complex, even contradictory backstage insight from day-to-day, on-the-ground work by symbolic creators. On the other hand, while cultural studies has long sought to foreground the issue of textual "meaning," it has done so in such a way that often privileges and even celebrates the resistant audience rather than the determinant producer; this set of literature has perhaps *overly* emphasized agency in theorizing power.

I answer Hesmondhalgh's call to bridge that gap and "revivify" the study of symbolic creativity by appraising "cultural *production* and *policy . . . in relation* to other key processes such as cultural consumption, identity and textual meaning."[118] In short, I apply the qualitative, interpretive tools that have long characterized cultural reception research—specifically, textual analysis and in-depth interview methods—to cultural producers, a group long theorized by political economists at an arms length.[119] Much like Todd Gitlin's pursuit of prime time television's backstage, I've captured, through interviews with symbolic creators, "the thinking," and, more specifically for my purposes, the "media logic" or "analytics of government" that makes guerrilla advertising what it is.[120]

Cultural production research specific to advertising similarly has room to grow.[121] Besides valuable historical efforts, critical advertising scholarship has more often rested on pillars like Judith Williamson's work—that is, insightful readings of the final product, but failures to truly account for the concrete workings and intentions of the producer.[122] The Barthesian-informed influence of Williamson has perhaps resulted in a "text-centered orthodoxy (and concurrent militantism against authorship)" that largely ignores the "encoding" moment of Stuart Hall's canonic model.[123] Yet we need to be studying that moment of advertisement encoding and the processes of creative producers who are involved in it.[124] For as Don Slater speculates, "Understanding this process [of advertising practice] might well lead us to reconsider assumptions about the way needs and consumers are formed which underlie the paradigm of communicative power."[125] I therefore raise questions about "how ideas are produced, how well the processes can be explained, [and] the influences (if any) that are at play."[126]

The project can be understood as an "analytics of government" in the realm of cultural production, in that it is "a materialist analysis in that it places these regimes of practices at the centre of analysis and seeks to discover the logic of such practices."[127] Such work falls within the neo-Foucauldian tradition: "to make explicit the thought that, while often taking a material form, is largely tacit in the way in which we govern and are governed, and in the language, practices, and techniques by which we do so."[128] A multimethod, multisource approach has been useful in delivering in multiple levels of "thick description" and rich detail.[129] A textual analysis of guerrilla advertising coverage in the popular and trade press first culled a useful sample of case studies and the industry's public representation and explanation of the techniques; subsequently, in-depth, one-on-one interviews with the practitioners involved with those campaigns further illuminated a more nuanced understanding of the beliefs and ideas that motivate and animate these forms, and the inspiration and decision-making involved. From the broad orientation provided by others' journalistic reportage to the unique insights of my own interview data, each method has yielded "webs of significance" to be synthesized for a kind of industrial understanding of the potentials and perils of consumer management today.[130]

In accordance with the "critical media industry studies" research agenda that Timothy Havens, Amanda Lotz, and Serra Tinic propose, I conducted "grounded institutional case studies that examine the relationships between strategies (here read as the larger economic goals and logics of large-scale cultural industries) and tactics."[131] Moreover, I take up their suggestion to "examine . . . how knowledge about texts, audiences, and the industry form, circulate, and change; and how they influence textual and industrial practices" so as to obtain "a 'helicopter' level view of industry operations, a focus on agency within industry operations, a Gramscian theory of power that does not lead to complete domination, and a view of society and culture grounded in structuration and articulation."[132]

In keeping with the metaphorical contrast they sketch, the "jet plane" or high-altitude approach of political economy to cultural production could have provided the underlying framework of governance as a way of understanding the way advertisers think about consumer audiences without ever needing to pick up the phone. Yet by opting for the "helicopter" view of this production (that is more informed by a cultural studies' sensitivity to meanings, identities, and lived experiences), it has afforded greater detail and complexity, and allowed me to see how that governance *actually tries not to seem like governance in relating to the subjects of its power.*

This research has been exploratory and inductive, based upon a textual analysis of hundreds of articles in the popular and trade press, and interviews with dozens of agency CEOs, creative directors, and brand managers.[133] The ensuing chapters answer these central questions from assorted sites and vantage points: How and why has the medium itself for advertising been rethought in the past decade? What do those strategies of governance reflect about emergent ideologies of audience engagement and consumer management? What role does pop content, subcultural capital, grassroots socialization, and networked interactivity play in organizing this media work? And how might these developments reshape branding, the media industries, and contemporary culture?

## 2

## The Ambient Governance of Advertainment

If you're creating a culture, you need to create content in order for people to interact or experience what the brand stands for. So, a 30-second commercial is content, but it's manipulated content that's supposed to persuade you to buy something. So people are conditioned to think of a TV spot differently than they are a piece of film on YouTube or a book or whatever. So I think ultimately if you want to get people on board, you have to give them tools, give them opportunities to engage, and come up with really creative ways of doing it.
—Scott Goodson, founder and CEO of StrawberryFrog[1]

The audience cannot notice the integration but must remember it.
—Jak Severson, managing partner at Madison Road Holdings[2]

As audiences have become more technologically and psychologically adept at evading traditional advertiser entreaty, branding has regrouped with ambitious new designs of its own. In the past decade, the explosion of product placement and branded content offers an entry point into how advertising context is being rethought and, moreover, suggests an effort at "casualizing" the exercise of marketing power. Cultural spaces like film, pop music, and video games furnish an ostensibly neutral ambience, whereas conventional advertising venues are now presumed to have conditioned subjects into anticipating the weight of manipulation, as Scott Goodson outlines in the epigraph. Borrowing the military terms from the first chapter, the commercial break announces the assault to follow. Yet entertainment (and even journalistic) programming can serve to obfuscate that project of power: with marketers self-effacing persuasive intent and embedding an ethos—not merely a message—into textual material that is sought out rather than forced upon. As a program for the "conduct of others' conduct," this kind of governance aims to manage subjects less deliberately (and therefore less candidly)—that persuasive force is, in a sense, arranged *architecturally* rather than foisted *explicitly*.

Unlike "newer" media tactics, advertainment relies upon the channels and genres of more traditional mass broadcasting. Yet motivated by many of the same pressures that cue the search for less blatantly commercial territory—TiVo, newspapers' waning relevance, cluttered markets, and a sense of rampant consumer skepticism—it nonetheless represents another step toward blurring those boundaries where audiences have customarily encountered advertising in their programming. What had been a more firm partition between commerce and content increasingly resembles a seamless blend, and the landscape that results could redefine the roles, norms, and financing calculus for advertisers, clients, and cultural producers. Coca-Cola president Steven J. Heyer stated as much at a 2003 *Advertising Age* conference when he told attendees that Coke now thinks of itself as a vessel for the delivery of entertainment and pop culture as much as just a simple soft drink: "The bottle is a medium, [Heyer] said, 'to open a movie, popularize and sell new music . . . and maybe . . . charge [the entertainment and media industries], like [they] charge us."[3] Recent figures highlight branded entertainment's market-share gains. As a broad category (encompassing product placement, advergaming, webisodes, and event sponsorship), it reached an all-time U.S. high of $25 billion in 2009 after thirty-five years of consecutive growth—including four years of double-digit growth.[4]

The guerrilla ideal (and paradox) of flying unavoidably "under-the-radar" gets echoed throughout the industry discourse about advertainment: from its trade group, the Entertainment Resources and Marketing Association, which stumps for a "'seamless' or 'organic' product placement [that] doesn't make a lot of noise by calling attention to itself" to former *Advertising Age* editor Scott Donaton's boast that, "Not only do entertainment tie-in's make the advertising more attractive, they make it impossible to avoid; you can't zap a product placement without zapping the very program you want to watch."[5] Yet this underscores a peculiar and contradictory tension for brands and products located in content: They need to be both inevitable and invisible; to have the audience "remember" the integration but not "notice" it, as Jak Severson enigmatically summarizes. As further irony, Mark Andrejevic warns that the same digital technologies that enabled ad avoidance—and help capacitate the agency of an "unruly" consumer subject for the commercial message—ultimately ensure that marketing will continue to creep farther into content that audiences actually *want* to see: "If the advent of interactive TV heralds the end of advertising as we know it—vignettes distinct from the program content—it simultaneously anticipates the transformation of all content into advertising."[6] Governmentally speaking, one might read this as a shift in mentality from domination to leadership—if subjects are resistant to direct summons (petitions from power partitioned off from "objective" texts), perhaps they can be shepherded through ambient appeals (petitions from power embedded and modeled in those texts).

Andrejevic's premonition comes at a precarious moment when the chaotic forces transforming television are also sweeping across other media industries. For burrowing into content is not just a retreat move on the part of advertisers fleeing the remote control or DVR pre-set; it is *also* part of an advance surge galvanized by new assumptions in marketing thought to increasingly stake out a wider swath of media space to generate brand identity. In that, the brand's textual creep outward from its 30-second spot "straightjacket"—as one branded content expert tellingly calls it—is part of a broader imperative to provide a (self-appointed) cultural "resource" to audiences and consumers.[7] This cues the search for terrain more expansive than that which has been traditionally zoned for commercial purposes during the programming break on TV and radio or surrounding editorial content in magazines and newspapers—especially at a time when those institutions seem to fail to inspire confidence in clients and advertisers as they once did. Ultimately, given the system of governance reflected in this strategy—to try to casualize the persuasive process, to influence consumption without it ever *feeling* like influence—pop culture content provides an appealingly "disinterested" space from which to make that case. In advertainment, a brand can belie its ultimate intention to sell products through the textual material that those products are embedded within. And by inventing or annexing pop culture forms, the brand displays its capacity to "transform, to adapt, [and] to transcend in order to take advantage of a virtually infinite variety of content and discourse."[8]

## Power and Agency in Branding

The marketer's push to engineer an ethos rather than simply issue a message is part of a long tradition of anthropomorphizing corporate identity; historians, in fact, date the first "brand" back to more than two centuries ago.[9] Increasingly in recent decades, the brand has become more central to business as an asset at once commodifiable if intangible. Liz Moor, who has chronicled this rise, notes that brands codify more than simply a name, logo, and trademark, and are meant to "embody 'relationships,' 'values' and 'feelings,' to be expressed through an expanded range of 'executional elements' and 'visual indicators.'"[10] Moreover, they "render a greater array of materials communicative and informational . . . attempt to give concrete physical form to abstract values and concepts . . . and try to influence the perceptions and behavior of customers and citizens."[11] We will see how a wide array of pop culture materials *already* "communicative and informational" is being repurposed for corporate ventriloquism.

Though manifestly a tool for marketer power, the brand is equally a project of governance brokered through the agency of the subject. For example, Celia Lury describes the brand variously as an "open-ended object," a "platform for action."[12] Taylorist marketing—ascendant for the first half of the 20th century—sought to "engineer" tastes and desires on command, "directed consumers as to how they should live and why their brand should be a central part of this kind of life," and issued paternalistic, "didactic" advertising appeals.[13] Such "marketing fiat" could certainly come across as "overly coercive"—a project wherein consumers were addressed more for their acquiescence than their agency per se.[14]

Against that backdrop, brand managers began to revise their focus from a direct and primary reference to the product to a *"context of [its] consumption."* . . . It is not the brand itself that counts, but what you can do with it, what you can *be* with it."[15] Such ambitious goals are not easily realized working within the traditional confines of promotional space. Thirty minutes of film provide a far more robust media platform for evoking that "context" than 30 seconds of advertising. Adam Arvidsson explains:

> Brand management is not a disciplinary practice. It does not seek to impose a certain structure of tastes or desires, not even a certain manner of relating to goods. . . . Rather, brand management works by enabling or empowering the freedom of consumers *so that it is likely to evolve in particular directions*. . . . Brand management recognizes the autonomy of consumers. It aims at providing an environment, an ambience, which anticipates and programs the agency of consumers. Brand management says not "You Must!" It says "You May!"[16]

These aspirations to lead through ambience and to stage discovery—again, seemingly contradictory notions—rather than execute a hard-edged discipline are especially resonant in the "invisible governance" of advertainment. For weaving the brand into content is not only a way of casually demonstrating that "context for consumption" (as opposed to conventional advertising spaces where that demonstration, by contextual definition, might be read as a deliberate contrivance); it is also meant to showcase what a seemingly autonomous agent (i.e., the popular storyteller) has "done" or "been" with it. It is a way of "authenticating" the act of governance, because it is (mis)directed through a third-party intermediary, a technique long since familiar to the PR industry. These autonomous representatives—film actors, TV writers, and pop stars who have been, more or less, sequestered to work for the brand—help "[define] the contours of what the brand *can* mean" rather than "aim at sending a 'message' about the product."[17] Contours "structure the possible field of action of others," while messages work less as "fields" and more as funnels—angling, unambiguously, toward a prescribed consumption outcome.[18]

Yet even if that promotional content worms itself into entertainment terrain, the problem remains. Marketers increasingly suspect audiences—and particularly millennials—will zap out anything that resembles advertising. This means that the brand has to perform an act of self-effacement: to market without selling; to show without telling. Douglas Holt formulates the obligation:

> The postmodern branding paradigm is premised upon the idea that brands will be more valuable if they are offered not as cultural blueprints but as cultural resources, as useful ingredients to produce the self as one chooses. . . . To be authentic, brands must be *disinterested*; they must be perceived as invented and disseminated by parties without an instrumental economic agenda, by people who are intrinsically motivated by their inherent value. Postmodern consumers perceive modern branding to be inauthentic because they ooze with the commercial intent of their sponsors. . . . Consumers will look for brands to contribute directly to their identity projects by providing original and relevant cultural materials with which to work. So, brands will become another form of expressive culture, no different in principle from films or television programs or rock bands (which, in turn, are increasingly treated and perceived as brands).[19]

Feigning "disinterestedness" is a way for marketers to accommodate the existence of and situate the opportunity for consumer agency even as an attempt at power is being implemented in soft, subtle, and sophisticated ways. Moreover, this nuanced distinction between a "cultural blueprint" and a "cultural resource"—the former being *operational* and the latter being *operable*—bespeaks the mode by which marketers seek to govern consumers through their freedom: a strategy of deploying an "impartial" cultural proposition (embedded, insouciantly, in pop content) rather than a pushy, vested imposition separate from it (protruding outward during commercial breaks).

George Yudice has, indeed, theorized culture as an instrumental resource as such and Liz Moor, building on Yudice, notes that "branding entails both

the management of cultural resources . . . and the management and mobilization of populations" to that end.[20] Stage-managing this perception of "disinterestedness"—this façade that the brand simply wants to put on a show
rather than move product off the shelf—represents one of the core tensions
with the advertainment space.

Yet the more cynical consumers become, the more corporations will cling
to that façade as the wellspring of brand equity. As one consultant claims,
"The primary objective is not to sell the product but to generate a fascina-
tion with the brand; to get the customer to identify with the world of the
brand . . . and provid[e] it with a deep emotional core."[21] Henry Jenkins dubs
this turn "affective economics"—a marketing strategy that strives to appreciate (both in an awareness and valuated sense) the "emotional, social, and
intellectual" meaning-making involved with consumption so as to exploit it
toward a "long-term relationship with a brand."[22] A useful fiction, this disavowal of "bottom line" in advertising—that is, moving inventory—is not
an uncommon refrain when it comes to guerrilla marketing. In my interviews with campaign creators, many shied away from the notion that a "sell"
was even taking place—preferring to think of their work, in more than one
instance, as "educational" in nature. For example, the director behind *America's Army*, an advergame recruiting tool for the U.S. military, put it this way:

> The idea was somewhat different from selling. So, we're not so much trying
> to change their tastes as we're trying to make sure they've got an adequate
> data set upon which to base their tastes. . . . We really think it's more in the
> field of education than actually marketing. That we're adding information,
> experience, and so forth to their mix, whereas classic marketing is a call to
> action involved. Usually, it's "I want you," which means you join. There's no
> call to action really in any of our [*America's Army*] products. It's kind of,
> try it on for size and see if you like it and, if you do, the logical action will
> arise, which is: Take the next step, learn more. So, it's a bit different than
> classical marketing, because classical marketing always has, just before the
> end, "Drink Coke" or "Become part of the Pepsi Generation" or something
> like this. And we actually think it's better for the Army and better for kids,
> if, um, it's more education and less marketing-oriented—that, if you buy a
> Coke and you don't like, big deal. Next time, you're going to buy a Pepsi,
> and, you know, well, I've wasted 75 cents or 50 cents, big deal. If you buy
> the Army and you don't like it, that's kind of a bigger deal.[23]

Here we find a practical application and articulation of this logic of invisible power: Foucault, for instance, defined government as "a right manner

of disposing things so as to lead to . . . an end that is 'convenient' for each of things that are to be governed" and "employing tactics rather than laws . . . to arrange things in such a way that, through a certain number of means, such-and-such ends may be achieved."[24] The colonel behind *America's Army*, here hoping that "such-and-such ends" would be achieved (i.e., recruitment), thus tried "employing tactics . . . to arrange things" (i.e., creating an adver-game, which is a format expressly predisposed to the participatory agency of young people) rather than issue a forthright "call to action," a la the Uncle Sam of old protruding his finger from a wall poster at the conscripted youth subject.[25] This passage also demonstrates the unstated legacy of a public relations mind-set: PR professionals, like guerrilla marketers quoted here, fundamentally see their task as one of education ("the public must be 'educated,'" ran the refrain of one pioneering 1913 campaign), which is itself a strategic self-effacement.[26]

Indeed, one early example of branded entertainment of just this sort came from Standard Oil's PR attempt to "anthropomorphize" its image by commissioning a full-length motion picture (*Louisiana Story*) from the acclaimed documentary filmmaker Robert Flaherty, which quite deliberately "did not *openly* promote the corporation": "The objective was not to sell oil, but to present the company in human terms, to evoke a silent identity of interests between [Standard Oil] and ordinary Americans."[27] Such a disavowal of the salesmanship component of corporate communications will be echoed throughout this book; it is a tactical recourse to seek governance of the consumer subject less explicitly and more casually by generating ambience that cultivates a brand halo.

This lack of an explicit "call to action" and the generation of ambience around a product rather than a frank exaltation of its attributes serve what I term a kind of "casualization" of that governance: a passive-aggressive strategy for trying to manage the (often youth) audiences by encouraging them to simply "discover" the message amid the legitimate and unbiased popular culture they *choose* to consume, as opposed to traditional advertising, which jams its message in through interruption of that content. This approach, then, constitutes that consumer in slightly different terms than did "modern or 'Fordist' marketing" in a way that is informed, if tacitly, by public relations' principles: "It is not about *imposing* ways of using goods, or behaving or thinking as a consumer. Rather it is about *proposing* branded goods as tools, or building blocks whereby consumers can create their own meanings."[28] To introduce those participatory propositions, rather than intrude with propagandistic impositions, guerrilla advertisers turn down the volume and directness of the hard/hot sell and embrace the "disinterested" sheen that popular culture affords, where the intent of governance might be self-effaced—a tactic best exemplified by product placement and branded content.

## From Innovative Integration to Branded Content
### Film and Television

Considering the deliberate, strategic, and highly profitable deployments of product placement today, it is interesting to note that the practice began as an ad hoc solution to film production needs. Although the term itself wouldn't come into vogue until the 1980s (thanks to a high-profile appearance in *E.T.*), scholars trace the first brand inclusions back to the Lumière films of the 1890s, with integration becoming more sophisticated and widespread from the 1920s on.[29] At that time, though it was primarily employed by filmmakers to offset prop costs or as a means of outsourcing promotion to manufacturers' ads (typically, a quid pro quo with little money changing hands), it was nonetheless regarded as a "somewhat sleazy practice," drawing the ire of exhibitors and film critics, and conducted so surreptitiously that "nobody openly admitted to practicing [it]."[30] Thus, from the very start, this form of guerrilla advertising was born of that under-the-radar impulse that characterizes the medium as a whole.

This, too, owes a debt to public relations, The use of branded products on-screen in the early film era was considered "publicity," and by the time it became routinized as a promotional process in the 1960s, half the companies overseeing the practice were PR firms (Hill & Knowlton being the most prominent) with ad agencies a "minority" player in the space.[31] Because of radio and TV's financial and regulatory structure—with federal limits on the amount of commercial airtime (even unpaid) and anxiety over giving away what networks were charging for during programming breaks—it took shape in those industries as even more of an "underground trade" than in film.[32] Nonetheless, in the case of sponsored broadcasts—as when Texaco, Jell-O, and Camel cigarettes would fully underwrite an assortment of variety programming or as with soap operas (so named for their detergent patronage)—on-air talent effortlessly oscillated between dual roles as entertainers and pitchmen with product mentions interlaced.[33] It is this wholly sponsored content that serves as the historic antecedent to more recent "branded entertainment" projects like BMW's *The Hire*, Rainier Beer's *Rainier Vision*, Nike's "Classic" pop song, and the *America's Army* game.

Following Reese's Pieces conspicuous appearance in *E.T.* and the sales increase that famously ensued, a host of companies across Los Angeles sprang up "that did nothing except to try and turn the products they represented into movie stars."[34] In the 1980s, in the midst of a broader climate of deregulation, TV networks interpreted less stringent enforcement of the limits on and identification of any paid or sponsored material.[35] The practice has, therefore, seen especially dramatic growth of late on both big screen and small: more firms peddling it; more programs using it; and higher costs for marquee placement. By 2002 *Minority Report* reportedly collected $25 million, or one-quarter of the film's budget, from products featured therein, and *Die Another Day* netted a then-record $120 to $160 million from estimated placement revenues.[36]

As such, *Variety* once amusingly likened product placement to "cocaine" for U.S. television, and the addiction, it seems, remains strong: Thanks to the explosion of reality TV opportunities, by mid-decade, Nielsen was counting 100,000 placement appearances in a single season of network programming—perhaps begging the question if content itself may one day be plagued with the same frustrations of "semiotic clutter" endemic to conventional advertising zones.[37] *American Idol* and *Survivor* have parlayed this opportunity conspicuously so, as Mark Burnett, producer of the latter, unsentimentally quips: "*Survivor* is as much a marketing vehicle as it is television show. . . . My shows create an interest, and people will look at them, but the endgame here is selling the products in stores—a car, deodorant, running shoes. It's the future of television."[38]

Moreover, this appearance of advertising, brand names, and commercial products in film and TV content has long been hailed and condemned along many of the same lines that endure today in newer manifestations of advertainment. From the beginning, firms pitched clients on the advantages of subtly cozying up to "captive" audiences (their term) whose attention was fully absorbed; on the potential for repeat viewing of a single placement; and, being embedded in content, on its fortitude against remote control and DVR ad-zapping threats. Moreover, being embedded in a "disinterested" space, product placement might serve to legitimize that effort at consumer governance through implicit, autonomous appeals. Echoing Arvidsson, the nonchalant ambience of "You May!" camouflages the bumptious intent of "You Must!"[39] Modeling that "context for consumption" (the brand's "operability"), James Bond is not *telling* you to buy a BMW Z3; he's simply *showing* you what he's done with his.

Because of that, product placement has also long endured two main criticisms: first, that such concealed commerce "destroys the illusion" of entertainment escapism to such a degree that the public would eventually come to resent it, and second, if indulged to the extreme, "[it] would result in having films made that were all mindless, content free, bland pap."[40] Consumer advocate groups have variously petitioned against the practice over the years: the Center for Science in the Public Interest (CSPI) labeled placement "an insidious form of advertising" and sought the FCC's intervention in requiring disclosure; later, the Center for the Study of Commercialism similarly asked the Federal Trade Commission to probe what they termed "stealth . . . plugola" to no avail.[41]

Compared to Western Europe—where product placement has histori-cally been more strictly regulated and even, in the case of the Germany, the United Kingdom, and Ireland, outright prohibited at one time or another—there are no federal rules restricting paid inclusion in U.S. film and similarly light enforcement when it comes to broadcast networks.[42] More recently, though, amendments to European television policy have liberalized some of those more stringent principles upholding the separation of advertising and editorial content. At the same time, the FCC, observing the recent preva-lence of advertainment and contemplating requiring disclosure, has called it "particularly insidious because viewers are often unaware that someone is trying to influence, persuade, or market to them."[43]

Such disclosure is, of course, anathema to a regime desirous of advertising without *seeing* like advertising so as to govern consumer choice without the subject sensing any "overly coercive" "marketing fiat."[44] Thus, one CSPI petitioner correctly worried in the late 1980s, "We are watching the fringes of a phenomenon that will permeate across several art forms like a disease. . . . We won't be able to recognize what is art and what is advertisement."[45] Such is the specter that hangs over each new "breakthrough" in brand integration: the potential for polluting the "original institution" (in this case, art, story-telling, popular culture) hosting the new promotional forms.

And even if *all* commercial broadcasting might ultimately, if cynically, be considered but a "marketing vehicle" (in the sense that every show effectively tries to create an "interest" for an "endgame" that is selling advertising space for the selling of products), Burnett's aforementioned vision for the future of television nonetheless heralds a transformation of the flow of that revenue model and a compromise of the "objective" of content in both senses of the word. Burnett has quipped that branded products are the show's "17th char-acter," plainly revealing an ambition worthy of QVC on a remote island. That said, the more that product integration runs aground of infomercial terri-tory—a format that telegraphs the sales intent so aggressively that it can hardly be considered "disinterested"—the more obvious the project of power will be to the subject it is visited upon. Balancing commercialization within content is, in fact, a question of the visibility of that governance. Scott Donaton, for one, savaged Burnett's failed venture, *The Restaurant*, as "nearly unwatchable by product placements that were aggressive, intrusive, and clunky—anything but the *seamless* blend that is necessary to make them bearable."[46]

In short, the product placement had not been "cool" enough—in the McLuhanian sense of low resolution; it had not self-effaced the ad component to a sufficient degree that it resonated *subtly* in the mediated ambience of the background. The commercial intent of a program like *The Restaurant* apparently "oozed" in such a crass way that its brand patrons hardly came off as "disinterested," much less "authentic." Consumer governance so obvious insufficiently allocates room for discovery; it betrays dictation rather than proposition.

Other observers have taken note of the growth of what Siva Balasubramanian calls the "masked news" or "masked spokesperson" approach that is emblematic of an "emergent hybrid" genre of advertising-cum-public-relations.[47] As an example of this trend, one can witness the marked uptick in video news releases since the 1980s: full-length stories created by PR firms "designed to be indistinguishable from genuine news . . . [and] without any attribution or disclaimer indicating that they are in fact subtle paid advertisements."[48] Elsewhere, others report that celebrities are being compensated for casually—and seemingly "disinterestedly"—referencing health care products on talk show appearances without disclosing their vested interests.[49] Part of the advantage of planting a drug plug in such an off-the-cuff manner is that it circumvents FDA requirements for conventional pharmaceutical advertising, which stipulate acknowledging a laundry list of potential side effects.

More recently, another approach in this arena of guerrilla spokesperson has been to enlist celebrities for "awareness" campaigns about public health issues that, either directly or indirectly, funnel customers into particular pharmaceutical fixes (here, again, a strategic recourse to education rather than a direct sell). For example, Rob Lowe "raising awareness" about febrile neutropenia while being on the payroll of Amgen, a company that stands to benefit from increased consumer anxiety about the condition.[50] Such unidentified commercial speech is similarly unregulated by the FDA; it, in effect, obfuscates—swallows, hides, or minimizes—the true aims of its persuasive intent. It seeks to govern choice without explicitly expressing preference: conducting conduct obliquely, "employing tactics" so that a given end unfolds freely rather than by unambiguous ordination.

Amy Doner, head of a PR firm specializing in this form of "Hollywood & Healthcare" guerrilla marketing, says that drug companies seized on these innovative approaches to message placement in the late 1990s when U.S. legislation deregulated direct-to-consumer advertising. The real goal here is less an awareness of the disease as much as an awareness of the *branded solution*—yet, in true guerrilla fashion, the audience is meant to serendipitously "happen upon" that conclusion by corporate communication strategized in a backdoor manner, for there is no direct and immediate call to action.

Digital insertion of product placement augurs another new horizon for innovative integration. Already rife in sports broadcasts, companies like Marathon Ventures and Princeton Video Image have developed technological capacities to "virtually" embed products and brands into already completed content. Jake Brenner, managing partner at Marathon, explains that this innovation was a way of recovering some post-hoc control over brand usage in the wake of the otherwise autonomous creative process: "[With product placement,] it's not like you're buying 30 seconds of your commercial and you get to do what you want. You're buying somebody's best effort, to the best of their ability, to represent your brand attributes in a positive light on the show."[51]

And for all of an advertiser's backstage machinations to win favorable space for their brand or product, its precise positioning is, ultimately, usually in the hands of the content provider (i.e., film or TV creative personnel). Virtual product placement, by way of digital insertion, can, however, guarantee brand appearance in a particular light because the creative act has already taken place. Moreover, as Brenner points out, it benefits the program owners and rights holders who can tap into a new revenue stream by repurposing, tailoring, and monetizing content space as needed: "Thus, that Coke can shown in the refrigerator of an original show can be bought by Pepsi for rerun syndication, and sold again to 7-Up for foreign markets."[52]

As for branded film, one of the most often-cited examples is BMW's 2001 short-film series, *The Hire*, which featured original plots, expensive production values, A-list creative talent, and a very noticeable automotive product as the real movie star. According to Anne Bologna, who worked as head of strategic planning at Fallon Minneapolis, the firm behind the campaign, the project was conceived as a response to a problem of unmanageable subjects: the fact that BMW's prospective consumer was thought to be increasingly unreachable through TV commercials. By opting for the online release of film vignettes through a dedicated micro-site rather than a broadcast channel, BMW not only addressed pragmatic financial challenges (i.e., the otherwise prohibitive cost of buying ten minutes of advertising space for each film) but also carved out a space for the expression of consumer agency in depending heavily on word-of-mouth and viral uptake:

> It's basically a short-film demo for the car and you were able to get away
> with things with the car that you could never get away with on television,
> because they wouldn't—the standards and practices and rules of what you

can and can't show in a commercial on television would never allow for all those car chases, because we'd have to be all like, "Don't try this at home." So the truth is that we really looked at the film as an engagement demonstration for the car. . . . One of the hallmarks of non-traditional media tends to be a little more often the consumer is choosing to engage with it as opposed to me just pushing it onto you. And the secret to engagement is not to hit people over the head with just your sales message because . . . it's just human nature—it's not how you want to engage with somebody.[53]

For Bologna and BMW, this engagement is predicated upon a proposition discovered as a way of trying to manage consumer subjects more subtly than conventional advertising. This becomes clearer as she delineates the so-called media logic they had invested in defining the consumer target thus:

It's sort of like the more evolved person: high income; high education; don't suffer fools well; don't want to be advertised to; like to make decisions for themselves. . . . When you're more discerning, it's: "Don't sell me. Like, let me make a decision for myself. I'm intelligent enough to do that." So the nature of the sell is counterintuitive: the less you try to sell, the more you're going to sell to this audience. . . . There's a confidence there that sets a very high bar for how they will allow themselves to be advertised to. Kind of like, "I'm too good for commercials."

The delicate, almost Zen balance of the cool sell articulated therein ("the less you try to sell, the more you're going to sell") underscores a kind of structured agency—a staged discovery—in these audiences' serendipitously encountering a casual marketing message amid content that's not predisposed to force a decision nor impinge on their sense of self-autonomy. It also, again, echoes the way in which marketer power might obfuscate its own objective to "conduct others conduct" by sublimating crude purpose—that vulgar "call to action" to *buy BMW*—for a higher brand calling; it attempts to govern consumer choice in a hands-off way without seeking to control it as blatantly as a 30-second spot might.

Interestingly, although the brand wholly underwrote the project, they reportedly had to abdicate "near-total creative control" to the talent involved, which meant tolerating elements that might otherwise make a client squirm—"like having a character bleed to death in the backseat of one of the vehicles."[54] Jim McDowell, BMW's vice president of marketing who oversaw both the product integration into the James Bond films of the late 1990s as well as the financing of *The Hire*, commented:

There were some things about [the Bond] scripts that made us quite uncomfortable, and through discussions back and forth we learned to deal with discomfort. Particularly the second James Bond film, which had a 7-series in the script that flew off the side of a parking garage and ended up in an Avis rental car showroom. We seriously had a debate about [this;] we didn't want to see our car falling seven stories and [get] destroyed. We began to learn that there were things that were more important about telling a good story than necessarily having it exactly the way that the car company wanted. . . . Did [*The Hire* directors] do things that we would have not done the same way if it had been ourselves? Yes. Would the work have been better if it had been changed the way we would have wanted it? No. Because we understood that boundary.[55]

The logic here is that brand management—by relenting the tight grip it has traditionally held over the advertised product context—believes it might have actually succeeded in spreading a more compelling message by outsourcing the content creation to those who could "authenticate" it by telling their own autonomous stories. (This will also prove especially true when it comes to word-of-mouth and consumer-generated efforts.) *The Hire* was, nonetheless, an exceedingly expensive endeavor at an estimated $15 million, but one that BMW justified as an emblematic model for success in the shift from "push" to "pull" media environments.[56] The attentive engagement to ten minutes of advertainment by a niche-targeted audience member who has *deliberately* downloaded the content (thereby expressing agency in ways *accommodated by* the program of governance) was determined to be worth higher cost per thousand (CPM) than a fleeting 30-second spot that the same person in a less differentiated TV audience might be avoiding or zapping anyway (thereby, expressing agency in ways *dissident to* the program of governance).[57] Considered the "gold-standard . . . [and] default king of long-form content" with more than 13 million views reported, *Advertising Age* named *The Hire* one of the ten best non-TV campaigns of the decade.[58]

Other agencies and brands have experimented with long-form content on television, in theaters, or online to greater and lesser success. To revive a Rainier beer label with a twentysomething demographic target, Cole & Weber United created 30-minute episodes of *Rainier Vision*, a *Wayne's World*–worthy late-night show (a slot more poised for "discovery" than prime time), which centered on the local Seattle brew in its plotlines. Such work, a page from the agency's old website claims, stems from a core principle they summarize in the phrase, "Let them say yes":

Advertising cannot force people to act. The difference between this old view and what we do is the difference between a screaming match and a conversation. Screaming works short-term, but what good is grabbing a few seconds of attention compared to someone experiencing your brand for hours at a time. Motivate people to tune into your TV show, link their blog to your viral film, replay your spot on their DVR, tear your ad out and tape it to their fridge. Now you're family.

*Let them say yes*: a tidy epigram for a marketing regime that strives to structure consumers' agency by luring them in through the mythology of a fully realized brand world (that "context for consumption"). It is also a useful metaphor for a communication environment where "push" media are increasingly giving way to newer (less "pushy") "pull" counterparts. Both represent paradigms of governance, but conventional advertising pressures by forcing obvious appeals while advertainment branding fosters by coordinating participation; the former presumes action upon a comparatively passive commercial subject, the latter anticipates action from an active one.

In order to orchestrate that discovery and participation, those agencies have to rethink their content creation in wider terms than the narrow spaces traditionally partitioned for advertising, which reconfigures the roles they have played. As Britt Peterson, director of business development for Cole & Weber, notes in an interview:

At the center of it, we are an ad agency, but I don't necessarily think we look like that anymore. Our real purpose is: how do we better connect brands and people in ways and in experiences that create longer-lasting relationships, allow more people to "say yes" to our clients' brands in a lot of different ways. . . . That's resulted in a lot more innovative thinking than just a standard—just to say a TV-spot is the answer or a print ad is the answer. . . . [With *Rainier Vision*], we said . . . let's actually develop a TV series that purposefully airs at one in the morning that is all about Rainier and use that as a kind of way to restart the cultural conversation around Rainier and bring more people into the brand. . . . We wrote each and every storyline. We produced every episode. And so, in that way, we almost became more of a TV production company than an ad agency.[59]

Similarly, in 2001, the sneaker company Vans financed *Dogtown and Z-Boyz*, a "legitimate and dynamic account" of skateboarding subculture, which also doubled as an extended commercial for the brand and won the (ironically titled) Independent Spirit Award for Best Documentary Feature.[60]

In 2007 Anheuser-Busch—historically, a prolific practitioner of the 30-second spot and an instrumental sponsor of the commercial structure of television that it underpins—mounted one of the most ambitious, albeit failed, attempts at branded entertainment to date, sinking an estimated $15 million into a project called Bud.TV, a kind of YouTube multichannel distribution network for original Budweiser-backed content.[61] And in 2008, working on behalf of the Sailor Jerry "lifestyle" brand of rum and apparel, Gyro Advertising, a company profiled in detail in chapter 3, spent $100,000 to produce a full-length documentary, replete with oral histories and interviews about the brand's titular character, which then aired at film festivals across the country. The chief executive of Gyro explicates the self-proclaimed "guerrilla" brand-building effort behind it: "[It's] basically an 80-minute ad for the brand. . . . It reinforces the authenticity of the figurehead behind the brand. And of course, when [people] see it and are interested, they'll Google the name. And then, boom, they *discover* our brand."[62] In an interview, he continues:

> It's not underhanded or devious, because it's a legitimate two-hour story about this person [Sailor Jerry] that has value for people so they don't feel like they've been conned into watching an ad. . . . People want stories and they want authenticity and they want things that are interesting. So, even with a client who hired us because of Sailor Jerry, what we do is spend all our time creating content and making the story richer, so that if people like the brand, they become part of the brand.[63]

Steven Grasse's project—crafting stories that engage audiences authentically rather than function like a con job advertisement from a figure of authority telling them to buy—articulates, once more, how advertainment tries to avoid the Taylorist discipline of salesmanship that nonetheless still must be its ultimate intent.

### Popular Music

If film and television once satisfied advertisers' desire to reach consumers through product placement in non-advertising content, the industry has been ravenously eyeing the promotional potential of other "new" spaces. For years, record companies and musicians have licensed songs for commercial use, re-igniting old debates about the tensions of art versus commerce.[64] For an industry whose financial model has been ravaged in the past decade—thanks to digitalization, peer-to-peer networks, and illegal sharing and downloading—an additional revenue source has become all the more enticing if not downright necessary. Yet that steady creep of song licensing has raised fears of commercialism "infiltrating the creative process."[65] Balasubramanian terms such a strategy "masked art": that is, "any work of art . . . that features branded products with deliberate (but usually not obvious) commercial intent."[66] It is worth noting that this commercial penetration seems equally an external effort by advertisers and public relations firms to embed brands in pop lyrics as it is an *internalization* of the brand as an operable "cultural resource" by artists that leads to a voluntary and thereby "organic" product placement.[67]

Hip-hop has played an outsized role in this trend—perhaps not surprising given its outsized role in pop music more generally in the past three decades—stretching back to "My Adidas," a mid-1980s smash by rap group Run-DMC. A gratuitous (in both senses of the word) paean to the sneaker, "My Adidas" features twenty-two mentions of the shoe; as legend has it, only *after* company representatives saw a performance of the track in concert did the group win a million-dollar contract licensing the song.[68] Since that time, the lyrical inclusion of trademarked names into pop music has pervaded to such a degree that Lucian James, a marketing consultant, created the "American Brandstand" list a decade ago: an index tallying all the brand mentions in *Billboard*'s top song charts each week.[69]

Few mainstream rap songs today, it seems, are complete without name-checking luxury goods ranging from Rolex, Mark Jacob, Bentley, Rémy Martin, and Versace, among countless others. On two occasions, actual sales impact has been alleged: When hip-hop cultivated an Escalade fetish, the average age of a Cadillac owner fell by a dozen years, and when Busta Rhymes and P. Diddy dropped "Pass the Courvoisier," sales for the premium liquor jumped by nearly 20 percent.[70] Some of this brand saturation is strategic: PQ Media estimates that the product placement market for pop songs represents $30 million of advertising spending.[71] Reported examples include McDonald's tendering financial bounty to any rap star that weaves the Big Mac into lyrics and Jay-Z inking a "poetry-for-pagers" deal with Motorola.[72] But a fair amount of brand saturation within hip-hop *does* seem voluntary. Over the course of an interview with James, he contextualizes this phenomenon:

A lot of brands [saw this development reflected in the "American Brandstand" tally and] thought, "This is sort of interesting," and how would they go about buying a place in the *Billboard* chart? What we pointed out is that it isn't that. If you appear in the *Billboard* chart, it's essentially a reward for strategy that's really hit a certain kind of cultural relevance. . . . Hip-hop talks about the here and now. [It] can be very reflective of what's going on in current culture. Chuck D from Public Enemy once described it as the "Black CNN." So it's got a kind of "currentness" that you don't have in rock music or pop music, which is much more often about eternal themes of love and happiness and sadness, so that's less good for brands. Hip-hop was very good for brands. . . . Using brands in lyrics is an incredibly poetic way to—it's a very concise way to express yourself. When 50 Cent is talking about taking a woman back to the Holiday Inn, you know exactly what the situation is about, so it's a very concise way of evoking a mood. . . . [Also], I guess, particular rappers over the past ten years have been incredibly entrepreneurial. It's pretty difficult to imagine that they weren't somewhat aware that there may be some payback in the form of mentioning certain things. It reached a point where rappers were kind of calling car company CEOs and saying, "Hey, look, I'll mention your car—send me a car." They were very aware of their power, so it became less innocent over time.[73]

Their "power" is, in fact, the ability to convert "cultural capital"—and more specifically "subcultural capital"—into "economic capital."[74] Moreover, James here unknowingly invokes what Arvidsson identifies as the source of a brand's power, both economically and culturally: its ability to foster "an *ethical surplus*—a social relation, a shared meaning, an emotional investment that was not there before."[75]

Brands have thus achieved, in hip-hop, what they have long sought more broadly: to function as a paralanguage of sorts. It is a sign that, if the brand *proposes* itself to youth consumers as a "tool," "building block," or "cultural resource" for the creation and circulation of meaning and identity—as "useful ingredients to produce the self as one chooses"—then these popular artists have accommodated that ideal and are relying upon it for their creative expression.[76]

Furthermore, those shepherding the brand-text—in its allegedly increasing "openness" and "flexibility" (see chap. 4)—seem eager to encourage rap stars' penchant for adapting or shortening the trademarked name. Thus, the formal "Cristal" is truncated to the more playful "Cris"; "Hennessey" goes by the apparently less corporate "Henny." Some brands have even started giving themselves nicknames in advance so as to conjure up a more chummy relationship with consumers: the luxury vodka brand Belvedere began deliberately calling itself "Belve," and Keystone Light is trying to get fans to refer to the beer as "Stones," believing that "a nickname can be a sign of affection and belonging, a proof of acceptance from those who bestow it."[77] These nicknames are meant to humanize what is an otherwise faceless corporation. One expert even proposes, "they remove part of the commercial character of the placement, and enable it to sound almost *natural* in the target audience's ears."[78] It is, then, a guerrilla play for street cred, a way of simulating an artist's (or a subcultural community's) appropriation of the brand, and a way of foregrounding organic agency rather than betraying the contrivance of power. And like other examples detailed here, this represents a mode of "casualizing" any exercise of authority.

As with film and television, brands are showing similar interest in playing a larger role in content creation—completing a transition from licensing recorded tracks to seeking product inclusion in the lyrics to financing the entire production from the start. The director of music at Grey Worldwide, a global marketing conglomerate, boasts, "We don't need the middleman, you don't need the labels. A lot of [artists] would prefer to associate themselves with a big corporation instead of a big label corporation."[79] Citing the music industry's financial woes, Scott Donaton notes: "You can't break new artists in the way that you used to be able to. . . . Brands have become the new A&R [artists and repertoire] department."[80]

This is not wholly unprecedented—airplay of licensed songs via commercials has long lured artists with the promise of promotion and exposure, and the hopes that TV advertising might serve as a "launching pad" to break unknown acts nationally.[81] The industrial reformulation here is that brands might increasingly incubate talent from the very start and distribute their music autonomously from traditional labels altogether. Recent examples abound: Bartle Bogle Hegarty, a London-based ad agency, starting up its "Leap" label for publishing unsigned musical talent; Euro RSCG acquiring a hot indie label; Mountain Dew and McCann Erickson imprinting their own (Green Label Sound and StayU Music, respectively); TBWA/Chiat/Day hosting new music showcases; Wrigley's financing songs by headlining acts that incorporate gum jingles; and London's Saatchi & Saatchi launching a "manufactured girl band" called Honeyshot that was open to hire for any brand that wished to employ them for covert, chorus-line shilling.[82]

Wrigley's campaign notably includes Chris Brown's Wrigley's-commissioned, top-ten smash, "Forever," which contains a chorus nod to a 1980s Doublemint jingle ("Double your pleasure / Double your fun"): "Label executives initially had qualms about releasing and promoting a song recorded at an advertiser's behest. 'But the song was so potent and strong. That overruled us maybe being a little bit hesitant.'"[83] As for Honeyshot, the first single, "Style, Attract, Play," by these commercial mercenaries was pulled from BBC Radio 1 airwaves when it emerged that the song was actually a "thinly disguised" commercial for Shockwaves hair gel. A radio spokesperson commented, "The track was presented to Radio 1 in the usual way, via a legitimate promotions company and we were not aware that it was a promotional tool for a hair product. As this is created by an advertising agency with the sole purpose of selling this product, and we do not play adverts, it is not something we would play again."[84]

Rob Stone, founder and CEO of Cornerstone, has been active in bridging this partnership of music and marketing. He won a Nike account for the campaign celebrating the twenty-fifth anniversary of the Air Force One sneaker by pitching the shoe company on an original track ("Classic") recorded for the occasion by hip-hop luminaries Kanye West, Nas, Rakim, and KRS-One. As with so many other examples considered here, Stone disavows the notion that the project (later nominated for a Grammy) was even "selling" something, in terms familiar for their "invisible governance" ethos:

> It wasn't about marketing to us, so *we almost had to market the sneaker without marketing it*. And celebrate the 25th anniversary in the same vein that Nike had grown Air Force One: organically. So we competed with some of the biggest agencies out there and I think what won it for us was the fact that we came with a very organic approach. We didn't talk about media buys and buying 30s or 60s or a creative campaign that way. We talked about creating something that would live in the culture, much like the Air Force One did. . . . I remember getting some blank stares [at the pitch], like, "What do you mean no time-buy?" . . . [Later in the interview, he clarifies this notion of "to market . . . without marketing":] The analogy would be that if you're going to court a certain female, your best approach might not be to just come out and say, "Hey, let's go to my bedroom," you know? That might work for some of them, but I think that you're probably going to turn 9 out of 10 if not 10 out of 10 women off. . . . You don't have to be so: "Buy our sneakers!" in the song. You can be a part of creating something and there's an appreciation—there's a very savvy audience out there and I think with appreciation comes respect and with respect comes sales.[85]

Mentioning the sneaker in lyrics was, Stone claims, entirely optional (though two of four artists involved did, apparently voluntarily, name-check the brand in their rhymes). The delicate calibration of credibility for a pop music track initiated by a brand indeed requires careful attention to maintaining that "organic" sheen lest it be judged as simply a crass ad jingle. To that end, Stone comments of a similar project for a Converse-backed pop track ("My Drive Thru"):

> When you look at what we did with Converse, there's no mention of the sneaker, but if you watch the video or read the reviews, it all points back to

Converse, where you can get the download. . . . So, yeah, there's a fine line and we push back very hard on the clients when they don't get it and we're not here to create a jingle. Like, the last thing that—the Nike song wouldn't have worked if we had tried to make it about Air Force One. You need to let the artist be the artist and you know what? When Nas says "Air Force Ones," it's a natural mention. He wanted to mention it.

Therein apparently lies the challenge for branded entertainment: to be involved in and unmistakably affiliated with the creative product without coming across as forcing itself into the limelight; to stage cultural content so as to appear to be "disinterested" and to "naturalize" the brand's positioning for the consumer to discover it serendipitously. Or as the *Wall Street Journal*, reporting on a branded webisode project by Unilever, frames that tightrope balancing act: "If the marketing theme is too discreet, customers can miss it altogether. If it's too overt, they might switch off."[86]

## *Publishing*

Perhaps no realm of promotional integration has drawn backlash quite so fervently as its incursion into letters—this despite the fact that product tie-ins can be traced as far back as 18th-century Japanese novelettes and Charles Dickens's *The Pickwick Papers* (whose title is taken from a carriage line company).[87] One estimate puts the value of the placement market in books at $27 million, with the most conspicuous—and controversial—recent appearance coming in Fay Weldon's 2001 novel, *The Bulgari Connection*.[88]

The Italian jeweler contracted Weldon—fittingly, a former Ogilvy & Mather copywriter before becoming a best-selling author—to provide a dozen brand mentions throughout the book for an undisclosed sum; the author ultimately delivered thirty-four, including title space, earning her a "firestorm of criticism" that variously derided the work as "*publitizing*," "*literatisement*," "*fictomercial*," and "*the billboarding of the novel*."[89] A chorus of critics castigated the partnership as "damaging to the credibility of all books and the integrity of all authors," and nearly two dozen dismayed literati wrote into book review editors requesting the work be treated as an advertisement rather than an artistic work.[90] Such deliberate bracketing would of course run contrary to spirit of "invisible governance," but it shows that as advertising redefines itself through guerrilla means, the contexts co-opted along the way have their own mores that cultural inhabitants there might jealously protect (like those censuring literati).

The project was the brainchild of Bulgari CEO Francesco Trapani, who explained his rationale: "When you take out an ad in a magazine, you only have a certain amount of space in which to speak. . . . You have to find a different way of communication."[91] The spatial rationale is instructive and echoes the quote from Scott Goodson that opened this chapter; it underpins a strategy that simultaneously seeks to overcome challenges in traditional advertising (ad-zapping, clutter, cynicism) while carving out a wider, more embedded, more "naturalized" expanse for the brand-text to reside than the tight confines that, say, a magazine ad affords.

Moreover, advertainment works *with* the agency of the consumer in being "chosen by" them rather than "chosen for" them (a subtle yet critical turnabout in governmental framing). In an interview, Nate Hahn, founder and president of StreetVirus, an alt-marketing agency, talks about branded content as a response to the frustrations of conventional "push" media. His firm created, for instance, an entire magazine, *Helio* (based on a Virgin Mobile brand extension of the same name), to reach that otherwise-unreachable hip youth demographic through cool sell understatement:

> They're not watching television commercials; they're certainly not reading the newspaper; they're online but I don't know how effective banner ads are online. So we wanted to get this magazine and *Helio*'s sort of ethos into people's hands. And I can put a magazine in a hip shop; I can put it in a salon; I can put it in a cool bar or a restaurant—I can't put a *Helio* brochure in there. And if you read one—it doesn't have a *Helio* ad in it. It's called *Helio*; it has their web address; the sections go along with how the phone works, the functionality—but it's sort of a subtle reminder that *Helio* is ingrained in this culture, whether it's art or fashion or technology. Then on our end, it's about access—I can't put a brochure in a bar and, if I did, no one would pick it up. So creating this content provides us with new ways to get that content in front of people, because a standard ad—I don't have any place to put it where this demographic is going to see it.[92]

Importantly, Hahn signals not only a frustration on the part of the marketer given contemporary media and (presumed) consumer psychology conditions but also the idea that, as Lawrence Wenner militaristically frames it, "programming has become the Trojan horse, with product placements playing the role of the armed warriors lodged inside."[93] The ease with which such innovations in product integration have been accommodated by creators of popular culture (who might otherwise be protective of the integrity of their workspace) needs to be weighed against the possibility that artists increasingly idealize *themselves* as brands. I gleaned this logic when the best-selling author Karin Slaughter was explaining her partnership with BMW in writing a short story ("Cold, Cold Heart") for the company's audio books site. BMW reportedly made but one request of authors for the series—that "each had to include a BMW car in their plotline, albeit subtly," of course, so as to ensure the cool sell.[94] In excerpts from an e-mail exchange, Slaughter explains why the transition from voluntary to contracted placement was an effortless fit for her:

> I have driven BMWs for the last twenty years, so I was already passionate about the brand. One of my series characters, Sara Linton, drives BMWs as well. I love the cars so much that sometimes when I am writing I have to hold myself back from talking about the performance or the soft leather. . . . Every book I've written has BMW in it. . . . BMW is all about innovation. It's an incredibly solid and reliable brand. *I think it melds well with my brand.* . . . We live in the real world. We have to put certain products in our stories. Coke, Band-Aids, Dumpsters—these are all brand names. I think when you find yourself contorted to force an element into a scene, you're walking down a slippery slope, but when it's organic, when you have the story and love the product, it can work out incredibly well.[95]

The author Bret Easton Ellis routinely skewers the vacuity buttressing this literary trope—defining human beings through brands—as in *American Psycho* where "characters are defined by the branded items they wear, use or otherwise endow themselves with, and the presence of one brand instead of another is often what defines a person."[96] (William Gibson also covers similar territory in *Pattern Recognition*.) Yet that "organicism" touted by Slaughter is a testimony to the "operability" (which prefigures interpretive agency) rather than "operationalization" (which simply dictates uses) of brands—a testament to BMW's presentation of itself as a "cultural resource" that she has, in fact, already used in her storytelling prior to getting paid for it outright. Moreover, this proposition of artist-as-brand is by no means a promotional self-conceit unique to Slaughter but rather reflects a cultural impulse common to other content creators.

Rap music, again, provides a conspicuous example of this consumption. From P. Diddy's "Sean John" and Jay-Z's "Rocawear" clothing lines to Jennifer Lopez's "Glow" perfumes and even Kimora Lee Simmons's "Baby Phat" medical scrubs and lab coats, few hip-hop moguls—as some of the most influential artists of our time—have *not* styled themselves as the synergistic center of a consumer goods constellation. (This trend was parodied, to very amusing effect, in *Tropic Thunder* by the fictitious rapper-turned-actor character, Alpa Chino, ever peddling his "Bust-A-Nut" candy bar and "Booty Sweat" energy drink brands.) When a producer of popular culture therefore considers herself as a trademark as much as an author in the first instance, the integration of other brands into her content is not a trying proposition. Indeed, it's more of a question of aligning the *right* brands as whether to partner up with corporations at all: "There was a very entrepreneurial spirit to everything in hip-hop. It was all about doing it yourself. Puff [Daddy] and I worked closely when I was Arista—he realized early on: 'I'm a business. This isn't just about music.' And that's kind of the beauty and the beast of hip-hop."[97]

Such a mercenary acknowledgement by a pop music artist is perhaps to be expected, but other cultural arenas have recoiled at the appearance of "masked art." Other than the *Bulgari* affair, one of the more prominent controversies of late came from the magazine business (whose brand and product placement market is worth an estimated $160 million) when the *New Yorker* sold out cover-to-cover advertising space to Target for an August 2005 issue.[98] The retailer not only plunked its peppermint logo in every nook and cranny of the ad well (via suspiciously "camouflaged" cartoons by *New Yorker* illustrators), but throughout previously sacred journalistic zones like the cover flap itself. As one critic observed, "For that week at least, Target was the *New Yorker* and the *New Yorker* was Target, their brands merged, their logos married, their content intertwined."[99] Though Target may not boast it (and the *New Yorker* certainly would be loathe to admit), the issue's advertising was *of course* intended to be indistinguishable from the editorial as part of the "camouflage strategy" that is the paradoxical essence of guerrilla marketing: a project of being "invisible" as advertising so as to actually be noticed by the audience.

Again, this porous leakage of the brand-as-text and extension of a promotional message across former borders that "corrupts" the church-state divide is nothing terribly new. Since the earliest mass advertising appeared in the 19th century, advertisers have hired journalists to write copy that blended in with the style and form of the nearby editorial content, and in trying to worm into news coverage, public relations has long been premised on its own "product placement" of sorts.[100] Yet more recently other forms of print media have been accommodating product integration in unexpected venues: DC Comics' *Rush City* finds the protagonist specifically behind the wheel of a Pontiac, and Marvel has sketched Nike logos into its *X-Men* panels; elementary school math textbooks by McGraw-Hill reportedly contain brand mentions like Gatorade and Nike; and a sportswriter for ESPN.com pioneered what might be considered journalism's first in-column product placement running feature called "The Miller Lite Great Call of the Week."[101] Moreover, countless brand incursions into "How To" consumption features populate the pages of *Maxim*, *Lucky*, and similarly advertorial periodicals. For an industry like publishing, which has, in some ways, been battered as hard as pop music by technological, economic, and cultural conditions, this retreat into "branded journalism" may indeed intensify if newspapers and magazines continue to struggle. Scott Donaton, as a prophet for and profiteer of *Madison & Vine*'s colonization of these new spaces, argues that such a shift in those business models would require an attendant alteration of values by content creators there:

> A lot of magazines when they hear "brand entertainment," that's what they think: You're trying to blur the line and confuse the audience and no doubt, some people who do that are. But I think there's a different play for magazines, which is just that for editors to kind of get past their egos and their kind of rules that have been in place for decades and understand that sometimes a brand has something as interesting to say to your audience as whatever you want to say. And I think as long as it's clear, again, that the content comes from a brand, then it shouldn't matter.[102]

Yet the issue of deception and disclosure—a tightrope walk of tension explored again and again throughout this book given guerrilla marketing's (often unstated) aspiration to advertise without seeming to advertise—is only part of the potential concern here. Lawrence Wenner reflects upon what he sees as problematic as innovations in product integration mushroom across the cultural landscape:

> When directors and screenwriters are pressured to "make room" for product placements in their script, even if they "theoretically" have veto power, the rights of the artist and the climate for creativity may have been impinged on. . . . The creative product had a key locus in the artist's imagination. A product placement infused arts necessarily filters cultural observations.[103]

The degree to which this is *concretely* being played out is one empirical area that "critical media industries" scholarship like this can continue to advance on the assumptions of political economy thought: to ascertain the degree to which, in fact, he who pays the piper really does call the tune (and just how precisely those notes are expected to be sung).[104] In the case of Slaughter's BMW-integrated short story, for instance, the car company apparently (and amusingly) had only one concern: "They were a bit nervous about the fact that the son in the story died in a car accident, but then they agreed that because it wasn't a BMW that everything was alright."[105]

*Video Games*

Finally, some brief consideration ought to be given to the recent surge of advergaming—a particularly relevant format of branded content because subject agency is quite literally programmed into its code (i.e., the "story" goes where the player chooses). Probably the most famous example of this approach is *America's Army*, online "militainment" that offers first-person shooter game-play while simultaneously indoctrinating military values and protocols.[106] In recent years, as the U.S. armed forces has strained to sustain personnel levels, they turned to gaming as a way to connect with millennials who were apparently "alienated or bored by traditional approaches to recruitment."[107] The first version of the game in 2002 cost $7.3 million to produce, and since then it has been downloaded more than 16 million times; in addition, about 20 percent of West Point cadets and 30 percent of new army recruits report playing it.[108] One market research firm, surveying high school and college students, found that 30 percent of respondents cited the game as a source of their pro-military views. Colonel Casey Wardynski, director of the army's Office of Economic and Manpower Analysis, was one of the creative visionaries behind the project. In an interview with *Fast Company*, he elucidates the cool-sell logic driving development: "The Army hadn't changed the way it communicated since George Washington. . . . *It was us telling you about things rather than you discovering them.*"[109]

This is a particularly emblematic shift given the image, as noted earlier, of the iconic Uncle Sam figure of yesteryear sternly enjoining a potentially recalcitrant recruit. (Uncle Sam may, indeed, be the perfect visual metaphor for the managerial, Taylorist discipline of the hot sell of old.) The army needed to structure "discovery" of its message—now a branded ethos wider than a simple, direct, finger-pointing Uncle Sam command—by embedding itself in a pop culture form that the army could itself author from the start. Research had shown that by the time young men and women were old enough to join the military, they had already formed impressions of the institution based mostly upon news coverage, feature films, and TV shows. Wardynski complained—not unlike Francesco Trapani's earlier lament—that traditional advertising did not allow for the kind of space needed to generate sufficient "ethical surplus."

Thus, the narrative of American military ideology is so extensively saturated into this form of branded content as to be invisible; the depth of engagement engineered by advergaming—"total submission" as one consultant claims—makes it "the sleeper of all non-traditional marketing approaches" and emblematic of branding's participatory regime.[110] The message of recruitment is, at once, everywhere and nowhere in *America's Army*. Thus, some critics fear that such advergaming is "more devious" for this reason, "because it relies upon the ambience created around an item rather than a frank exaltation of a product's virtue."[111] Indeed, the advertainment strategy is a project of governance through ambience; for marketers keen on trying to exercise power over subjects without being seen as the source of domineering authority—especially youth subjects presumed to be particularly resistant to discipline—this ambience (rather than overtness) is precisely the draw. In an interview, Wardynski points to the strategic benefits of interactivity inherent to the medium that allow for customization and, hence, an optimal architecture for engagement:

> We can sort of create an experience that learns on the fly and delivers information that's more relevant to the user about the Army. So, it's like, a tool for us to learn and a tool for them to learn at the same time. We don't learn about them in specific, because they play under a *nom de guerre*—so we don't know who the players are—but we learn in aggregate what parts of the Army they are interested in. . . .[112] And then we took it to the next step, which was: We built technologies in the game where we could deliver a message tailored to the user. . . . So they began to change their environment based on their interest so that they see more of what they're interested in and less of what they're not interested in. And now you're looking at . . . the polar opposite of TV advertising which is—TV is a dead end in my mind, because you're shouting at the world and very few people are actually interested in your message because your message is too generic and there might be something in your product they're interested in, but all you're able to say is, "We got a product over here." . . . I think [this] is a two-way street: Young folks learn about the Army, but the Army learns about what kind of Army we really have to be relevant to young folks and the Army begins to adapt itself to the expectations of young Americans in terms of what do they want to get out of the Army. . . . It's much different than traditional marketing where it's like shouting at everybody—with this one, you ought to be listening.

Thus, Wardynski frames TV advertising ("shouting at everybody") as overbearing and indiscriminate in its efforts to try to discipline subjects as opposed to the more ideal exercise of casual, nuanced, adaptive power that is soft, subtle, and sophisticated. For *America's Army*, as with the other examples of advertainment discussed here, the aim is to market without selling and show without telling.

### Advertising, Authorship, and Autonomy

For corporations seeking to co-author a richer, fuller "context for consumption" for themselves, the move from product placement to branded entertainment is rather natural. It not only achieves the goal of becoming "another form of expressive culture" on par with film, television, or music; it is a way of enacting a scheme of governance that offers even greater control over that "context" (i.e., the story) while still *appearing* to be autonomous from it.[113] Brands might thus usurp more and more of that middleman role traditionally played by media companies or advertising agencies and become, as one consultant told me, "publishing arms of themselves . . . [that can] create messages, promote messages, and direct messages of their own."[114]

As technological and economic upheavals destabilize the business model that both entertainment and advertising have relied upon for decades, the two industries may be forced to reconsider their roles in, rules for, and relationship to content. Donaton states this more starkly: "To ensure their mutual survival, these industries have to overcome distrust, often-divergent agendas, and creative conflicts and collaborate by forming alliances that benefit both."[115] In the past decade, major media-buying companies have invested aggressively in developing branded entertainment divisions.[116] No longer able to depend on the publishing apparatus that traditionally supported them, popular artists and entertainers—perhaps not unlike journalists—need a patron. Conversely, no longer able to depend on traditional advertising contexts to either get their message across or to tell a story sufficient to build brand equity, sponsors need a vessel.

A common lament about these advertainment trends tends to assume that creativity, once pure and autonomous, is now being hijacked and defiled by sponsorship interlopers. "Control," after all, sits at the heart of advertiser worry, yet curiously enough, the same might be said for consumer advocate critics and cultural aesthetes when they hear about product placement innovations, albeit for opposite reasons.[117] Advertisers fret about not having enough control over content; these critics fear they'll exert too much.[118] Indeed, Donaton notes that he has seen, among Hollywood creatives, what others describe as a "sea change" from product placement opportunities "already in the script" to product integration "becoming the script":[119]

> This is going to be a gross generalization, but if you go back five years ago, the view of most people on the Hollywood side was essentially: "Oh, so, wait a minute, this is going to be another funding source that we haven't tapped into and we might be able to now? That's awesome, write a check and stay out of my face. I'm the creative guy, right?" And, again, this is gross generalization, but two years ago, I think the feeling was, "Ok, listen, I understand that because you wrote the check, you need a seat at the table, but it's probably best if you just sit there quietly and don't say anything. We'll let you in the room, but don't talk." And now it's almost to the point that content creators are saying to brands: "Hey, if you don't like this ending, I'll write another ending"—to the point, where you almost have to say, sometimes, "Hold on." You know, "I need you to maintain some level of artistic integrity so that we know this thing has audience-value." Because there are brands that would be tempted to just kind of turn everything into much more of a sales message and I think everybody loses when that happens.[120]

Such is the aforementioned specter: the transformation of all content into advertising. Yet this critique of advertainment, I think, might mistakenly conflate the independence of 20th-century pop culture creators for the independence of a long-lost folk culture. Film studios, TV networks, and music labels have certainly been as meddlesome and commercially inclined as, say, BMW, Nike, and Bulgari could now become here. This is not to exonerate, much less celebrate, the guerrilla commercialization of these cultural spaces; it is simply to acknowledge that an artist needing to get paid has never been fully "free" in the creatively absolutist sense of the word. Perhaps a continuum of autonomy—from an idealized, unfettered producer of content on one end to an utter brand-slave or media corporation–slave on the other—is a better way of framing this; a continuum, whose extremes are likely never fully borne out in practice, rather than an either-or proposition of selling out versus staying true to one's vision, for such binaries seem less salient in our current era. Indeed, in a sense, the movement from product placement (i.e., characteristic of content that is more artist-initiated) to branded content (i.e., characteristic of content that is more brand-initiated) might well map onto such a continuum.

Oddly enough, too, the logic of invisible governance may actually mediate these supposedly polarized loyalties (i.e., art versus commerce): As client patrons like BMW found in according creative license with *The Hire* or when a company like Cristal or Hennessey allows rappers to truncate a corporate nickname, they're indulging appropriation and encouraging autonomy—in other words, abdicating control—so as to authenticate a "disinterested" appeal and casualize any semblance of the exertion of influence. This becomes ever more apparent in later chapters as the brand is rethought as more and more of an "open work"—and, moreover, an *operable* "open work," which in this case refers to the way the promotional interlocutor is granted agency to use the product as she wishes rather than come across as pop culture puppet to a backstage patron.

More important, still, the ongoing development of such advertainment may be a harbinger of how media industries are funded and managed. If many of the frustrations outlined in chapter 1—technology, clutter, and skepticism—have driven advertisers to explore the creative or editorial space of mass media as a site for locating promotional messages, the possibility of constructing a wider brand identity by filling out the content that they alone author there has enticed them to stick around. Rather than dictate an ad message and seem like they're imposing goods on the consumer as marketer disciplinarian, advertainment seeks to *suggest* a cultural context (in this case, storytelling) where no "call to action" visibly appears. Unlike the 30-spot, branded content casually governs its consumer target through ambience rather than articulation; the source of force is not the typical sponsor's voice of authority but the filmmaker or pop artist who isn't *telling* us what to do with the brand but is, rather, *showing* us what has been done with it. Persuasive force is, hence, diffused into the cultural ether surrounding the product. Rather than prescribing behavior dictates unambiguously, as a "hot sell" fiat in a conventional advertisement might, product placement and branded content slyly model a context for consumption to achieve those desired ends. Before turning to word-of-mouth marketing and consumer-generated advertising, the following chapter examines branding's chief nemesis—culture jamming—and shows how forms of alternative-outdoor guerrilla marketing have re-routed its resistance, co-opted cool, and simulated subversion.

# 3

## Street Spectacle and Subculture Jamming

Youth cultural styles may begin by issuing symbolic challenges, but
they must end by establishing new sets of conventions; by creating
new commodities, new industries, or rejuvenating old ones.
—Dick Hebdige[1]

As a rule, we get off more on the culture jamming aspect of what
we do for clients than the actual advertising aspects.
—Alex Bogusky, creative director and co-chairman of Crispin
Porter + Bogusky[2]

As branding has become a ubiquitous social force, it has run up against
political reservations and, at times, outright contestations. "Culture jamming" often serves as a banner for the ideology and diverse tactics of those
who would protest branding's incursion into everyday life and popular
culture. It is also culture jamming that, some believe, represents the social
movement most intellectually and expressively equipped to undermine the
ambitions of corporate advertising and whose subversive zeal is fueled by
much of the same brand management strategy that has been carving out
otherwise "disinterested" spaces (see chap. 2). And, yet, when Alex Bogusky
revealed the impulse animating Crispin Porter + Bogusky, his comment
bespoke a revitalized logic of co-optation that characterizes some of the
most celebrated guerrilla-marketing work of the past ten years—notable
given that his creative powerhouse won *Advertising Age*'s top "Agency of
the Decade" status, and Bogusky himself was named *Adweek*'s "creative
director of the decade."[3] Culture jamming may have set out to issue to
"symbolic challenges" that call into question the very premise behind the

corporate symbolism that so clutters contemporary environments, but it seems to have also partly succeeded in "rejuvenating" the industry that it was born to parody.

This chapter offers a study in the sociology of recuperation to understand how dissidence might be productive and, in fact, necessary to the work of this particular form of governance. Foucault articulates the function of resistance—and the locus of individual agency here—as such:

> At the very heart of the power relationship, and constantly provoking it, are the recalcitrance of the will and the intransigence of freedom. Rather than speaking of an essential antagonism, it would be better to speak of an "agonism"—of a relationship that is at the same time mutual incitement and struggle; less a face-to-face confrontation that paralyzes both sides than a permanent provocation.[4]

Advertising represents one such "power relationship" whose attempt to govern the consumer subject has to work with her freedom and, as necessary, finesse a "refusal to submit" that can take shape through an assortment of "counter-conducts."[5] These characterize the project of culture jamming—one whose self-conceit and often "clandestine" political action, whose anti-commercial "objectives and methods" "struggle against the processes implemented for conducting others" in the hopes of "an alternative to governmental direction in the form of another form of conduct" (i.e., not "buying" into consumer society).[6] As the expression of resistance, culture jamming's counter-conduct seeks to be "antagonistic" toward advertising as an institution of governance and intends to reclaim authenticity as an experience *external* to marketed culture. And, yet, contemporary advertising remains a receptive institution when it comes to symbolic impudence—particularly when "cool" is precisely what's for sale to youth consumers.

Thus, the "agonistic" interplay of branding and culture jamming might aptly be framed.[7] Governance of free subjects in the marketplace must allow for that "compromise equilibrium" that Gramsci identified—a practice in which power "has continually to be renewed, re-created, defended and modified" even as it is simultaneously "resisted, limited, altered, challenged by pressures not all its own."[8] One of the ways that governance channels that defiance is by posturing as defiance itself: guerrilla advertising, here, self-effacing its own power through an anti-establishment ethos and dissident aesthetics, which attempt to absolve any pretense of marketer authority. And for an industry always on the prowl for authenticity, given the perceived cynicism of millennials, that defiance represents a key source of credibility.

Even the trade press seems to recognize some of the imbricative parallels between these oppositional gestures and incorporated practices. In 2001 *Brandweek* interviewed the street artist Shepard Fairey, noting that his famed "Andre the Giant Has a Posse" viral sticker project is "arguably the longest-running guerrilla campaign, albeit not one devised for any actual campaign," and Fairey himself has capitalized on his own street art success to become an "alternative marketing whiz" for Pepsi, Sony, Ford, and Levi Strauss.[9] More recently, the magazine named Banksy, a prolific pseudonymous British street artist, its "Guerrilla Marketer of the Year."[10] One of my interviewees remarked, "A lot of guerrilla marketing techniques were nothing more than offspring of street art."[11] And, tellingly, Fairey boiled down for *Brandweek* how guerrilla marketing works in McLuhanian terms evocative of the spirit of the cool sell:

> A portion of the public is skeptical of big corporations and the typical big billboard or print ad approach. They're the tastemakers, the person probably 15–25 who is willing to take risks with fashion and art and music and everything having to do with popular culture that then ends up influencing everyone from 10–50, the mainstream. . . . [With guerrilla marketing], when someone sees it, they're curious and they ask someone else, and they're curious and everyone's talking about it. It's a whole effect of an image that has a certain charm, memorability, gist, pop, whatever, *that generates interest because it isn't explained.* With guerrilla marketing, *the medium is the message.*[12]

A word or two is in order, then, about what I mean by guerrilla marketing here (relative to advertainment, word-of-mouth, and consumer-generated formats). In fact, when guerrilla marketing is specifically discussed in the popular and trade press, it most often refers to the kinds of tactics analyzed here (although other approaches equally merit conceptual claim to the guerrilla label). According to one industry estimate, "alternative ambient advertising, which includes guerrilla, street teams and other non-traditional approaches," and which exist primarily in pursuit of youth demographics, has now grown to a market value of $550 million.[13] These street spectacles invent or appropriate outdoor settings and arrange theatrical tableaus in ways characteristic of the guerrilla approach: unpredictable, serendipitous, ambiguous, and, most of all, not circumscribed by the traditional boundaries of road signs and storefronts. As rebellious, even illicit promotional displays on behalf of a commercial product in that space, many require a surreptitious execution and thus telegraph a subversive undertone not far removed from the tactics of culture jammers and street artists who violate similar conventions or improvise with urban environments in order to cast their work. This provocative approach is meant to be a way of demonstrating distance from the image of a didactic, domineering marketer and, like advertainment (see chap. 2), communicating through an unconventional space in which that persuasive influence might come across more casually. It, too, might be thought of as ambient governance but of a more "street" variety, both in the sense of an out-of-home context and a connotative form of resistant identity imprinted on it.

## Contesting the Brand

In recent years, branding has emerged as an explicitly contested political terrain for leftist thinkers and social activists who view the practice as wasteful fetishism—not only in whitewashing environmental degradation and labor inequalities but equally in its pervasion of *mental* conditions (e.g., its presumptive arbitration of shared meaning; its aims to engineer social dependency; its replacement of a more "authentic" lived experience with a new set of commercially oriented, irrational obsessions). Perhaps none make this case more emblematically than Kalle Lasn and Naomi Klein, whose books have both precipitated and chronicled the rise of culture jamming—branding's most expressive ideological nemesis amid late capitalism.[14]

Lasn, the co-founder of *Adbusters* magazine, has been at the intellectual forefront of shaping the movement, which he places in lineage with Situationist *détournement*: that "perspective-jarring turnabout in your everyday life" that comes from "rerouting spectacular images, environments, ambiences and events to reverse or subvert their meaning, thus reclaiming them."[15] Led by Guy Debord, Situationism idealized independence from the "'spectacle' of modern life": "Everything human beings once experienced directly had been turned into a show put on by someone else. . . . Immediacy was gone. Now there was only 'mediacy'—life as mediated through other instruments, life as a media creation."[16] Increasingly, brands *themselves* seek to furnish that "mediacy" through cultural spaces of their own creation or annexation, and Lasn's call to arms therefore represents a reaction to what he sees as that "most prevalent and toxic of the mental pollutants"—advertising—as it oozes out from previous confinement in all the usual places (e.g., TV, print, etc.).[17] He thus advocates "invad[ing] enemy territory and [trying] to 'devalue the currency of the spectacle'" in his culture-jamming manifesto:

We will take on the archetypal mind polluters and beat them at their own game. We will uncool their billion-dollar brands with uncommercials on TV, subvertisements in magazines and anti-ads right next to theirs on the urban landscape. We will seize control of the roles and functions that corporations play in our lives and set new agendas in their industries. We will jam pop-culture marketers and bring their image factory to a sudden, shuddering halt. On the rubble of the old culture, we will build a new one with a non-commercial heart and soul.[18]

This approach owes a distant, metaphorical debt to Gramsci's thinking on cultural resistance; "adbusting" is, in effect, an attempt to recover "good sense" from "common sense." The latter represents a form of consciousness and conceptions of the world "superficially explicit or verbal, which [one] has inherited from the past and uncritically absorbed."[19] Common sense, as the site at which bourgeois ideology is constructed, "contribute[s] to people's subordination by making situations of inequality and oppression appear to them as *natural and unchangeable.*"[20] Lasn might argue that advertisers' daily challenge is to graft arbitrary product associations into our "common sense" (e.g., a brand logo signifying social status), so that consumer audiences mindlessly scramble for the baubles of capitalism. The culture-jamming project is, then, an endeavor to carve out that "good sense" in popular consciousness—that critically endowed awareness of those commercial machinations that people "already 'feel' but do not know'" (i.e., that scramble, which ad-busters posit, ultimately leaves one feeling empty and exploited).[21]

For these culture jammers—again borrowing Gramsci's terminology— this necessitates not a "war of movement" but rather a "war of position"; the former characterizing a "frontal assault on the state" (or, in this application, advertising) while the latter more usefully representing the need to contest, appropriate, and subvert the message of branding on the same terrain upon which it initially secures consent and derives its social power.[22] Although their actions are diffuse and decentralized—unique in texture, though united in philosophy under that banner of ideological refusal—one particular pioneering pamphlet presaged primary practices: "media hacking, information warfare, terror-art, and guerrilla semiotics," which includes "billboard bandits, pirate TV and radio broadcasters, [and] media hoaxers."[23]

For culture jammers, the shrewdest way to undermine and sabotage the machinery of contemporary marketing is by "peeling away the brand veneer" so as to expose the unseemly "backstage" machinations behind the glamour and artifice of the advertisement and to destabilize branding's claim on becoming some kind of "authentic" cultural resource.[24] This peeling away leads to the kind of iconic "subvertisements" for which *Adbusters* is probably best known: mocking Calvin Klein's emaciated archetype as dangerously deranged, by foregrounding the image of a bulimic model hunched over a toilet bowl (i.e., "Obsession"); subverting Marlboro's rugged and masculine ethos with comparatively flaccid white-collar workers sneaking a drag, addictively, outside their office. Such "semiotic Robin Hoodism" can also be executed at a street level, with jammers known to deface the billboards of prominent brands by re-contextualizing their hype, teasing out that ugly reality beneath the slick chicanery.[25] The PR theatrics of the Yes Men and the sonic artistry of Negativland equally fit within this tradition of "vandalism of mass media, the activist arm of our remix culture"—the former, a prank troupe impersonating the spokespeople of powerful organizations to espouse *reductio ad absurdum* pro-globalization rhetoric; the latter, an experimental music group specializing in sound collages that rework and undermine commercial jingles.[26]

Fundamental to these divergent expressions is a common project of reclaiming public and social space from corporations, divulging the real-world upshot behind advertising's fetishized values, and doing so through the kind of playful, parody-based "semiotic jujitsu" that is culture jamming's "stock in trade"—and that makes culture jamming an irreverent heir to Hebdige's punk *bricoleur* (his term for one who engages in the subversive appropriation of available materials).[27] It is, in sum, an endeavor toward awakening: a bid to snap the sleepwalk of shopping culture, this (to culture jammers) slumbering trance of consumerism, this consensual hallucination that ultimately contributes to brand equity's bottom line. Indeed, the more that marketers seek to shape conduct implicitly (and even invisibly), the more semiotic grist for the ad-buster's mill—for the more that advertising self-effaces its operation, the more that culture jamming seeks to bring those machinations to light.

If, however, advertising—and, for that matter, capitalism, a specter of broader ideological menace to jammers—has proven anything over the course of its history, it is that today's rebellion is tomorrow's mall fashion; what starts as controversial content ends up at Hot Topic. Thus, one scholar rightly remarks, "The assimilation of skepticism toward advertising not just in terms of [consumer culture's] *content* but in terms of its very *form*" means that "the rise of such alternative marketing techniques such as 'gonzo', word-of-mouth, viral, etc. . . . *also* make a claim to rebellious authenticity."[28] Put simply, culture jamming seems to offer guerrilla marketing not just a subversive message to annex but also a subversive *medium*.

Repairing the Rupture

> Many anti-marketing activist techniques were derived from advertising
> principles—Lasn, for example, used to work in advertising—just as many
> of the marketers . . . have organically adopted anti-marketing strategies
> into their marketing plans out of a genuine discomfort with traditional
> marketing. Those who work in advertising are most capable of subverting
> it, the conventional wisdom goes. Culture jamming has often been said to
> dismantle the master's house with the master's tools—*and then provide the
> master with blueprints for a better house and better tools.*[29]

Culture jamming might thus style itself as the "appropriation" of brand
identity for political subversion, but the guerrilla marketing I introduce here
seems to represent the *expropriation* of that political subversion for brand identity: the corporate feigning of an unsanctioned paradigm; a dominant culture's
incorporation of dissident practices and aesthetics; commerce appropriating
the resistant appropriation of commerce. Thomas Frank's *Conquest of Cool*
foreshadowed much of this in his account of how the 1960s business-thought
subsumed the anti-establishment stirrings of that era as bohemian cultural
style traversed from adversarial to hegemonic so as to "[replenish] . . . the various culture industries' depleted arsenal of cool."[30] What Frank excavated from
the 1960s, I probe from turn-of-the-millennium promotional thought, and
just as Frank documents how that era's advertising incorporated rule-breaking
content, I show how contemporary alternative outdoor advertising more and
more accommodates nonconformist *form.* To wit, Frank describes one creative
director's principles in a manner that prefigures the thinking behind guerrilla
marketing (and unknowingly echoes Guy Debord): "Creativity was defined as
an embrace of what he called the 'the unexpected,' a general contrariety that set
an ad off from the mass-cult bubble surrounding it. . . . '[Advertising] must be
interruptive, disquieting, challenging, surprising and unsettling.'"[31]
Whereas in the 1960s "the unexpected" meant innovations in substance—for example, the clean minimalism and witty self-deprecation of
Bill Bernbach's legendary Volkswagen "lemon" ad—today this might mean
innovations in the intermediary employed: guerrilla media that opts out
of conventional corridors like the 30-spot or the freeway billboard. Urban
youth-seeking advertisers who take these steps toward innovation seem to
believe that that "mass-cult bubble" has so fully inflated that "contrariety,"
much less eye-catching transgression, is difficult to achieve in traditional
media; that the spaces designated for commercial appeal have become

structurally deficient, their semiotic soil poisoned from years of overuse. Or, one managing director at a guerrilla firm complains, "A lot of advertising that happens today—whether it's billboards or TV or radio ad mentions like that—it's just a giant swirl of white buzz."[32]

Not surprisingly, then, fetishizing "the unexpected" is at the core of *both* culture jamming and guerrilla marketing. Some have already noticed marketers experimenting with guerrilla tactics that have "overtones of social movements created by the Situationists."[33] Just as *Adbusters* became an "underground hit with the young scions of the advertising industry," so, too, did Pabst Blue Ribbon's marketing manager think that *No Logo* contained "many good marketing ideas."[34] And, perhaps most amusingly, *Advertising Age* named Kalle Lasn one of the ten "most influential players in advertising in 2011," thanks to his viral stewardship of the Occupy Wall Street crusade.[35] There is surely some irony to be found in advertisers appropriating an appropriational movement; this models the fluidity with which "any hegemonic process must be especially alert and responsive to the alternatives and oppositions which threaten its dominance."[36] Such is the "dialectic" of resistance and appropriation in cultural production:

> The industry co-opts and denudes the resistance of any symbolic force, converting revolt into mere style. The sanitized symbols are then mass marketed back to the many followers who want to buy into the form of the resistance without committing to its subversive potential. . . . Much of what is taken to be subcultural resistance is manufactured by the consumer industry.[37]

Guerrilla marketing is particularly emblematic of such prefab resistance, not just in the content of the sales pitch but in the context of it (i.e., a rebellious delivery). For example, one agency CEO defines guerrilla marketing as "getting consumers seeing things that they aren't used to seeing, creating something that lives in the context of what they do but that is out of context with what they are used to."[38] This characterization bears uncanny resemblance to *détournement*, for the project romanticized by culture jammers—producing something "so unlike what surrounds it on the commercial-TV mindscape that it immediately grabs the attention of viewers"—is, of course, precisely the same scenario that *advertisers* idealize.[39] This is because (perhaps surprisingly, given their polarized aims) marketers, in fact, *share* with culture jammers a frustration with that "media-consumer trance"—this zombie-like repose within "mass-cult," that Lasn alleges—which is habituated by a steady flow of commercial messages.

Some reductive critical theory (e.g., the Frankfurt School's canonic texts) might maintain that advertisers, collectively, need this "trance" because it dulls the inertia of potential social resistance and displaces any notion of systemic change or participatory refusal (whether that be flipping off the TV or agitating to overthrow the foundations of capitalism). Yet singularly, for any given advertiser who wants to stand out amid clutter to alter the buying habits of the (supposedly) narcotized masses, the lethargy of this "trance" is an impediment and awakening the ideal. And whereas culture jammers pursue awakening to revive consumers from the overall "false consciousness" of branding—to activate some more authentic lived agency—advertisers pursue awakening to revive consumers from the "false consciousness" of their product competitors. Think different, for *Adbusters*, means questioning the imagery and symbolism grafted onto, say, personal computers, thus parodying the farcical notion that an operating system could somehow encompass and represent a person's identity. Think different, for Apple, means questioning the dominance of Microsoft's market share—parodying those who would choose to remain a "square" PC when they could be a "hip" Mac instead.

## The Resourcefulness of Resistance

Advertising has long sought after "breakthrough" work—creative copy that cuts through a cluttered communication context. But these guerrilla strategies seem to proffer solutions that *literally* break through the confines of traditional media placement—strategies like "brandalism, vandalism committed as an advertising campaign," and "graffadi, or graffiti that is advertising," that shatter the boundaries that once circumscribed outdoor commercial spaces and utilize fonts known more for their opaque dissidence.[40]

Gyro Advertising, a midsized Philadelphia agency (now known as Quaker City Mercantile) that offers buzz, guerrilla, and viral among other services, explicitly diagrammed a "Life Cycle of Hipness" on its website—a step-by-step model of the movement of trends from fringe to mainstream, from oppositional to incorporated, from the street to the mall. Gyro postures as archaeologist of authenticity, conquistador of cool—unafraid to articulate aloud its coldly calculating ideology of co-optation:

Like the pop-cultural equivalent of a rapacious 1980s leveraged buy-out firm, Gyro Worldwide bought up cultural capital on the cheap from the second "alternative" network, broke this content down into its most fundamental cultural tropes, then retailed it to the first "mainstream" network at a significant premium. But where buy-out firms consumed, digested and finally excreted the rudiments of capital into the global marketplace, the maw of Gyro chewed up and reconfigured something far more elemental and powerful—the essence of culture itself.[41]

Gyro is by no means the first firm to cannibalize culture so crudely; it merely offers a conveniently recent, lucid, and unsentimental expression of such scheming. The rapacious foraging for symbolic material by commercial prospectors makes genuine subcultural statements—most especially oppositional ones—intrinsically ephemeral, because they are so enticing and useful as emblems of dissent, particularly for a governmental force, marketers, trying to relate to cynical millennial consumers without the usual trappings of authority. This speaks to the "resourcefulness" of resistance in a dual sense: There is, of course, resourcefulness exhibited in the creative appropriation of commercial products and texts from the mainstream so as to express unorthodox, even oppositional meanings (à la Hebdige's punk *bricoleur*). But resistance is also "resourceful" for power, because it is a display of agency that can then be co-opted by the very structure that it acts out against. Because this signification of resistant values can be recuperated into the commercial establishment, however dexterous the defiance, absorption is ultimately somewhat inevitable. Yet that "cool" is also, in some ways, dead on arrival—a quality with an inexorable half-life—because by the time it shows up in Madison Avenue practices, its semiotic status is precariously accessible, further demonstrating that compromise equilibrium between seller and marketplace.

This is also why "authenticity" is such a preoccupation in advertising and, even more so, guerrilla advertising: Authenticity accounts for the experience of the active subject whose (consumer) conduct does not feel conducted as such by marketers. "Authenticity represents the struggle between the will of the individual and the determinism of the commodity structure," Robert Goldman and Stephen Papson declare. "[And] the dilemma of authenticity in the age of the consumer sign is that no sooner does something become recognized as a mark of authenticity than it gets appropriated and transformed into a popular sign."[42] Authenticity therefore derives its power from its apparent distance from mainstream mediation.

For advertisers, then, the key is to know how and where to locate this "authenticity" as it is continually produced, which makes it a project of cultural reconnaissance. "Cool hunting" represents one recent solution to this: a form of industrial epistemology whereby inquisitive agencies and colluding consumers deliver on-the-ground intelligence about social patterns back to brand headquarters.[43] Sputnik, for example, emerged in the 1990s as one cool consulting firm with this capacity; the founders' textbook subtitle (*How Today's Alternative Youth Cultures Are Creating Tomorrow's Mainstream Markets*) neatly summarizes the philosophy behind this work.[44] Cool hunting is, moreover, representative of the excavation of "subcultural capital" and that assimilation of cultural practices from "authentic" to "phoney," "hip" to "mainstream," and "underground" to "the media."[45] The willfulness of this original expression of individuality, as located in "cool" creativity, is precisely what makes it valuable to the exercise of power and authority: It exudes an ineffable vibe of "bottom-up" authenticity, which can be pressed into service from the "top-down" commercially.

Advertisers have cycled through (and continue to employ) a host of knowledge-gathering techniques meant to paint a picture of the demographic imagined and targeted in a particular campaign. As "the counterculture movement legitimated the 'street' as a source of authenticity, sexiness, and coolness," that kind of research has increasingly taken an ethnographic turn with participant-observers "hanging out with teens, and looking in their closets, lockers, and cupboards for clues to the values that would be most culturally relevant with consumers."[46] Urban Outfitters, for example, eschews questionnaires and focus groups altogether in favor of stalking city habitats in search of such style: "We're not after people's statements. We're after their actions," the company president reveals.[47] In an interview, Adam Salacuse, a graffiti artist-turned-advertising CEO, tries to express how street culture impresses itself upon the cool hunter's task:

A lot of it goes back to my childhood, growing up in New York City—specifically, Brooklyn in the 1980s—in which I found most if not all advertising irrelevant. I don't think a billboard even to this day has inspired me to do anything, let alone buy a car or wear a certain type of clothes. It was pretty much the street culture—meaning friends, the local DJ shops, skate shops, the power of, you know, the cool kids on the block—whether that be a basketball player, a skater, or what have you. You know, you kind of learned about it through the streets. . . . The streets are where it's at, if you ask ALT TERRAIN [his agency], and what we try to do is try to figure out a way of integrating brands and the streets in street culture in a way that people might actually like it.[48]

The "street" enables subculture to speak back to commercial creators on its own terms. Such a shift stitches together two earlier themes: First, it carries forward the ambitions charted in chapter 2 whereby the brand conceives of itself as an operable "cultural resource" rather than simply a blueprinted, "trademarked shorthand" for product attributes or status connotations. (In other words, to construct itself as a true "cultural resource," a brand needs a form of knowledge that is more field-oriented than focus-grouped—from those who are already modeling that cultural resourcefulness in the "streets".) Second, as a testament to that flexibility that is hegemony's "compromise equilibrium," it presages the increasingly negotiated nature of brand meaning that seems a byproduct of the two-way flow of communication (epitomized by buzz agency and consumer-generated advertising).

Note here that the word "urban" has long served as code word for race among marketers.[49] One youth market research CEO, writing in *Brand Channel*, specifically traces "urban" marketing's roots to hip-hop, a subculture originally born of economic inequality and socio-cultural frustration among a minority underclass in New York and Los Angeles.[50] To say, then, that guerrilla marketing is simply "the offspring of street art," guerrilla marketing of this sort is also, in effect, the co-opted offspring of black culture; one might further contextualize the discourse around and fetishizing of the "street" (and even "cool" itself) as equally racialized. After all, graffiti—that alternative outdoor advertising par excellence—was initially the avant-garde expression of underprivileged young people of color; when the "coolhunters" for Nike and Tommy Hilfiger, for example, as depicted in Malcolm Gladwell's reporting, go looking for insight into edgy taste, they show up first in African American neighborhoods. In some ways, this pattern might be traced as far back as Norman Mailer's sociological deconstruction of the "white negro"— those proto-hipster, "urban adventurers who drifted out at night looking for action with the black man's code," his slang, music, and clothing styles.[51] Indeed, Mailer posited a hip/square binary (wherein the source of "hip" was African American culture) that—in the former's bohemian rejection of the latter's bourgeois conformity—distantly echoes guerrilla advertising's danger-courting self-regard in contrast to traditional advertising's obedient orthodoxy. In pursuit of the "street," Gyro presents a tidy, eloquent summation of this mentality: "Hire cool. This isn't as easy as it sounds. It takes years to build your cool pipeline, beginning at the deep, dark pools of cool that form around last call at the seamiest dive bars and ending with barrels of cultural capital pumped out all over the world."[52]

A "cool pipeline" aptly encapsulates a trickle-up model of mainstreaming, where the brand appropriates the productivity of subcultural capital, the ethical surplus that is style. Andrew Loos, head of Attack!, an agency that specializes in guerrilla and nontraditional promotions, spells this out in more detail when he explains how his firm seeks to "geo-target" cool based upon a "TVH" (trends, venues, and happenings) database they maintain. What

Loos envisions might be termed a kind of "panopticon of cool" as the data-gathering ideal—a model of surveillance in which nothing ever escapes the gaze of the marketplace and no meaning autonomously survives the "giant harvesting machine" that is advertising, because advertisers are in constant competition to chart and reap the latest frontier of fads for youth brands.[53]

This is, at once, an adherence to and a departure from Foucault's conceptualization of the panopticon.[54] Surveying the historical trends in penal-reform thought and the techniques of discipline and supervision that emerged from them, Foucault highlights Jeremy Bentham's utilitarian prison design as a more general "formula" of power that "spread throughout the social body" by virtue of its capacity for inducing "a state of conscious and permanent visibility."[55] This panopticon represents an apparatus of surveillance that assures obedience through visibility—symbolizing techniques of "power/knowledge designed to observe, monitor, shape and control the behavior of individuals situated within a range of social and economic institutions."[56] As Foucault diagrams:

> Knowledge follows the advance of power, discovering new objects of knowledge over all the surfaces on which power is exercised. . . . In order to be exercised, this power had to be given the instrument of permanent, exhaustive, omnipresent surveillance, capable of making all visible, as long as it could itself remain invisible. It had to be like a faceless gaze that transformed the whole social body into a field of perception: thousands of eyes posted everywhere, mobile attentions ever on the alert, a long, hierarchized network.[57]

On one hand, these "thousands of eyes posted" seems to aptly evoke the pursuit of omniscience through market research techniques like Loos's "TVH" cool-hunting database. It is through this "permanent, exhaustive, omnipresent" monitoring and generation of "cool" knowledge that power (here understood as youth consumer governance) might flow. Yet unlike Foucault's schematic, resistant practices are here actually *desired* and co-opted for their resourcefulness rather than confronted and disciplined as a *regrettable* breach of conformity. Moreover, the "normalization" that results from bringing them to light (i.e., mainstreaming them) immediately degrades their value as authentic and hastens the need for *more* panoptic monitoring (because agency and authenticity will have moved on to the next hip thing). Whereas dissidence is an *impediment* to governance and the source of anxiety in Foucault's panopticon, dissidence is the *solution* for governance and the source of value in the "panopticon of cool"; if obedience is sought in the former, *disobedience* is actually sought in the latter. In an interview, Loos elaborates on the constant, frantic challenges of maintaining that omniscience:

One of the areas of intelligence that we provide is that trends and attitudes and consumer-types change every mile across the country we feel, especially in places like Los Angeles where it changes every *half-mile*! But you've got—what's cool, where's cool, what's not cool is changing very rapidly. . . . Our database . . . it's a moving target. It's never stopped in nine years, because I think one of the lamest things you can do . . . is to sit in a cubicle somewhere in the country and try to guess what is cool in a major market that you're not a part of or don't have someone there. . . . It's like, man, you've got to get back in there and do [this] stuff. . . . Get in and do some like hard-core raw intelligence using people who know—and that's another thing, is that a lot of people claim to know, but very few actually do know where the relevant spots are. . . . It [takes] nonstop, around-the-clock recruiting and program management and communication with our army of people across the country. . . . We also lean on them for local intelligence, and we also rely on people at college campuses that allow us to get into student housing places, into dorms, into Greek Life. . . . The one thing that we do is we admit to not knowing everything in-house. We are students of trends in research, and we will commit to always being that; we will never admit to any client that we've got it all figured out. Which is why we rely on kids in your demographic to get us information and to reward them with things that will actually speak to them to give us that information. . . . Again, [that's] a moving target.[58]

His point here about the innate ephemerality of cool (and the intractable agency of that youth consumer) has been echoed by Gladwell as a kind of riddle of epistemology ("the act of discovering cool causes cool to take flight")—a burdensome paradox of Sisyphean surveillance that guarantees an advertiser's work is never done (and also offers a self-serving justification when billing clients). This requires delicacy with which hipness has to be plumbed for fear of it taking flight in response to hegemonic incorporation: "The better cool hunters become at bringing the mainstream close to the cutting edge, the more elusive the cutting edge becomes."[59]

It is not coincidence, moreover, that the cool sell, one of the central theories threaded throughout this analysis, shares a term with that of the "cool" hunt. Being low-definition and therefore demanding higher engagement of the audience, cool *media*, in the McLuhanian sense, is conceptually analogous to the reserved exclusivity of cool *content*. By definition, cool culture *would* eschew loud, accessible, *broad*-cast channels in favor of what some describe as more authentic, higher integrity, micro-media. For corporations seeking to bestow that "subcultural capital" and an underground ethos upon their products, "mass" channels squander this potential through the inherently "mainstream" connotation that accompanies diffuse and therefore indiscriminate popularization.

## A Work of Advertising in the Age of Media Reproduction

"If 50 million people watch something, how cool can it be?" quips Scott Johnson, the executive creative director of Tribal DDB Worldwide.[60] His question suggests that a kind of "credibility hierarchy" of media might impact the way that brand management operates. By credibility hierarchy, I am arguing, in the tradition of Harold Innis, that each medium has a bias on a scale of inherent "qualitative core values" from obvious to hidden, from mass to niche, and from hot to cool.[61] Jonathan Bond and Richard Kirshenbaum, advertising executives who wrote a trade text advocating the use of covert methods to reach cynical consumers, plot out a scale of just this sort—with media ranging from "the most uncommercial, believable, under-the-radar" vehicles (e.g., word of mouth, public relations, product placement, guerrilla media, Internet) to "the most artificial, contrived, and highly commercial" forms (e.g., magazines, radio, newspapers, outdoor advertising, television).[62] What they propose seems to essentially be an inversely proportional relationship between gross rating points (a standard measure of audience size within the advertising industry) and message integrity, whereby ubiquity comes at a cost of authenticity and vice versa; or, put in Sarah Thornton's terms, the more mass mediated, the less subcultural capital preserved.[63]

A representative example from the under-the-radar end of the scale would be something like ALT TERRAIN's pull-tab wild posting ads for New Balance sneakers that function as a sort of micro-media: hand-written, photocopied flyers with a set of informational strips that could be torn off at bottom—the kind of posting common to college campus bulletin boards. Adam Salacuse, the company president, delineates the media logic informing the campaign in an instructive manner:

> We liked those more because they look noncommercial. And people are—the more commercial something looks, the more slick it is, the less relevant—the more someone thinks, "It's not going to be relevant to me. It's a mass produced item." And, so, if it's homespun, homemade-looking, and creative, sometimes it'll attract more attention than a really highly designed piece in a magazine—an ad in a magazine, let's say. So they went

with black-and-white—it looked like it was Xeroxed copies with photos pasted on that. . . . We went out to a bunch of different markets and we saw—we'd repost every week and we'd go back and we'd see all the tabs gone from the posters, which is a very good sign that people are picking them up. It's almost, like, as good as a click on a banner—you can't get any better than that. Actually, we think it is better, because when you interact with media, it makes a huge, huge difference. I'm not a brain scientist, but, again, when you smell it, touch it, pull a little tab off a poster, it gets registered somewhere different in your mind. . . . That is where you end up having the most impact.[64]

Thus, according to Salacuse, this deliberately noncommercial format was intended to simulate something homespun, rather than the conventional advertising context that a major corporation like New Balance could otherwise afford by throwing up a huge, expensive billboard. By not seeming to be mass produced, it was presumed to communicate a more authentic message on behalf of the brand—one that, the agency hoped, youth audiences were less likely to filter out because homemade and noncommercial seeks to govern consumer choice more casually than mass produced. One might call this the "aura" of an advertisement in Walter Benjamin's terms: the sense that an authentic, unique message has been handcrafted and distributed to a limited group of receivers (thus maintaining that insider taste-knowledge that, Thornton notes, supplies subcultural capital).[65]

I hear a refrain similar to that of Salacuse in the words of Joe Earley, the executive vice president of marketing and communications for Fox, who discussed a summer teaser-campaign for *House, M.D.* meant to stir up confusion and intrigue, and that relied, initially, on an ambiguous symbol similar to the caduceus (but featuring House's signature cane rather than the traditional staff), which was spray-painted onto city streets around the country. The "graffadi" icon prompted a flurry of online buzz (that was, of course, monitored) as to its meaning and origin: Was it promoting a new film? Was it propaganda for that summer's federal health care reform initiative? Earley notes that, in keeping with the essence of the cool sell, less (information) begat more (participation):

If we'd gone right from the beginning and put that [*House*] logo on [the caduceus], you know, maybe *House* fans would have immediately stayed tuned and watched [the campaign unfold], but I think by *not* putting it on there, this way we were able to probably entice and entertain some people who would have otherwise just moved on from it.

This again bespeaks a rationality of governance that obfuscates intentions—driving engagement through restraint by withholding the "conduct of conduct" being sought after. Earley further explains how using graffiti as an advertising medium is not only fiscally sound but, he believes, retains those connotations of integrity:

> The cost of hiring a street crew to chalk—spray chalk on a sidewalk is, you know, fractional compared to what you would have to spend on outdoor [billboards]. It is also more credible. . . . When you see it up on the big board, you immediately know that it's a big company that has enough money that is buying that ad. When you see it [sprayed] on the side of a building, on a window, on the ground—it can cut through your media filter. We're bombarded by so many images every day, consumers are absolutely sophisticated enough to know when something is a marketing message and it's much easier to tune it out. When you're walking and you're hit with something on the ground that wouldn't normally be there, that doesn't look slick, that isn't that highly produced, and that's a little more raw—it can get past that filter.[66]

It can, in short, fake that credibility. The dissidence intrinsic to the aesthetic—most graffiti and street art is, after all, *illegal*—is presumed to purport toward a purity of purpose even if, in this case, the brand message was hardly "underground" but rather teasing the upcoming season of a top-rated network show (not exactly a beacon of cultural exclusivity). Yet integrity is not just a product of deploying a renegade channel; equally important, it seems, is *uniqueness* when it comes to the outdoor guerrilla medium. The publishing apparatus of mass media, by virtue of its mechanized, standardized (historically Fordist) output, cannot churn out that credibility so convincingly, not off its "culture industry" conveyer belt production line. Guerrilla marketing, on the other hand, being more nimble, offers outdoor alternatives to brands striving for subcultural capital. These small-scale micro-media icons like stickers, flyers, and graffiti tags—as opposed to mass-produced billboards—serve the self-effacement of the cool sell: being hand-created, seeming noncommercial and therefore addressing consumer conduct more subtly and serendipitously.

## Establishing the Anti-establishment

One of the blue chips in the economy of youth cool over the past decade has been Pabst Blue Ribbon, whose brand renaissance serves as a compelling case study in how the anti-establishment might be simulated. After years of decline, the down-market beer label suddenly, rather inexplicably, achieved sales growth a decade ago when it was embraced by otherwise ad-weary skater and punk twenty-something tribes in hipster havens nationwide from Brooklyn to Portland: "the kinds of people who can't be fooled by marketing and in fact tend to detest it."[67] This turnabout occurred despite the fact that PBR had long focused most of its marketing on a very different, blue-collar, fifty-something demographic target.

Alex Wipperfurth, head of a brand consultancy, was brought in to demystify and harness the newfound enthusiasm from the otherwise "anti-corporate" and "anti-brand communities" who, unexpectedly, now acted like "America's most logo-loyal consumers."[68] Brushing up on the work of Naomi Klein, Thomas Frank, and Kalle Lasn, Wipperfurth concluded that, in an era inundated with semiotic clutter and goods overwrought with deliberately marketed (read: governmentally forced) meanings, PBR's distinct *lack* of an image (read: power disinterested) provided consumer-fans with a kind of brand tabula rasa from which they could ply their own meanings. Again, take note here of the presumed efficacy of governance-without-machination: a brand that had set out to manage a particular population wound up appealing to a very different one because it wasn't *trying* to manage it. In the case of PBR, guerrilla strategy was mobilized to precipitate participation from those thought to be deeply averse to traditional, didactic, Taylorist advertising petitions:

> Within [today's] complicated cultural context, the no-frills aesthetic of PBR fits right in. It's perfect for the self-mocking, "anti-brow" attitude of critics and rebels intent on expressing disdain for mass commercialism. . . . This reading [of Klein, Frank, Lasn, etc.] proved a great platform to identify PBR's battle cry as the "anti-badge" brand. It helped us understand some of the fundamental trends and drives of the skeptical, anti-corporate modern-day consumer. And, most important, it enabled us to create some marketing rules so that Pabst Brewing would remain the brand of choice for an audience that uses "consumption as protest." . . . People consume PBR as an expression of their attitudes against mass marketing and hype.[69]

The irony of annexing Lasn's ideology—fundamentally, *a protest of consumption*—to chart new and more clever ways of stimulating "consumption as protest" should not be lost here, nor should the program of governing *through* resistance and working with the elitist discrimination within underground subcultures that disdain anything mainstream. Had PBR consciously sought after this psychographic, the brand would have more than likely repelled them; recall the cool sell balance Anne Bologna articulated in chapter 2: "the less you try to sell, the more you're going to sell." In a lucky twist of history, then, PBR stumbled upon the utility in a brand obfuscating—backgrounding—its actual intentions within a field of disinterested cultural output. Or, as Cole & Weber earlier encapsulated it, arranging for a way to "*let them say yes*":

> Pabst was careful never to force the brand on to a market. For instance, when sponsoring bike messenger races, it would refrain from hanging banners all over the place and it made sure that competing beer brands were served. This counterintuitive move allowed the various subcultures to *choose PBR rather than having the brand chosen for them.*[70]

The logic of this power relationship ("Discover! You May!" rather than "Learn! You Must!") once more underpins the policy strategy of what some call "bottom-up branding" that is thought necessary "to establish street credibility" with a generation of young people.[71] Rather than trying to *compel* a demographic that is assumed to be otherwise resistant to invocations (consumer governance by force), the brand *seduces* participation by stage-managing impartiality—playing down its sponsorship role and serving competing beers at events (consumer governance through freedom).

Wipperfurth coined the term "brand hijack" to explain PBR's unlikely success. The phrase is tellingly evocative of that staged discovery—that furnishing of a space for agency that is so vital to engagement-oriented marketing today: "Brand hijacking is about *allowing* consumers (and other stakeholders) to shape brand meaning and endorse the brand to others. . . . [It is] the consumer's act of commandeering a brand from the marketing professionals and driving its evolution."[72] To orchestrate a successful brand hijack, the marketer must temper a cautious cascade of media exposure: from early, delicate, patient seeding in credible (even, as needed, illicit) teaser venues to establish integrity through to the eventual mainstream and mass market blowout.

If the process of discovery needs to *feel* unforced to (that is, "chosen by") the targeted demographic, the staging and coordination of that consumer agency ("chosen for") perhaps makes this form of advertising more sophisticated and challenging than ever. Or, as Richard Kirshenbaum, co-author of *Under the Radar*, pithily puts it, "It takes a lot of work to get accidentally discovered by the right people in the right way at the right time."[73] Yet this brand hijack is not only predicated on a simulated revelation, it must also be agile enough to accommodate unforeseen audience appropriations: "If your brand is hijacked, the consumers may take your product or service in unexpected directions: They may choose to reinterpret how the brand fits into their lives . . . or use the brand for social commentary. Learn to trust them."[74]

The American Legacy Foundation's "Truth" anti-smoking campaign represents another telling case study. One can find in the work of Truth a project to conceal the "call to action" portion of the marketing message beneath seemingly objective content (as part of that larger imperative to market without selling and show without telling) and, moreover, to frame such content rebelliously in opposition to the dominant commercial imagery emanating from Big Tobacco (not unlike *Adbusters'* politics and approach). In an interview, Eric Asche, the senior vice president of marketing, describes the intransigent millennial subject who represents the center of focus for Truth:

> An "at-risk" teen or "open to smoking" teen is generally at risk in some other areas as well. There's sort of this parallel of activity of pushing the boundaries of risky behavior . . . testing the boundaries on a lot of fronts. . . . A teen that is a little bit more rebellious . . . [He later adds] You're talking about the most skeptical, the most cynical—probably the hardest group that we could get to. But they are at the same time, the most at risk. So how we effectively engage with that consumer is a very delicate dance, for lack of a better term.[75]

"Delicate dance" actually represents the perfect visual metaphor for the approach to governance being deconstructed here, for it is one that attempts to exercise power over active and, in this case, outright resistant subjects by choreographing a graceful give-and-take that never betrays overstepping their agency (while still seeking to lead their conduct). Courting that at-risk teen and trying to compete with a tobacco industry that supposedly spends more each day than Truth does in a whole year—"we literally have the slingshot against the Goliath," Asche claims—the public service crusade uses prank activism that seeks to "subvertise" against smoking ads in a way that's deeply reflective of guerrilla marketing and, for that matter, culture jamming: "Unlike Nancy Reagan's 'Just say no' campaign that was, by most accounts, a dismal failure in the 1980s, Truth invites young people to assume a subversive posture that is far more active than just impotently saying no to tobacco."[76]

And so rather than overtly instructing kids not to smoke (a disciplinarily clunky "hot sell" in terms of obvious behavioral administration that the former First Lady tried and failed), Truth advertising "trains young people to practice their own brand of Situationism, by confiscating a small space from commercial advertising and using it as a site for rhetorical invention."[77] Asche further elucidates the governmental logic behind the encoding of this campaign; he is worth quoting in full for what he reveals about how this strategy thinks through—and tries to disguise—its own position of authority when relating to millennials:

> We may want to tell the consumer in the language, "Don't smoke. Do not smoke." But if we literally package the message in that way and tell the consumer not to smoke, that's going to be falling on deaf ears. In many cases, it may perpetuate them and cause them *to* smoke, because it's something *we* want to tell them versus speaking to the consumer in their own language. . . . How do we actually communicate with them in a way that's productive, not counterproductive? . . . In many cases, smoking is a way to take control and define who you are, and it's a very powerful tool that teens still use today as a means of self-expression. Most public health officials would look at that and say, "Let's tell teens not to do it. Let's show them the harms and tell them not to do it." Well, teens are filled with "dos" and "don'ts" and rules, and what they're really looking for, in many cases, is a way to take the information and make their own decisions. So what we did was really—instead of fighting against the rebellious nature of the teen . . . our goal has been to work—it's almost like a judo approach—where we work with the momentum. Teens are going to rebel; teens are going to self-express; and tobacco has traditionally been a very powerful way for them to do that. So how do we move with that momentum in a positive way? And the way that we've done that is shine a light on the activities of the [tobacco] industry, and our hope early on was that when teens actually see that as they think that they're making this independent choice to smoke cigarettes and it's a tool for self-expression—that they are actually falling into the trap of a well-concocted industry plan.[78]

Several key themes reemerge here. First, Asche reveals a reverse-psychology appeal at the core of that delicate dance of governance—a challenge that is particularly acute to guiding the conduct of an age cohort constantly confronted with overbearing discipline (those dos and don'ts and rules that structure the teen experience) and is therefore thought to be allergic to it. Thus, Truth obfuscates its own intent (trying to cultivate "good sense," à la Gramsci) by attacking cigarette smoking as an act of false agency—unmasking its "common sense" as a gesture of pseudo-resistance, prefigured by Big Tobacco, rather than being an authentic and autonomous expression of individuality (as Big Tobacco would purport it to be). Second, for Truth, this also means striking that "disinterested" pose of persuasive self-effacement by simply providing information rather than pushing a message, as befitting the PR-recourse to education echoed in the comments of creative personnel behind *The Hire* and *America's Army*. Finally, Asche cites judo tactics (so clearly reminiscent of Lasn's jujitsu), which work to harness that rebellion and shine a light "backstage" so as to expose and disrupt the slick veneer of tobacco's pop culture image.

"As soon as we position ourselves as the all-knowing, all-being public health official, we are dead in the water with teens," Asche adds. "In the early days, we talked about a sort of guerilla feel and the idea being that Truth was . . . and is this subversive counterculture. . . . We don't want to be "The Man," for lack of a better term." These days, few advertisers aiming for engagement would either. "The Man" (in the authority sense of the phrase) sought to discipline through the aggressive force of direct messages and interruptive mass media; "the man" (in the colloquially "cool" sense of the phrase) solicits by staging discovery, engineering participation, and naturalizing persuasion such that it hardly feels like persuasion at all.

Selling Cool

Advertising is, fundamentally, a constant sell: not just in the communication produced on behalf of companies for their products, but in the communication produced on behalf of agencies for *their* products. In other words, agencies are simultaneously pitching clients on messages, audiences, and *themselves*; it is for this reason that Katherine Sender reminds advertising industry researchers to treat these texts "as invested, if in different ways and with different ends in mind."[79] The self-styling of guerrilla agencies should, therefore, not be taken at face value, because the edgy, subversive angle often pitched through these methods must appear consonant with those same firms' self-conceit.

For example, Wieden + Kennedy, a Portland-based creative firm that gained national renown for their Nike work, projected such an image to clients during its rise to prominence in the late 1980s: an "in-house atmosphere [of] 'T-shirts and jeans, long hair and insouciance, the meeting-was-supposed-to-start-an-hour-ago-where-are-they'" attitude meant very consciously to stand "in sharp contrast to the 1950s ad man, the man in the gray flannel suit."[80] To pitch in this rebellious style is to project an air of authority about the group the advertiser is claiming knowledge of; it is a way of "acting" like the youth target, which is particularly useful in the event that the target's rebellious disposition needs to be harnessed through a campaign program.

Gyro—and, more specifically, its head Steven Grasse—also presents a rich portrait of this cocksure contrivance. In an interview with *Adweek*, Grasse boasts, "Our clients work with us because they buy into the Gyro cult thing. They drink the Kool-Aid. . . . It's like a party you feel cool that you were invited to. We make our clients feel like they're one of us."[81] This is a strategic institutional disposition, cultivated to corroborate Gyro's credentials and also designed for contrast with those competing "gray flannel" suitor squares. The advertising "pitch" is then, in a sense, not contained in the campaign peddled but in fact spills over into the account manager's pose struck beside it. To that end, a photo caption in their company history reads: "Gyro's black pirate flag waves over Walnut Street, announcing the day of punk rock reckoning to Philadelphia's white-shoe, tea-and-crumpet advertising world."[82] Later in the book, the firm brags:

> Much like the style of their work, Gyro's pitch methods were intended to shock even the most jaded of executives and involved tactics that frequently offended the fearful and the uptight. . . . "We would do anything to get a piece of your business. . . . Anything. We'd fax you a phony ransom note, leaving a flaming bag of shit on your doorstep. Send you nutty junk from our basement. We'd keep coming until you either said, "Okay, we give up, we'll give you something," or, "Don't you ever call this fucking office again."[83]

The impudent style of Gyro's pitch meshes with the self-professed content of it: "use humor and/or offensive content to secure the target's attention."[84] This is true whether the "target" is a client or an audience the client is hoping to reach. To be certain, this could clearly not work with all clients and all audiences (one would expect, say, a life insurance company to be less amused by the antics), but Gyro can take this license because their partners have included, over the years, Converse, Hot Topic, Mountain Dew, MTV, Puma, and Urban Outfitters—corporations, in other words, hoping to stake out the same edgy space so as to win over the hearts, minds, and wallets of a particular youth demographic. Similarly, the tagline for Andrew Loos's guerrilla firm ("Your agent on the inside") works as a "double-sell":

> It means something different—it's to our clients and our [buzz agent] contractors. To our clients, it means we are the people who know where the cool is; we know how to engage your demographic, and we know how to speak to them. In a world where people are being bombarded by traditional media, we know where your consumer is working and playing and shopping. . . . And then, "your agent on the inside" with

our talent means: We're the company out there finding the coolest agencies, finding the best brands, finding the best programs—if you register with us, you're going to have the inside track to the coolest promotional opportunities in the country.[85]

The slogan is, in short, a statement of knowledge-power; a testament to their task of poaching from the underground. It is meant to draw attention to the firm's "pipeline" (to borrow Gyro's term) of subcultural capital, to substantiate their status as arbiter of cool flows. The image sells the methods, but, conversely, the methods also confirm the image. Again, some of this kind of guerrilla marketing stands on wobbly legal footing—so the "bad boy" posture (as one interviewee put it) is not only a calculated scheme for cultivating cool but also a product of the fact that such tactics could, indeed, get one arrested. Adam Salacuse of ALT TERRAIN adds that the subversive feel also derives from its flouting of industry convention—that is, the fact that most other advertisers have to *pay* for their media space:

> Everyone else is paying for a traditional billboard spot and you're going, putting something below it or on it or whatever. So it is subversive to the other paid media. . . . It gives campaigns that edge. That—for people to stand up and take notice and say, "Oh, that wasn't there yesterday," or, "Is that supposed to be there or not?" and you're pushing the limits. . . . People just tend to ignore things that they saw there the week or month before, so if you—no matter how creative the billboard—it has to be a damn creative billboard to get someone to say, "Hey, take a look at that." But if you put up a static-cling poster somewhere on the streets and you realize that wasn't there yesterday on your way to work, it's like, "Oh— what is that here? Is that a real sticker? What is that?" So it is that element of—you could call it subversive media, guerrilla media, whatever you want to call it.[86]

Andrew Loos notes that while many guerrilla and street tactics are not legal per se, they're tolerated "the more you can sort of add to a cityscape and the more it's not sort of overt branding."[87] Thus, the cool sell is apparently a way of dodging vandalism fines—and, by contrast, the larger the logo, the hotter the sell, and the more likely its illegal placement will draw fire. But a subtle approach—presumed to confer subcultural status anyhow—stands a better chance of being overlooked by disapproving authorities and being noticed by urban hipsterati. This, of course, does not always happen. As Sam Ewen acknowledges, "We've had our fair share of people arrested, a lot of citations given. We've done a lot of college guerrilla marketing where you end up getting thrown off campus and are asked to never come back."[88]

## Corporate Street Art and Branded Flash Mobs

Sam Ewen should know these risks better than any other guerrilla marketer. As CEO of Interference, he heads up the firm responsible for the most notorious incident in recent memory.[89] When the agency launched its *Aqua Teen Hunger Force* street art campaign on behalf of the Cartoon Network in January 2007, it whipped up such a frenzy that some advertising executives called it "the largest ruckus they had ever seen from a guerrilla marketing stunt."[90] The incident offers a window into how advertisers deploy ostensibly transgressive formats while, in actuality, safely corporatizing outdoor aesthetics that had once served as a site of subcultural dissidence.

In pursuit of the millennial demographic that the show targets, Interference hired performance artists to place hundreds of flashing electronic light boards across major American cities. Fans recognized the light boards' otherwise undefined image to be that of an *Aqua Teen* character (posed, naturally, with middle-finger extended), but when officials in Boston mistook the covert "street art" advertisement for potential terrorist explosives and shuttered main thoroughfares for bomb squad investigation, the agency and network were forced to pay $2 million in fines. Adding insult—or ingenuity—to injury, the performance artists arrested for the stunt held a "mock news conference" outside their courtroom and opined, Dadaistically, on the evolution of men's hairstyles. (One can read this, too, as an effort to avoid the appearance of being an advertising campaign at all costs.) Video available from the website of an artist arrested shows his crew planting, in the dead of night, the glowing Lite-Brite icons—not unlike something Banksy, the esteemed street artist, might fashion—almost like Easter eggs hidden among the corners of the Boston cityscape.[91] As one of the "most cost-effective campaigns of all-time," it upstaged the "world's biggest ad showcase," the Super Bowl, sucking up the promotional media oxygen for forty-eight hours during that annual week of hoopla.[92]

Moreover, by contributing ambiguous iconography to the streetscape, like *Aqua Teen* campaign did, the disciplinary message ("Watch this show") was cloaked in content less blatantly forceful and more (seemingly) disinterested; it raised a vague visual question rather than issue an exclamatory literal declaration. Robert Goldman and Stephen Papson write of a similar phenomenon emerging in TV advertising by the late 1980s: "Where advertisers once sought to maximize the transparency of their framework, they now try to jar viewers into interpretive quandaries as a way of keeping them engaged in ads"; such tinkering is "designed to deny the existence of pre-digested meanings and create a hunt for meaning."[93]

In the wake of the *Aqua Teen* incident, a censuring *Boston Globe* editorial observed, "Such marketing is an odd descendent of guerrilla theater, the outrageous performances that were staged in the 1960s to freak out the Man. But the cartoon ad stunt did not shake the foundations of capitalist society."[94] The *Globe* is correct in noting the *détournement* lineage here; the exercise of techniques such as these show that countercultural fonts, like street art and graffiti, can be conscripted by those who would author a commercial message. And whereas the guerrilla theater of the Situationist movement—the *Aqua Teen* stunt's aesthetic ancestry—might have attempted to "shake the foundations" of capitalism with a "perspective-jarring turnabout," advertising such as this actually endeavors to fortify those foundations by engaging disenchanted consumers to watch and spend more.

Interference's campaign on behalf of Le Tigre, an apparel company, offers another instructive example. For this, Interference created nondestructive static cling stickers featuring the brand's tiger logo and disseminated them to staff, who placed them on *other* advertisements and billboards in urban settings (not unlike the "billboard banditry" of culture jammers described earlier). A booklet handed out to field staff during the training offered tips for furtive implementation like, "Are there people directly around me? If so, move."[95] Ewen charts the "media logic" he employed to try to fulfill his marching orders from brand headquarters ("to stay as irreverent as possible"):

Just by using these tigers, we could make everyone in every advertisement that we see, basically be wearing Le Tigre. . . . We didn't have a lot of money really, and we wanted to brand a lot of different stuff. We had an icon which I think worked in our favor in the sense that—and I think this is part of the guerrilla nature of it—for people who are maybe going to get pissed off at it, they wouldn't really. It wasn't like we were putting the brand name on there—we were strictly using an icon. *You actually had to work to find out who did it.* But for the people who knew, it had a very tongue-in-cheek feel—you know, there's someone on the side of a movie poster and now suddenly they're wearing Le Tigre. . . . We can put these things anywhere; we can do it overnight; no one needs to see it. . . . We were sort of creating this *underground* opportunity for people to notice it. You know—we didn't champion it; we just wanted to put it out there and see what happened.[96]

The cagey execution evokes that which a graffiti writer must also abide by; the creation of a riddle, not unlike the *House, M.D.* caduceus, "you actually had to work to [figure] out," rather than an overt, hot sell, "official" appeal (explicitly "champion[ing] it" as a Super Bowl ad might) shows a proclivity for bottom-up mystery (obliging agency) rather than top-down proclamation (presupposing passivity). Moreover, Interference's use of existing commercial materials (the advertisements they defaced) to refashion a message of their own seems to echo Dick Hebdige's *bricolage* exemplar—albeit Interference's "theft and transformation . . . appropriating a range of commodities [i.e., existing ads] by placing them in symbolic environments which served to erase or subvert their original straight meanings" was done not to advance the cause of resistant subculture but rather in the service of further commodification.[97] That is, whereas the Billboard Liberation Front, a culture jamming outfit, sabotages outdoor advertising with an anti-corporate attitude, Interference was here enlisted *by* a corporation to sabotage its competitors in much the same way. For the second half of the campaign, Interference wielded a stencil of the tiger logo, but rather than spray-painting it directly onto streets, the agency used a special industrial cleaning substance to spray *clean* the grime and graffiti on previously defaced sidewalks and buildings around the stencil such that only the *logo* remained—formed out of extant filth there. And here is an almost perfect metaphor of Madison Avenue's co-optation of the "street": Hegemonic forces scrub clean the resistant ideal of graffiti but retain and expropriate just enough of it to extend a commercial message.

In a similar act of "pre-emptive *bricolage*," a billboard campaign for Neon endeavored to build "signs of cultural resistance" into its own ads by graffiti-tagging them *in advance*—a "wink-wink" simulated contestation of the ad; an effort to "recode" the meaning as part of the initial coding.[98] More recently, a senior manager for youth and urban communications at Nissan also reportedly commissioned preemptory tagging as part of his guerrilla marketing push. He defends the approach in terms by now familiar: "It's about discovery, letting people discover you, rather than [you] yelling at them."[99]

Street stunts showcase much of the same subversive simulation but add in a dash of surprising live performance. Marketers here treat the banal procession of everyday life as a blank canvas upon which a commercial message might be sketched with hired bodies, creating in the spirit of *détournement*, that "perspective-jarring turnabout in your everyday life" through unexpected spectacle. One noteworthy campaign in this regard arrived in January 2009, when T-Mobile organized hundreds of performers dressed as normal commuters to descend upon London's Liverpool Street station and break out in an elaborately coordinated—though seemingly spontaneous—dance medley. As one of the more famous branded flash mobs to date, the stunt was captured and uploaded to YouTube and, within two years, had garnered more than 21 million online views—making it a bona fide "viral" phenomenon at a moment when advertisers are increasingly venerating that as a metric for success.

In recent years, such flash mobs have grown thanks to social networking contagion; in their organic or authentic form, they refer to a mass of otherwise anonymous strangers converging "spontaneously" upon a designated time in a public place to perform or engage in something quirky or rebellious without warning or explanation (like pillow fights, naked bike rides, "silent" disco dances, or, in some instances, senseless mayhem). A kind of performance art—and not without overtones of political demonstration, yet deliberately opaque in pinning down precisely what it is that participants are agitating for—they are meant to jar the perspectives of passersby with their silly, absurdist character. Improv Everywhere, a culture jamming troupe, has played a key role in developing flash mobs, as part of a larger "prankster movement" meant to "jolt strangers out of their routines, shake up the monotony of urban life and create mildly awkward moments that play well on YouTube."[100] Given those aims of disorientation and awakening—and noting the ideological proximity to Situationism—it should come as little surprise that marketers also find them an appealing alternative to break through a traditional media environment cluttered with advertising competition.

In the case of T-Mobile's flash mob, Gareth Ellis, Saatchi & Saatchi's UK-based planner on the account, explains that the execution centered on an organizing idea: "Life is for sharing." Over the course of an interview, Ellis reaffirms the idea that the brand should represent a "cultural resource"—an operable tool presented to a target of governance presumed resistant to anything that resembles overt discipline:

> Suddenly people were starting to share with strangers. Sharing has become open-ended, and there were new types of sharing and flash mob is one manifestation of that. . . . This gave us a role in the culture. And basically our role as a brand is to encourage people to come together, to get close together, to collaborate more and to be part of this "we" movement—you know this movement from "me" to "we" seems to be a profound kind of cultural shift that was going on. . . . Our view is that if you make an idea incredibly interesting and compelling, people will remember who came up with the idea. You don't need to rely upon obvious visual signifiers or cues to do that. So I think you treat people—you treat customers as being very, very sophisticated and I think they are very sophisticated now. . . . I think

you—not demean, but you actually do people a disservice if you make clumsy advertising because what you're saying is: "We don't think you're sophisticated enough to get this."[101]

For a telecommunications company, this "sharing" makes "cents," of course, as an organizing idea, because "sharing" is the crux of their revenue model: The more "sharing" that happens, the more profit that T-Mobile sees (especially in the event of data overages). Ellis also acknowledges a debt of influence to Improv Everywhere, principally as a visual reference to explain the project idea in their pitch to T-Mobile. Furthermore, he mentions that, in that pitch, Saatchi had to convince T-Mobile *not* to outfit all the participants in branded garb, in what would have been a "hot sell" strategy error, quite obviously impairing their ability to blend in and stage a surprising spectacle that invited attention rather than annoyed passersby. The brand that chooses guerrilla marketing as a strategy is choosing to resist coming straight out and "dominating" the demographic target with an unavoidable ad message and instead seeks to craft a way of governing through freedom: "letting" visitors to Liverpool Street station (or YouTube) "say yes" to viral collusion.

Other campaigns have toyed with this kind of performance art advertising. For example, to mark the twenty-fifth anniversary re-release of Michael Jackson's *Thriller* album, Sony BMG choreographed paid performers to "randomly" break out in the distinctive music video dance in European public venues like subway cars and city squares (with fingers crossed for eventual YouTube viral replication, of course). A vice president for international marketing explained to the *New York Times* the cool sell logic: "It's really guerrilla marketing. . . . You go in, do your thing and leave as fast as you can. There was never any intention to hand out leaflets and say '*Thriller* is coming out again.' It's just bringing '*Thriller*' back in the minds of people, but without the hard sell." This is, once again, advertising without seeming like advertising—consumer governance without force—and the "do your thing and leave as fast as you can" modus operandi is precisely the same conditions that a subversive street artist has to operate within. Moreover, this particular *Thriller-détournement* built upon a (noncommercial) culture jam stunt known as the "zombie walk." Even Charlie Todd, founder of Improv Everywhere, sold out a prankster stunt (the "freeze mob," whereby a mass of people stay frozen in place in a public site) to Taco Bell as part of a viral marketing push and he's begun accepting "corporate sponsorship" for his subversive exploits: "If I work on a corporate thing, there's going to be a certain percentage of my fan base who thinks it's evil. . . . It's been a very difficult thing for me to figure out."[102]

Agency, Authenticity, and Assimilation

Culture jamming seems to fantasize that through superficial subversion—
not in a disparaging sense but literally at the level of surface contestation—
dissenters might lodge a contrarian counterpoint to consumer culture. Yet
oppositional ideologies—expressed not only through but also *as* aesthetic—
can be emptied out and altered to accommodate safe and commodified ends.
Such was the mechanism intrinsic to Gramsci's theoretical blueprint for
hegemony: an unceasing incitement and struggle between force and resistance, co-optation and escape, with neither side ever establishing a totalizing,
permanent advantage over the other. Because these oppositional gestures
can be subsumed as incorporated practices (and vice versa), authenticity—
the expression of individuality amid and against the determinism of branded
commodities—is constantly dying and being reborn again. Cool, much like
capitalism itself, is "an order of endless flux and change," and because "the
act of discovering [it] causes [it] to take flight," it is also a fickle resource—a
"commodity" that must be increasingly tracked with a panoptic insatiabil-
ity.[103] Yet for culture jammers who view their practices through a true political lens, to homologize the aesthetics of this resistance (e.g., graffiti) is to
"sell" them out.

This ideological back-and-forth, played out across urban surfaces, succinctly captures the complex strategy of action and reaction between culture
jamming and guerrilla marketing: the former ever scavenging for new forms
and expressions to be fashioned out of remix; the latter, hot on the heels
of the former, "selling out" the supposed integrity of the new postmodern
medium forged—and then the cycle repeating itself once again. The notion
that a resistant style could ever "hijack" (to borrow Wipperfurth's term) a
cultural space that cannot be subsequently recuperated by the marketplace
is pure illusion—a chimera of romantic longing for "aura" that has persisted
throughout the history of the industrial production of popular culture.[104]

Joseph Heath and Andrew Potter contextualize this longing as part of a
wider—and, in their estimation, misguided—propensity of "countercultural
rebellion" to see itself as a means of escape from consumer capitalism such
as that which Lasn advocates. Yet "rejecting the norms of 'mainstream' society . . . [has] become the new aspirational category," now available for sale in
the same marketplace that the culture jamming rebel fancies herself somehow autonomous from and antagonistic toward.[105] Cool, not conformity, they
argue, is what ideologically drives capitalism today (a proposition certainly
in evidence here), and that system has long accommodated purported ene-
mies in this regard because "advertising is more or less impotent in selling

cool" without gleaning "market signals" emerging from social margins.[106] Indeed, the central argument here—reflected in Heath and Potter's assertion that "advertising is less like brainwashing and more like seduction"—is that audience agency (and, more specifically in this chapter, resistance) is the crucible through which marketers have to negotiate their designs on power.[107]

However, the dichotomization proposed by those who resist branding— corporate on one hand, independent on the other—does not likely reflect the experience of most consumers in advanced Western economies. Rather than thinking through this in binary terms, a more fluid model—a "compromise equilibrium," for example—seems to better express that complicated interplay of mainstream and underground, commerce and authenticity, guerrilla marketing and culture jamming. The methods of *détournement* cannot be assumed to have an intrinsic ideological allegiance even if they were originally developed for specific political ends.

Flash mobs are a superb example of this interplay—developed initially not to protest war, poverty, or civil rights but (not unlike a *Seinfeld* episode perhaps) to be a kind of "show" about nothing, as Bill Wasik, a flash mob originator, himself readily acknowledges.[108] Similarly, Shepard Fairey's legendary "Andre the Giant" street art campaign was a phenomenological experiment in much the same fashion—apolitical simulacra, masturbatory virality for its own sake. What, therefore, could branded flash mobs even "sell out"? What integrity is really being compromised when an advertiser uses stickers like Fairey did? Gyro's Steven Grasse admits as much in recalling a campaign for Reactor blue jeans that pasted Reactor's models in other advertisers' motifs (e.g., borrowing the font and Mountain West iconography of Marlboro just as *Adbusters* does in its own subvertisements):

> I think it was probably being too dumb to know that's illegal to do what we were doing. But it was also a way of getting a small brand that didn't have a chance in hell, sort of—trying to get them mentioned. . . . I didn't think it was political—it was just really fucked up. And I think that—it's interesting, because the same tactics that anarchists use are the same tactics that I would use, but that's only because they're just tactics. It's just ways of getting the word out; they're not politicized. They're not saying something culturally if you put up a wall poster. It's just a form of communication.[109]

Corporate street art and branded flash mobs are not, then, the de-politicization of street spectacle as Kalle Lasn might decry; they are simply part of a larger, ongoing process of resistance being generated, harvested, and generated anew—in this case, resistance found in the shape of the letters of cultural expression rather than what they necessarily spell out. And if you do share Lasn's anxieties about social justice (e.g., environmental, labor, etc.), as I do, perhaps consumerism is not the optimal site at which the fate of political consciousness might reside.[110] After all, consumerism, Conrad Lodziak contends, is sold to audiences—both for commercial products and readers of cultural studies—as encouraging an "active, creative engagement in the pursuit of difference and individuality."[111] Yet all that talk of "freedom" (also much in evidence here) seems to ignore "a field of dependence by virtue of the alienation of labor."[112] To Lodziak, it is "freedom within unfreedom"—that is, freedom available to those who have gainful (much less meaningful) employment to participate in "the only game in town."[113] I hesitate to endorse that full and disdainful dismissal of "freedom," as Lodziak scare-quotes here, but I do concur that political focus on the consumption-side is but an afterthought if the distribution of wealth, on the production-side, continues to migrate to less equitable, more rarefied niches. The 1 percent are more "free," yes, but that does not make 99 percent "unfree" by extension. It might seem silly—as culture jammers (correctly) toil to point out—that brands have managed to cultivate the arbitrary associations they've achieved in our minds, but even if consumers no longer bought into those commercial myths, would ours suddenly become a more fair society in terms of meeting collective needs? Until we address economic injustice and properly politicize the opportunity to produce wealth (i.e., the need for good jobs), unmasking advertising's machinations toward a purposed "false consciousness" of consumption (based on those branding schemes) is not exactly a world-changing agenda.

The alternative outdoor advertising highlighted here has demonstrated how guerrilla marketers strategize the expression and experience of agency by working with, rather than against, the productivity of defiance. To seek to exert power over the most intransigent of subjects (Truth's "at-risk" teen or PBR's "anti-brand" bike messengers)—jaded youth subjects who cling fiercely to their own sense of autonomy, especially in the marketplace—the vestiges of power cannot be seen exerting any kind of deliberate, palpable influence lest they be turned away. Once again, the advertising cannot seem like advertising. What was the function of "disinterestedness" in chapter 2 is here executed through "antiestablishment" means. Having shown how brands fend off those disaffected consumers bent on rebelliously talking back *at* them, the next two chapters explore how—in that restless pursuit of orchestrating a regime of engagement—brands are getting deeply consensual consumers to talk *for* them with the rise of word-of-mouth and crowd-sourced advertising.

# 4

## Buzz Agency and the Regime of Dialogue

We now have a greater opportunity to move beyond transactions to relationships than ever before, but to do so requires that we strike the right balance between being in control and being in touch. Ironically, the more in control we are, the more out of touch we become. But the more that we're willing to let go, the more we're able to get in touch with consumers.
—A. G. Lafley, CEO of Proctor & Gamble[1]

It's not about, "I wanna be like Mike"—Michael Jordan. It's about, "[I wanna be] like Steve"—and Steve's the kid around the corner. Because they have a hell of a lot more credibility. And you can get 10,000 Steve's for the price of one Mike. . . . It's about getting someone who's authentic in my peer group that will endorse the product. And that's what "real life product placement" was about—it was about getting *real* people to use *real* products in *real* ways.
—Jonathan Ressler, CEO of Big Fat Inc.[2]

[Friends] are better at target marketing than any database.
—Steve Lynch, creative director of Digitas[3]

Amid abundant advertiser anxiety about conventional communication channels, a significant number have begun turning to the oldest medium of all: word of mouth. Since casual conversation with friends and family has long represented a trustworthy space, it tenders fertile and unspoiled territory for marketers who claim to be routinely rebuffed in their effort to break through traditional media fronts. In this chapter and the next, I demonstrate how commercial promotion is adapting to and working through practices of "the crowd," both online and off, in an attempt to embed structural objectives in pliable, autonomous, grassroots social flows: "[getting] in touch" (so as to exert more power) by, paradoxically, "[letting] go" (and exercising less control), as Proctor & Gamble's CEO puts it. Power is, in fact, foremost a project of *flexibility* here, and it is through that flexibility that power—the way in which conduct is conducted—can appear both democratic and authentic (or "*real*," as Jonathan Ressler ironically states).

Advertising has long venerated "authenticity" as an ethical ideal; zealous and conspicuous pursuit of it belies the true and polar opposite nature of the industry's project: contrivance.[4] It is for this reason that "brand evangelism," like other forms of guerrilla marketing, self-effaces any affect of disciplinary authority so as to blend in with that which is not typically contrived. Dave Balter, who founded what has become one of the nation's largest word-of-mouth companies, BzzAgent, characterizes his firm's approach in ways that bear a striking resemblance to Che Guevara's fluid, boundless, and unpredictable combat paradigm (see chap. 1):

> [Word-of-mouth marketing] is not scheduled. It doesn't "come on" at any exact time. You can't turn it on or turn it off. Sometimes it moves very fast. Sometimes it moves slowly. It's not contained in a single medium. It takes all kinds of forms. . . . *Word of mouth is often all but invisible.*[5]

Thus, not unlike guerrilla warfare flouting the conventional rules of military engagement, "[Word-of-mouth] differs from [traditional advertising] text precisely in its lack of boundaries: it exists in the everyday real world."[6] This requires a dynamic industrial "reinvention," in the words of Proctor & Gamble's CMO Jim Stengel: "What we really need is a mind-set shift that will make us relevant to today's consumers, a mind-set shift from 'telling and selling' to building relationships."[7] When the world's biggest corporate client talks up reformation in this way, recipients of its $11 billion in global advertising and media money surely take note.

Word-of-mouth marketing has, in fact, enjoyed one of the fastest growth rates of any marketing segment of late—from $300 million in spending in 2003 to $1.5 billion in 2008, and PQ Media expects that figure to double by 2013.[8] According to some estimates, more than 85 percent of the top 1,000 marketing firms now exercise some kind of word-of-mouth strategy to "penetrate the no-marketing zones people have erected around their lives."[9] A recent survey commissioned by a London-based agency noted a similarly "dramatic rise" in the use of buzz marketing campaigns by brands in Great Britain.[10] One CEO spins this growth as a "natural" progression, given larger social and technological trends:

The majority of our conversations are sponsored in some way—they're a means to an end and so, you know, I think this is the natural evolution of marketing. If you're saying that media is moving to the people, well, if people are now creating all the media, then, you know, *the people become the platform.*[11]

## How Buzz Agency "Works"

As one of the largest and perhaps best-known of all word-of-mouth advertising operations, BzzAgent offers a useful point of entry to detail, empirically, how it is that these buzz campaigns are executed. With more than a half-million volunteers in its stable by the close of the decade, BzzAgent had assembled a network of individuals who, simply put, try out free products, talk them up with friends, and report back to the company on that dialogue.[12] By the middle of last decade, the firm had raised $14 million in venture capital and was reportedly growing its revenue 350 percent annually.[13] A single campaign that utilizes 1,000 agents and runs for twelve weeks was said to cost a corporate client about $100,000 and delivered, on average, five to seven "interactions" per agent about the service or product.[14] Like others before me, I signed up for BzzAgent hoping to observe firsthand how the marketing network operates and manages intelligence in what is a flexible, interactive form of decentralized commercial engagement.[15] While I was not, regrettably, invited to participate in any "full immersion" campaigns (those in which the BzzAgent receives a free sample of the product to buzz about), several salient themes emerged in exploring the company's website, member materials, and overarching ideology.

First, all activity points toward and subsequently rewards the giveaway of personal information. This explained why, to my chagrin, I never got offered a chance to buzz about free swag: I had not given enough of my (consumer) self. In an interview with Balter, the company CEO, in which I disclosed my role as an underutilized participant-observer in his network, he explained that with only a dozen or so campaigns going on at any one time, my status as a BzzAgent novice put me at the back of the line for campaign invitations, behind more "senior" BzzAgents: "The more you fill out profiles, the more you do that type of stuff, the more you get opportunities for campaigns."[16]

Indeed, scarce as the actual samples may have been during my six months of poking around as an agent, there was no shortage of opportunities to vocalize consumer preferences. From the start, I was subjected to an endless battery of surveys, both on BzzAgent's homepage and via e-mail from

MyPoints.com, an affiliated "shopping rewards" program—poked and prodded on habits, interests, and expertise. My "status level," which would have earned me benefits like campaign invitations, could have been improved by even more active participation either contributing to the Frogpond (a user-generated index of "hot" websites) or BzzScape (an assortment of social media "brand communities") parts of the BzzAgent site. If I had been invited to join a campaign for, say, Mahatma jasmine and basmati rice, Ultra Palmolive dishwashing detergent, or Neutrogena Clinical Anti-Aging Skin Care rejuvenator (to name just a few of the participating clients who passed on my assistance), the site laid out precise recommendations for crafting the perfect BzzReport feedback about my word-of-mouth interactions almost as a journalism textbook might instruct: "Describe exactly what happened so we can imagine we were right there. To make your report shine, include some direct quotes. Remember when you had to answer the '5 W's Questions' in grade school? Who, What, Where, When and Why? If your report answers all those questions, there's a great chance we'll love it and show our appreciation accordingly."

Reflecting on the utility of panoptic discipline as a means of population management, Foucault theorizes, "[It is a] system of power . . . [that] firstly, [tries] to obtain the exercise of power at the lowest possible cost."[17] Such an economic (in the sense of efficient) approach to governance is illustrated concretely here in BzzAgent's outsourced observational apparatus. The buzz firm's exhaustive profiling before, during, and after campaigns is a means of achieving the omniscient ideal of anthropological surveillance that brands and companies covet and, by getting agents to report back in minute detail, the agency can "imagine [it] was right there," without really having to be *right there.*

"Let us know about your experiences—good and bad—so we can keep BzzAgent fresh and exciting," the company's instructions cheerfully cajole. "After all, you're our eyes and ears." Subcontracting cool hunt reportage to the insiders under study is advantageous because, as any ethnographer knows, producing knowledge from fieldwork can be a slow, painstaking endeavor for one small slice of cognate community, much less 600,000 heterogeneous agents. But with those hundreds of thousands of participants mobilized to be independently monitoring on behalf of the company, such proxy panopticism perhaps begins to resemble what Foucault described as that "faceless gaze that transformed the whole social body into a field of perception: thousands of eyes posted everywhere, mobile attentions ever on the alert, a long, hierarchized network."[18]

One of the ways that BzzAgent legitimizes this workload is by hewing to a myth of brand democratization: "Know anyone who'd have fun as a

BzzAgent, too? Refer your friends and enjoy spreading word of mouth and influencing your favorite brands together!" Corporations, the meta-message runs, are not using us; rather, we are influencing *them* and thereby making them better for us. This giveaway of personal information—sold under the guise of obedient and responsive brands just "eager for your opinion," as BzzAgent claims—undergirds the "customer relationship management" that advertisers increasingly strive to perfect.[19] Anne Moore skewers such pretense: "It's like a work-for-hire contract, except no one is hired but everyone works anyway . . . a strange social space where every communication reflects a sales pitch and is preowned; where labor is called 'sharing' and remuneration is not an option."[20] It is framed as opportunistic for the buzz agent, without actually being rewarding in a conventional financial sense.

Every conversation, under these circumstances, may indeed reflect a sales pitch, but as BzzAgent and other word-of-mouth marketers go to great lengths to emphasize, the conversation is not technically *scripted* as a sales pitch. Rather, corporate messages are meant to be insinuated "authentically" into everyday discourse, not written out expressly. It is for this reason that BzzAgent claims on its website, "We're not into writing dialogue. So be yourself—share the positive and the negative. While we won't provide you with a script, we will provide you with info on the product and some suggestions and tips." The "BzzGuide" arrives as an "educational" booklet with "suggestions on who, when and how to spread the word" in "bullet point format to help you spread the Bzz quickly and effectively" and featuring "anecdotes and behind the scenes information on what makes the product worth talking about" as well as "contexts and situations when Bzz might be appropriate."

There is, apparently, a fine line between "writing dialogue" and providing "bullet point format" talking points, although I do take Balter and his company (as well as many others in the word-of-mouth industry) at their word when they emphasize that they want buzz to be authentic and appropriate to the social situation—neither forced nor predetermined. After all, marketers' stories that appear in traditional advertising are, as Balter acknowledges, always "sparkly perfect tales," which would fail the guerrilla smell test of blending in with the surroundings (in this case, a person's natural conversational cadence) and ring hollow to listeners anyhow.[21] Product stories woven into the social fabric by what would appear to be an objective, trustworthy interlocutor (the BzzAgent) stand a better chance of keeping an audience's attention because the conceit is contextually naturalized; the attempt at discipline—getting you to buy—is governance "casualized," contrivance "vernacularized."

The Roots of Word-of-Mouth

Word-of-mouth traces a notable and revealing proto-history. During World War I, the U.S. Committee on Public Information mobilized "Four-Minute Men" opinion leaders around the country to sermonize for war support and "provide guidance for conversation" among their neighboring communities ("in a manner calculated to suggest spontaneity" not unlike the "serendipitous" ethos that informs today's guerrilla marketing).[22] These "bellwethers of local thinking" acted as distant forerunners to those working in the word-of-mouth industry that has grown sharply in the past decade. Indeed, the "Four-Minute Man Bulletin" newsletter, with its suggested talking points, sounds very much like the ancient antecedent of today's "BzzGuide."

Edward Bernays, credited by many as the founding father of PR, famously sought to persuade *indirectly* through the intermediary of "third party authorities"; for example, promoting Beech Nut bacon not by "reiterating [the message] innumerable times in full-page advertisements" (think: hot sell), but rather by coaxing thousands of physicians into recommending bacon to their patients.[23] Through such endeavors, "every moment of human interaction became a suitable venue for publicity," as Stuart Ewen concludes, and public relations began "moving beyond the borders of journalistic press agentry, attempting to encompass the ether of human relations itself."[24]

Word-of-mouth marketing probably represents the guerrilla marketing form most indebted to PR's legacy; the simulation of grassroots fervor even has its own neologism, astroturfing, which, as defined by *Campaign & Elections* magazine, refers to "the instant manufacturing of public support for a point of view in which either uninformed activists are recruited or means of deception are used to recruit them."[25] It is this $500-million-a-year PR subspecialty that represents "a calculated simulation of enthusiasm" through ostensibly "spontaneous" phone calls, letters, and faxes; staged rallies; phony interest groups; and other outward trappings of an authentic social movement.[26] Gramsci might well have recognized astroturfing's technique of "gaming consent" through such "corporate grassroots strategies . . . designed to mobilize the masses while keeping effective control of actual political debates concentrated in the hands of a select few."[27] Though this diagnosis sounds politically Machiavellian, the "corporate grassroots" *consumer* scheming analyzed here seems to genuinely accede more autonomy to the conscripted intermediaries.

Word-of-mouth marketing is, in fact, a contemporary incarnation of many time-honored PR principles including Bernays' formulation of public relations as a "two-way street," which reciprocally calibrates public interests and elite exigencies (a forerunner to the contemporary "regime of dialogue," to be deconstructed shortly); the exploitation of opinion leaders and third-party intermediaries (today's buzz agents); and a fundamental comfort with less control over the details of the "message" than traditional advertising demanded (now extended to the brand as a whole in thinking of it as more of an "open work"). More fundamentally, though, buzz marketing—not unlike the ideals of public relations—is about working through the "bottom up" in order to achieve structural objectives (like selling goods) that emanate from the "top down." At a grassroots level—the field of practice in which peer-to-peer influence like that of word-of-mouth operates—governance can be more subtle and spontaneous than the comparatively deliberate and conniving contexts of traditional advertising.

While it wasn't until 2004 that industry growth finally necessitated the formal formation of a Word-of-Mouth Marketing Association (WOMMA), complete with an Ethics Code, buzz strategy itself claims a much longer trajectory. Some scholars trace the use of brand evangelists as far back as the 1920s, when Macy's reportedly cleared out a backlogged inventory of white gloves by hiring elegant women to don them on subway trains so as to stir up conversation.[28] Alissa Quart reports on the use of "teen peer-to-peer marketing" on behalf of Frank Sinatra in the 1930s, Hires Root Beer in the 1950s, and Converse sneakers in the 1980s, when the shoe company refined a technique known as "'seeding,' which involves giving away merchandise to a high school's most popular cliques in the hopes that the brand will spread like wildfire among the in-crowd's teen fashion followers."[29] By midcentury, landmark research by Elihu Katz and Paul Lazarsfeld on this "two-step flow" model had advanced the notion that interpersonal networks tempered direct, seemingly all-powerful mass media influence.[30] Yet Katz and Lazarsfeld were, as Susan Douglas caveats, universalizing their findings as representative of the entire population based on a specific study of *women's* networks in the Midwest.[31]

The gendered context here is not inconsequential. By that time, the California Perfume Company (later renamed Avon) and Tupperware had already long been utilizing women's interpersonal relationships and social capital in order to push products.[32] For these firms, an all-female sales force offered a shrewdly useful contrast with the sleazy door-to-door salesman archetype—and a way of insinuating advertising into grassroots social flows rather than having it be seen as an external imposition. "We train our girls . . . to be genteel, not too aggressive," one Tupperware representative claimed, unknowingly presaging the future "light touch" of the cool sell through which word-of-mouth marketing governs contemporary subjects.[33] Avon similarly sought out interpersonal "confidants" rather than social itinerants whose reputation and network of contacts could be harnessed to commercial ends. As a means of distinguishing his representatives from consumers suspicious of that roaming, door-to-door (male) huckster, Avon's founder, David McConnell, also consciously recruited an all-female sales force and deliberately relied on "the social skills of the representative [and] her community reputation" to gain entry into homes.[34]

Decades later, the interactivity of guerrilla marketing broadly—and the advantageous familiarity of buzz agents specifically—offers much the same contrast with "one-size-fits-all," aggressive, untrustworthy commercial appeals emanating through traditional media channels. Given this gendered legacy (i.e., that talk about shopping has long been stereotypically associated with women), the "hot" sell—with its blunt, disciplinary insistence—might be coded as conventionally "masculine" in contrast to the more socially pliant and structurally reciprocal accommodation of the "cool" sell, whose temperamental inheritance is from the historically "feminized" sphere of public relations.[35] Moreover, McConnell's encouragement that representatives should "make business an integral part of their personal lives by incorporating their families, friends, and even their churches, into their selling activities . . . to make their social networks serve their business" further illustrates an early example of word-of-mouth's strategic conversion of social capital into economic capital, at a moment of financially and politically limited potential for women.[36]

Alison Clarke highlights the strategy invoked in Tupperware's groundbreaking "party plan" for "informal salesmanship [sic], networking and 'friend-finding,'" in which "women were dissuaded from adopting a corporate image and encouraged to use their own social skills to 'create incentive or change excuses into a positive party date.'"[37] (Unlike most of the contemporary word-of-mouth firms, Tupperware's vendor guide apparently actually scripted dialogue scenarios outright.) This effacement of "a corporate image" underlies the tactics of not just buzz but guerrilla marketing as a whole, for in the pursuit of "invisible governance," context is as important as content. The hostess party, with its reliance on "strong female networks and kinship structures," offered an "antidote" to "the stigma attached to unscrupulous, masculine, door-to-door sales practices" (just as buzz marketing pitches itself today as a subtle alternative to the 30-second-spot, barging into living rooms uninvited).[38]

Today, the gendered framework of these traditions has been drawn into new forms of word-of-mouth marketing. Moreover, the same structure of "authenticating" commercial contrivance through organic and credible social patterns persists in the rhetoric hyping these methods. Because advertising is fundamentally perceived as self-serving, peer recommendations have long represented a pliable alternative vehicle for marketer address and this, again, heightens the importance of a brand striving to produce seemingly "disinterested" content (here formulated as a conversation, not unlike a short film or pop track). It is this credibility and trustworthiness that buzz marketing seeks to co-opt—a brand evangelist's apparent independence from a commercial entity relative to traditional advertising, an ostensible autonomy from the operation of power.[39] One interviewee who runs a word-of-mouth firm phrased it this way:

> A broadcast commercial innately is something that you put your defensive guard up against, because you know you're being sold something directly and it's not necessarily pure sentiment. It's a paid endorsement. . . . Broadcast is purely push, right? . . . You're not typically going to solicit a commercial. Word-of-mouth happens pretty naturally in your day-to-day life. . . . [You're] just not being guarded because you know you're preparing yourself or bracing yourself for some pushed medium. You're pulling— you know, you might—it's like a word-of-mouth endorsement comes in through something that's already happening naturally in your day-to-day.[40]

This reframes that conundrum of "authenticity" endemic to word-of-mouth strategy: the task of engineering that which is otherwise organic. Because we do not (generally speaking) filter out friends, this kind of guerrilla marketing is a way of harnessing that trust placed in peer influences— peers who, in the social media era, are thought to be more productive and interactive than ever before—and flexibly accommodating decentralized, interpersonal, commercial appeals within a new media environment.

### Astroturfing Subcultural Capital

Buzz implementation is, in a sense, the obverse of cool hunting, and anthropological surveillance and grassroots seeding often work hand in hand—a cyclical pattern of cultural trends being absorbed through young opinion leader "insider informants" and commercial products then being tested out via those same vanguard market communities. Music promotion, has, in particular, played a key role in the "astroturfing" of subcultural capital.[41] For example, Sam Ewen, head of Interference and the author of the *Aqua Teen* stunt (see chap. 3), credits his background in music marketing with teaching him "how buzz happens and how word-of-mouth . . . can cause big change."[42] Having drummed up guerrilla buzz for various rock acts over the years, Gyro also professes on its website that, "We believe brands can learn a lot from bands. That's because bands have been doing the whole viral thing forever." As part of Gyro's "viral music program" for their Sailor Jerry lifestyle brand (see chap. 2), touring bands are encouraged to stop by the agency, where free apparel is exchanged for subcultural exposure, with the agency carefully culling buzz acts from mainstream headliners: "Because we pick bands that have huge underground cult followings, their legions of fans find their way back to the Sailor Jerry website, which ultimately results in sales. . . . We actually say, 'no!' to a lot of great famous bands that our staff doesn't believe are 'cool enough' to represent the Sailor Jerry brand."

The romantic mythologizing of an esoteric and exclusive underground—and, conversely, the scarlet letter that comes with being labeled a "sell-out"—is perhaps more acute in pop music than in any other arena of consumer culture and gives rise to the sort of snotty hipster elitism echoed earlier. "Club undergrounds see themselves as renegade cultures opposed to, and continually in flight from, the colonizing, co-opting media," writes Sarah Thornton. "To be 'hip' is to be privy to insider knowledges that are threatened by . . . general distribution and easy access."[43]

This presents the music marketer with a puzzling conundrum given that popularity and purity are, in typical subculture framing, not only antithetical but inversely correlated with each other: The "bigger" the act, the less "ownership" a fan supposedly feels of it. A member of the hardcore-rap group, Insane Clown Posse, hypes their own music to this end:

> Everybody that likes our music feels a super-connection to it. . . . They feel so connected to it because it's exclusively theirs. See, when something's on the radio, it's for everybody. It's *everybody's* song: Like [someone who says], "This is my song" [of a radio hit]—[I'd reply] "That ain't your song, it's everybody's song." But, to listen to ICP, you feel like you're the only one that knows about it.[44]

Again, gross rating points seem to be inversely proportional to message integrity—Walter Benjamin might have dubbed this the "aura" of the underground.

Because pop music culture traffics so heavily in identity (and, in particular, youth identity) as part of its "product," it lends itself especially keenly to word-of-mouth, "the consummate medium of the underground."[45] This, then, is the music industry's mode of "astroturfing" promotion: simulating the bottom-up from the top-down through street teams and the sort of "graffadi" and wild postings analyzed in chapter 3; obfuscating the corporate record label source of hype through more authentic "real-life" intermediaries that "'communicate sincerity' better, faster, and cheaper" than patently commercial contexts like billboards and TV spots.[46] Subcultural capital centered on pop music might then trickle up through such grassroots networks:

> The bragging rights around identifying music as, you know, being an early adopter of music, a certain artist or a certain genre—and then having the bragging rights of being the first person to tell your friends about this discovery—with music, it's almost more powerful than any other form of media. . . . [It's that kid who] wants to be the first person to tell everybody that they're his favorite band or her favorite band and, "You gotta check them out," because in a year when they're selling out stadiums around the world, they want to have bragging rights to say, "I told you so" and "I was the first one to know about them."[47]

Todd Steinman, COO of M80, mentions "discovery" here—a central component of this scheme of consumer governance that I emphasize throughout, because discovery is the means by which subjects might be "shepherded" rather than "disciplined" (that is, discovery rewards their agency). Steinman's firm, one of the earliest to specialize in word-of-mouth and social media marketing, got its start, like others, in the music promotion business in the 1990s, by recruiting young, "proactive fans" for M80 clients like Pearl Jam, N'Sync, and Marilyn Manson—trading promotional gear in exchange for their buzz agency.[48]

Fan communities have long been shown to exhibit so-called productive tendencies, a phenomenon ably demonstrated in the cultural studies literature.[49] Word-of-mouth marketing seems to take its cues from these hives of grassroots activity, channeling and capitalizing on crowd-contributions. This "free labor" is, at once, gratuitous and also autonomous, both of which help make it a ready resource for a structure of governance (advertising) ever in need of authenticity and, with it, legitimation on the cheap. Steinman further explains how this equity co-creation is meant to feel effortless to those whose conversation is conscripted, as "empowerment" begins to function as "employment" (albeit without the remuneration):

> These people [were] publishing about Neil Young or the Red Hot Chili Peppers or Green Day all day long. And so we aggregated them into some existing, rudimentary platforms at the time and put them to work basically. . . . These were people who were willing to work for free, because they would do anything for these artists—the passion was behind it. And

you can't buy that level of enthusiasm so it really became a matter of using [it]. . . . It was, "What can I do with this crowd that I've sourced?" . . . It was really a matter of what to do with them.[50]

Nate Hahn, founder and president of the buzz firm, StreetVirus, also got his start in music promotion and phrases this logic similarly:

[It] really sort of started with the idea of empowering fans. So, let's say in the mid-90s, all these bands sort of got together and said, "We have these legions of fans. *Let's sort of empower them to do our marketing*"—whether it be putting up posters or going online and telling their friends or sharing their music. That's sort of the synthesis of where we started: How do we empower people and engage people on a very grassroots level? . . . We call that a sort of grassroots upswell. And that goes back to the music in that people were so passionate about these bands that they would, for free, go put up posters or tell their friends or start MySpace pages dedicated to the band or start fan pages or e-mail everyone they know. And we try to take that approach to those brands that don't have that kind of fanaticism.[51]

Thus, *idle* chatter *about* a band can be channeled to function as *productive* chatter *on behalf* of a band (and soon enough, buzz marketers schemed, any brand as well). Moreover, Hahn here emphasizes the "grassroots" ideal—the means by which independent agents, communities, and networks can be mobilized and orchestrated for their autonomy while assisting in a project of power. If cultural phenomena—even consumer culture phenomena—emerge with the righteous stamp of grassroots appeal, they are presumed to be authentic, democratic, and artless; to achieve that populist status for a brand or product is the goal of many a guerrilla marketer (not to mention, political strategist). And yet, at the same time, cultural industries, the mass media, and institutions of advertising do not easily manufacture grassroots appeal:

The marketing machine has changed. The marketing machine is, now, everybody's trying to engage the consumer and get the consumer on their side. Whereas before it was like . . . "We're going to talk and you're going to listen." . . . The power has gone back to the people. The power's gone back to the consumer.[52]

Here Jonathan Ressler opines emblematically in straw-man terms, summing up the philosophical shift in brand management from authority to partnership (the marketer's onus), from compulsion to discovery (the advertising ethos), and from passivity to agency (the consumer's proscribed role). Such egalitarian rhetoric is admittedly convenient—if the people are "empowered," as Ressler frames it, ad dollars should flow to a buzz marketer like him—but, even so, the mythology does help explain that growth in the word-of-mouth sector in the past decade.

It is also worth noting that the word-of-mouth industry would not have made such strides in that time if not for the emergence of the Internet; this rendered palpable (and noisily so) what had previously been the "invisible networks" that structure our lives and the communication that courses through them.[53] Pragmatically, it introduced a scalable platform for harnessing all that social energy.[54] Connectivity in the online realm and the ensuing social productivity of user-generated content, whether that be chat-rooms, ratings sites, video uploading, blogs, and the like—apparently spurred interest in utilizing social productivity *offline* as well.[55] Interactive media and the contemporary culture of everyday opinion sharing "in public" through Amazon and iTunes reviews, Facebook and Twitter status updates, and YouTube commentary piqued marketer interest; to rephrase Todd Steinman, "It was really a matter of what to do with [it]." Dialogue that had been diaphanous could now be archived and was, indeed, almost impossible to avoid; peer-to-peer influence that had been ephemeral and estimated was now definitively demonstrable and quantifiable.

### Instrumentalizing Power through Grassroots Agency

Earlier chapters have show how this invisible governance has taken shape through diverse means as a technique of self-effacement amid disinterested spaces and authenticated interlocutors (advertiament), or as a program for obfuscating authority by way of dissident aesthetics and an anti-establishment ethos (alternative outdoor). Here, we see how this same governmentality sets out to orchestrate a complex set of unpredictable relations in the service of broad, albeit adaptive, commercial objectives. By instrumentalizing their autonomy to useful ends, those individual agents, networks, and communities can work both simultaneously independently and within macro-level goals. This hinges, foremost, upon the mobilization and operationalization of that which might be tagged "grassroots."

As the term for an organic, spontaneous, and often local social movement assumed to be self-organizing and free from distant, dominant interests, grassroots evokes a form of populist authenticity admittedly more often associated with politics than consumption. Yet it is precisely *because* of those characteristics that the grassroots ideal is fetishized—and, here, strategized—by structural interests: those selling not just candidates but goods as well. In other words, the grassroots field functions as power because, like earlier articulations of resistance, it seems to operate farthest from the appearance of it; constitutionally, it seems to "rise up" *from* the people rather than being imposed *upon* them. One might frame this as ratification through decentralization—managing sentiment and action organically and autonomously, without any semblance of discipline or force (an example of which would be the traditional marketer contrivance of a 30-spot). Freedom is the lynchpin of this mechanism of power, as one neo-Foucauldian scholar proposes: "Certain ways of governing, which we will broadly define as *liberal* modes of government, are distinguished by trying to work through the freedom or capacities of the governed. Liberal ways of governing thus often conceive the freedom of the governed as a technical means of securing the ends of government."[56]

The use of that which is stamped as grassroots is an incisive example. Grassroots social flows and, more importantly, their ethos of credibility and self-determination offer a means through which one might authenticate the machinations of power—embedding the intentions of (commercial) governance in the sovereign agency of the governed (consumer) subject. The grassroots apparatus is, therefore, also representative of public relations' incumbency: "naturalizing" the exigencies of rule through the leadership of opinion-leaders modeling (and thereby proctoring) the desired managerial outcome. Indeed, the very label "guerrilla" connotes a grassroots uprising against a power structure seeking to impose itself undemocratically. It is against this backdrop that brand management increasingly hails a "democratization" of its relationship with consumers—a shift not unrelated to the network overtaking broadcasting as the organizing principle of today's media environment.[57]

For networks are, by their very nature, ways of instrumentalizing grassroots agency. They represent the means of "working through" the social capital (or, more simply, "connections") of individual agents. As Pierre Bourdieu states, "The social capital possessed by a given agent thus depends on the size of the network of connections he can effectively mobilize and on the volume of the capital . . . possessed by . . . each of those to whom he is connected."[58] Thus, the more sociable an agent, the more grassroots power they might be able to marshal on behalf of an interested third party. Various buzz firms, recruiting prominent influencers who are socially productive both online and off, are an example of this social "capitalization": using participants for their "possession of a durable network of more or less institutionalized relationships of mutual acquaintance and recognition." And thanks to social media, the highly visible productivity emblematic of user-generated content has put "buzz"—that form of grassroots output—front and center on the agendas of governance, be they political or consumer.

Seeding buzz is, however, an uncertain exercise of power and a highly improvised terrain of governance. Grassroots flows—like those of the word-of-mouth agents or the consumer-generated content creators (see chap. 5)— cannot be "managed" in a formal, Taylorist sense; they can only be negotiated. Foucault tendered a useful analogy in his discussion of "pastoral" power: "The shepherd's power is exercised not so much over a fixed territory as over a multitude in movement toward a goal. . . . It is a matter of power that individualizes by granting, through an essential paradox, as much value to a single one of the sheep as to the entire flock."[59]

Although Foucault does not employ the term "grassroots" here, his phrase "a multitude in movement toward a goal" certainly evokes it. Moreover, he visualizes an "openness" in conducting that movement rather than a "fixedness" of ends that will be made concretely apparent, from a marketing perspective, through interviewees' comments. The environmental shift from mass media to interactive media that individualizes encounters with audiences rather than interpellating them as homogenous flocks makes this all the more possible.[60] I call this program of flexibility and authenticity that endeavors to instrumentalize power through grassroots agency "the regime of dialogue."

The Regime of Dialogue

A supposed democratization of consumer dialogue is perhaps the central myth animating guerrilla marketing's brand evangelism. I use the term "myth" here not to cast aspersions as to its veracity—indeed, at first glance, there *does* seem to be a great deal more information flying back and forth between brand and consumer than in earlier decades, though it remains to be seen whether this merits a label like "democratic"—but rather to understand its function in establishing a model for certain kinds of institutional behavior.[61]

Responding to industry pressures that privilege engagement over impressions—a shift in governance from presuming passivity to activating agency from the subject, a shift that clients seem to increasingly demand—the word-of-mouth marketer ballyhoos this participatory gesture as magnanimous (giving the consumer a "voice"). That act of empowerment, though, is equally a play for dependency: a way of burrowing ever deeper into our interpersonal affairs, a means of materializing the brand as social tissue. Word-of-mouth marketing does not *script* conversation—practitioners are very righteous and adamant on this point—but it does *conscript* conversation in attempting to funnel interactions (and, if possible, relationships) through branded contexts. And this reframes how the marketer addresses the consumer subject because it requires a more contingent, negotiated exchange than traditional advertising has accommodated.

Hence all that rhapsodizing about dialogue, one of the most common thematic refrains throughout my interviews, and perhaps second only to "engagement" as a buzzword. Even when not referenced by name, it seems to be at play in the logic of the work conducted. Over the course of an interview, Dave Balter of BzzAgent claims that this is part of a central and profound transformation in media as well as marketing—the product of that public sociability at the grassroots level that is almost constantly on display in today's information environment:

> [It's this] idea of authenticity being the cornerstone of dialogue in many ways. We're at a moment in time where we've shifted from being spoken *at* by brands to have to communicate *with* consumers to ensure that brands have effective dialogues. . . . Consumer-empowerment is becoming critical—and social media has really come along and put a scale around that and allowed—given consumers an even broader voice than they had before. . . . Communication between consumers about a brand isn't a fad, and this is a monumental shift that I think they'll look back on in fifty years and say, "You know, this is the time—can you believe before this everybody was sort of these drones watching what media producers wanted to put in front of folks? And they actually watched! That's crazy." . . . The future's going to be about what people want to be doing and the ways that brands are going to get involved in that instead of the other way around.[62]

Note Balter's "history of the present" as captured from a futurist lens. It (again, somewhat self-servingly) frames an evolution from "drones" fed static, top-down content to self-determining individuals participating actively in an "authentic" dialogue.

This shift, as Alex Wipperfurth suggests, rewrites the job description from brand *manager* to brand *"facilitator"*—a less deterministic, domineering, and more agile, accommodating spin on professional practice and, hence, consumer governance.[63] To facilitate is to acknowledge the fundamental autonomy of the subject more so than to simply manage her. Indeed, Wipperfurth's brand hijack paradigm is predicated on the utility of that dialogue, for by "allowing the consumers . . . to shape brand meaning and endorse the brand to others," corporations are abiding by another oft-cited, strategically "true" myth: "Marketing managers aren't in change anymore. Consumers are."[64] I heard a similar exhortation from Britt Peterson, director of business development for Cole & Weber, who situates this transition—this movement from "pitch" to "conversation" as a way to, as earlier celebrated by her agency, "let them say yes"—in the context of a shift from hot to cool media, a shift from "aggressively shouting at everybody at the same time" to now whispering "occasionally to a few individuals":[65]

> If you think about traditional broadcasting—that's what it is. It's a broad-cast of a message sent out to millions of people. And, in that way, it does become a screaming match for who can say what the loudest; who can break through that number of commercials; whose message is more important than others; what's more unique about this than that. But it's very much from a marketer's perspective on: "What is it that I want to tell you about this, that I think will motivate you?" A conversation is more about: "Hey, I want to share this with you—what I think is interesting to you about me, but *I also want you to share what you find interesting about me to you.* Because I want to have that dialogue about how we can be more connected." . . . You have to find ways to actually involve people in your brand or at least show empathy enough that it says, "'We get it. And we understand the conversations you're having in the world and we want to be a part of them."[66]

Brands that coordinate this kind of evangelism *do* seem to be fundamentally more uncertain about themselves, as ambiguity is written more and more into their narrative DNA. In other words, as texts, they seem to be authored in a more flexible, conditional way than in earlier decades when marketers constructed product meaning more definitively with the brand intended to be a kind of stable idea-widget, which came churning off the advertising assembly line. At a moment when millennial consumers, especially, are thought by marketers to recoil at the authority of semantic designation—those contrived proclamations imposed upon audiences through interruption—postmodern branding tries to accommodate a pre-programmed polysemy, to be more things to more people by getting more people to interpret and promote those various meanings on the brand's behalf.

Brands conceived so culturally conditional so as to rely upon evangelical structure for their promotion *need* the consumer-cum-producer to do the work—and not just the work of word-of-mouth or consumer-generated advocacy but also the work of basic self-definition. That is, buzz agents not only tell others about the brand, they also tell the brand about itself;

participation in this system is, therefore, part annotation, part proselytiza-tion. Such a move is emblematic of the larger post-Fordist shift in advanced capitalism where industrial output is streamlined to be agile and customized, and the advertising pitch can be produced, per Six Sigma manufacturing line ideals "just-in-time" as the conversation presents itself rather than stockpiled as media inventory. (Inventory that is, in any case, comparatively wasteful and inefficient with its one-size-fits-all message composition that might just get zapped by the remote control.) Ted Murphy, founder and CEO of Izea, a buzz marketing firm that specializes in social media, speaks to the ideal of this flexibility in an interview:

> If you give ten different bloggers a laptop and ask them to talk about it, each one of them is going to come up with their own slant. . . . Different people are going to value different things about your product and by giving them the freedom to create the ad unit instead of saying, "Here's what we think is important, so here's what we want you to say," you have the ability to create hundreds or thousands of permutations of that ad message, each of those being relevant to the audience that's consuming the message.[67]

A brand that presents itself as lithe in this way accommodates a host of unique, personalized interpretations of it (i.e., messages) and that move from monologue to dialogue, in terms of brand philosophy, is frequently celebrated in rosy populist terms. Two-way interactivity, be it online or off, is somehow more of a democracy where one-way mass media messaging was really autocracy by comparison. A word-of-mouth message from a corporation can be humanized just for me, because it comes from a con-tact in my social network that can tailor it effectively, knowing the audi-ence of one. Consumer governance from that corporation thereby flows through a more casual, less confrontational (read: flexible, even invisible) touch-point.

## The Unmanageable Subject

Embracing this myth of dialogue is not, however, just an egalitarian affirma-tion of agency; it is equally a consignment to the perception of lost control: "Behind this 'surrender' is advertising and marketing professionals' increas-ingly widespread belief that the consumer masses have become unfortu-nately unmanageable."[68] Encouraging more freedom for their consumers is not a course of action that marketers would freely choose if they did not feel forced toward it, given an unease over uncontrollable audiences (particularly for those targeting younger consumers). I heard this refrain—resignation to the empowerment of those once thought mastered—expressed frequently in trade and interview discourse; even if it did not always take shape as a lament, it must nonetheless be understood as that, because it is an acknowledgment that the Taylorist project of advertising—in short, the disciplining of want and need on command—has fizzled.

Buzz agency is, then, a way of harnessing what was once frustrating disobedience to the "pre-digested meanings" meant to structure interpretation (i.e., the brand-text as closed, permanent, and definitive) and to the media institutions meant to structure commercial exposure to those meanings (i.e., 30-spots we were supposed to stay tuned for, pop-ups we were not supposed to block).[69] By rethinking consumers in this way—less as subjects to be engineered and more as agents for potential collaboration—power becomes a matter of facilitation rather than management, to borrow Wipperfurth's terms. And that power, recalling the shepherd parable earlier, becomes more "pastoral" in nature. Jonathan Ressler, CEO of Big Fat Inc., a guerrilla buzz firm, states this emblematically in an interview. It is worth quoting him in full, for he summarizes the recalibration of marketing thought and closely echoes Foucault's articulation of "structuring the possible field of action of others" that is the essence of contemporary liberal governance:[70]

Ten years ago, and even five years ago, and even today a lot of brands believe this: that they actually own the brand. And I don't believe that at all—I believe the consumer will drive the brand in the direction they want it to go. And today more than ever with the social media explosion, you can be out there thinking your brand is one thing and it's something completely different. People are talking about your brand—pick any brand and go out on YouTube, and I guarantee there are hundreds if not thousands of videos about that brand where people are using the brands in their own way, where people are saying things about the brand that are not consistent with the brand message. So a company, a brand today has to look at what's going on in this quote-unquote "guerrilla" world and this social media and take cues from that. Before it was all about, "Ok, we're going to develop our brand plan and here's our core brand values and everything we execute has to live within those core brand values," and today I think it's more about open-source marketing. The consumer owns the brand. You can start a message but you can't control the message anymore. . . . The smarter brand people know right now that they don't control the brand anymore—they're, for lack of a better term, shepherds and they have to try to guide the flock. Or they're a cattle rancher: they have to try to get the cattle to go the way they want them to, but at the end of the day, if all the cattle go left, you gotta go left. You gotta go left! It's just the way it is because there are too many pieces of the puzzle that the consumer can control. The consumer doesn't control TV, but the consumer controls social media; we control the blogs; we control YouTube; and we control what the world knows about the brand.[71]

If power relations are, as Foucault suggests, "strategic games between liberties," then the image of a marketer shepherding a wily flock of consumers is both a concrete application of those theorized power relations and a redefinition of the advertising industry as it blends more and more with PR (which has long acknowledged that "you can't control the message").[72] Yet there is also an intriguing contradiction of agency and passivity in this metaphorical conceptualization of the brand audience by marketers. Consumers are, at once, considered creative and autonomous yet still resemble a mass of sheep or cattle that has to be herded by marketers; the brand manager is sketched as deferentially bowing to the will of these newly emancipated *individuals* on one hand yet still has to regard them as an aggregated, tamable *collective* on the other.

As a template for power working through an open-source, interconnected media environment, Ressler's "quote-unquote 'guerrilla' world" offers a new mode of thinking about managing subjects. Such governance "presupposes rather than annuls their capacity as agents; it acts upon, and through, an open set of practical and ethical possibilities."[73] It is the advertising industry's way of making lemonade out of lemons: working with, rather than against, the exasperating trends of audience empowerment and consumer cynicism outlined in chapter 1; reconciling disobedience by channeling that agency to productive ends as opposed to redoubling the typical disciplinary effort; and harnessing flows rather than building fences. As Adam Arvidsson suggests, "Brands work by *enabling* consumers, by empowering them in particular directions. This is different from Fordist advertising . . . which was primarily directed at imposing a particular structure of needs and tastes on consumers."[74] It is, once more, how marketers "let" us say yes. Dialogue is the cornerstone for this form of power—the method by which the intransigent independence of the consumer can be recuperated into the regime of the now-pliant brand. Take, for instance, Scott Goodson, head of Strawberry-Frog, who, in an interview, summarizes this shift:

People are smart; people are truth-junkies. They're aware; they want to know the truth and today they have access to information that they didn't have five years ago. . . . It used to be that you'd lob an idea out into the world and people would stand back with their mouths—jaws dropped—and say, "Ooh!!" And that's just not the way anymore—now, it's about a combined brand building, you know, where the consumer is building the brand together with the brand owner.[75]

Goodson no doubt greatly overstates the heyday of advertiser power.[76] Today's fondness of and nostalgia for the golden days of mass media when an advertiser could (supposedly) elicit hushed reverence for her work clearly overhypes the docility of earlier audiences; as early as the 1920s marketers were fretting about the supposed cynicism of their consumer targets.[77] Yet constructing history from the present in this way, wherein audiences are said to have evolved from tame to resistant, lends itself to a particular set of practices: by defining the consumer in such-and-such a manner (that is, otherwise unmanageable), it inevitably defines the course of action (specifically in favor of Goodson's methods). For brand managers, in-house exactitude increasingly gives way to an embrace of outsourcing for that authenticity and adaptability:

In the traditional ad world, the agency or brand creates a message, and then they pay people to reproduce that message via commercial or via display ad or whatever it may be. In our world [of word-of-mouth marketing], you create kind of an introduction, and the individuals are creating the message on your behalf. And so you have to kind of be willing to put your product in the hands of other people and put your marketing campaign in the hands of other people and recognize that those people will either do a good job or a better job than you can do on your own.[78]

Such is the creed that the buzz agency facilitator repeats to herself as the brand she manages is set "free"—let loose in the rough-and-tumble arena of word-of-mouth and consumer-generated advertising. (And such was the same creed in advertainment that, for example, BMW clung to when it saw a character bleed to death in one of its cars in *The Hire*.) The myths spun about the lost control of brand meaning therefore legitimizes, rationalizes, and naturalizes the presumed inevitability of choosing to outlay the advertising budget in this direction; the client is theoretically supposed to recognize, as Dave Balter tells me, "Ok, I no longer have any control—what do I do to be a part of this dialogue that's happening with or without me?"[79]

This notion of lost control pops up repeatedly in recent advertiser discourse. At a 2006 national conference, *Advertising Age* reported that, "Marketing heavyweights such as Proctor & Gamble, Wal-Mart, MasterCard, Burger King, and Yahoo heralded a common theme considered heresy just a few years ago: Consumers control the brand."[80] In an article for *Brandweek*, "Lose Control: It's Good for Your Brand," Sam Ewen of Interference writes, "The days when you were able to exercise 360-degree control over your brand communications have ended. And . . . when the brand lets go a little, consumers start to open up a lot."[81] And Emmanuel Rosen, author of *The Anatomy of Buzz*, contends that

> Word-of-mouth represents an elusive concept. When you buy advertising, you see it in the newspaper. It's harder to see or measure buzz that spreads from network hubs to others. . . . It contradicts a nice, linear paradigm: the idea that buying advertising, marketers can spread messages directly to an accepting public. It's hard for some marketers to accept the fact that information spreads in nonlinear ways they can't always control.[82]

And Bob Garfield, a critic for *Advertising Age*, makes "lost control" the centerpiece for dramatic changes in commerce, marketing, and media: "The consumer (and voter and citizen) is in control: of what and when she watches, of what and when she reads, of whether to pay any attention to you [the marketer] or to make your life a living hell."[83]

Lost control equally ratifies the related principle that treats the brand as an unfinished text: inviting and, indeed, obliging the engagement and unique tailoring provided by the evangelist and their conversation partner. In such a disorderly, improvisational space, marketers have, admittedly, less control over the brand's reputation—in the narrow, traditional sense— but can hope that they've achieved broader reach into what had been commercially dormant zones (and therefore avoid the emblematic ad-zap trap of TiVo). A. G. Lafley's quote that "the more that we're willing to let go, the more we're able to get in touch with consumers" cuts to the heart of the fulcrum of guerrilla power: conducting subjects not directly but through tactics, arrangements, and, here, intermediaries. The challenge is, quite simply, to conscript conversation without scripting it; to precipitate what comes naturally without forcing it; to govern without seeming like governance. And the problem, as Garfield points out, is that "to actually, intentionally, simulate WOM"—one of the fastest growing sub-fields of advertising nonetheless—"historically, has been about like trying to control the weather."[84]

## Making the Invisible Transparent

The contradiction of word-of-mouth marketing stimulating what is seem-ingly spontaneous and organizing what is otherwise organic alights directly upon the dilemma of disclosure. "Undercover" word-of-mouth market-ing—sometimes called "shill" or "stealth," whereby buzz interactions are *not* revealed as the product of agency affiliation—has cropped up intermittently throughout the decade to the ethical chagrin of WOMMA membership (and in violation of their charter which expressly forbids it). One of the more notorious instances of this "black ops" approach to buzz was part of a $5 mil-lion campaign in 2002 in which Interference hired dozens of actors to pose as tourists in U.S. cities, soliciting other tourists to snap their photo using a new camera-phone product from Ericsson. The agency also planted a simi-lar number of attractive actresses as bar "leaners" to conspicuously toy with their phones, the intent being that "onlookers think they've *stumbled* onto a hot new product."[85] As one executive involved averred, succinctly encapsu-lating the cool sell commercial logic of disciplinary obfuscation and staged discovery, "If you put them in a Sony Ericsson shirt, then people are going to be less likely to listen to them in a bar."

This is, of course, because the Sony Ericsson shirt would evince authority, rather than "allowing" the *consumer* to feel like the authority through their freedom to serendipitously encounter—to "stumble" upon—the promo-tional message rather than being subject(ed) to it. The stunt, which attracted national attention when covered by *60 Minutes*, drew the ire of the nonprofit consumer advocacy group Commercial Alert, with one observer critiquing the covert effort thus: "They are trying to fabricate something that should be natural." Interference countered that the effort wasn't really a sales pitch: "[They were] just to demonstrate the product. We were never supposed to pitch anybody. If the product created desire because of what the product did and people pulled the information from us, then that's where we wanted to be."[86] In an interview, Sam Ewen lent further insight into this logic of "shep-herding" subjects:

I very specifically instructed and trained people [the actors] not to solicit. And so, what happened at that point—you're letting the consumer drive the conversation. . . . What ended up happening was—at the time [people had] never seen a camera on a cell phone before, so there was instant won-der. And also the fact that people aren't shilling them in the sense that: "Oh, you can go buy it right there." You know: "This is the best thing in the world; you have to have it; everyone has it." It was very much like, "Uhh,

I just got it; I'm still learning about it myself." Which was true. And, you know, literally, if they said, "Where can I get it?" [The actors] would say, "I don't know where you can get it, because I'm from out of town." The person had to go find it for themselves and that was only if they wanted it.[87]

To marketers like Ewen, "discovery" supposedly legitimates a scenario whereby the consumer is enticed to draw out information without feeling like it has been forced upon her. As such, Interference "managed" to conscript conversation without ever really seeming like it was dictating dialogue. As another firm defended its own similar stealth seeding, with no apparent trace of irony: "Marketers love [this] idea . . . because it offers what no other medium can: a candid conversation with potential consumers."[88] The "candidness" of a covert marketing interaction is perhaps in the eye of the beholder (and ultimately the FTC, which prohibits outright deception).

Interestingly enough, Jonathan Ressler, the CEO who earlier hailed the emancipated consumer in some of the most exaggerated overtones ("the consumer owns the brand . . . the power has gone back to the people"), has also been one of the more prominent stealth tacticians. Indeed, Ressler's Big Fat firm pioneered what it called "real life product placement" as a way of strategically seeding word-of-mouth on the sly—netting more than $4 million in billings within two years of the company's founding:[89]

[The agency] has paid bar "leaners" to casually talk up the merits of certain liquors, doormen to pile up packages from a particular online catalogue company in the lobby of their building, mothers to talk about a new laundry detergent at their kids' little-league games, and commuters to play with a new PDA on the train home.[90]

Such interaction seems to conflate real life with "reel life": treating humdrum exchanges between common folks as an opportunity to script product placement as though life were a James Bond film—even if precise scripting is, to be certain, not really feasible. Indeed, Ressler demurred at my characterization of his work as "brand theater":

You can't write a script. So you're trusting that they're the right person and that they're going to deliver somewhat of the right message. It is improv to some extent. . . . It's not so much brand theater as it is more about finding the little ways to creep into the lifestyle landscape. . . . So putting it in people's hands and letting them create their own theater, letting them use it in real ways, is so much more relevant and so much more powerful.[91]

Ressler's use of the term "improv" here is telling. Improvisation, as opposed to scripted theater, is much more spontaneous, organic, and "authentic" (however tortured that term has become the more that advertising has pursued it). As a tool for governance, improvisation is less deliberate and has compromise and flexibility built in, accentuating the opportunity for independent agency. Yet there remains a fundamental tension with this philosophical approach: "If you do it right, people never know [they've heard a marketing pitch]. It's just a matter of presenting stuff in a different channel and trusting consumers to be smart enough to make their own choices," says Ressler.[92] The contradiction of assumptions in evidence here—the consumer "not knowing" about the marketing pitch and yet at the same time being treated as "smart enough to make their own choices"—isn't clearly resolved; it is, in fact, a contradiction that cuts to the core of word-of-mouth marketing.

On one hand, buzz agencies tout their ability to bypass those "advertising schema" filters that stymie traditional media approaches with rhetoric that borders on—and in some cases, openly hypes—the under-the-radar merits of going word-of-mouth. These firms argue that although individuals increasingly ignore or avoid old forms of advertising, they are still influenced by peers, especially at younger ages, and that such a seeding strategy can usefully intervene through those casual channels of interpersonal influence. But if buzz firms request disclosure of their agent-participants, as many agencies obedient to the WOMMA charter do, the subtlety and "cover" of that guerrilla intervention is blown. Disclosure—ethical as it may be—by acknowledging that buzz stems from a formal campaign source *denaturalizes* the otherwise "natural" cadence of conversation and weakens the premise of efficacy that word-of-mouth firms sell to their clients. Dei Worldwide, a social media marketing company that specializes in what it calls "conversational outreach" boasts: "We deliver your messages *seamlessly*, integrating them into the context of the conversations that are already occurring."[93] Given those benefits espoused, disclosure would seem to be fundamentally antithetical to the buzz act; it exposes the "seams" of socializing commercially. If word-of-mouth works because, as Dave Balter claims, it is "often all but invisible," isn't transparency an inherent impediment to its own competitive advantage?

Responding to these anxieties about covert buzz, in 2005, Commercial Alert, an advertising watchdog group, asked the FTC to investigate the legality of Tremor, Proctor & Gamble's teen buzz marketing unit, which had 240,000 young people on its rolls (alongside some 600,000 mothers in P & G's Vocalpoint buzz unit) and did not, at that time, require disclosure during promotions, leaving it up to the participant's prerogative.[94] Commercial Alert argued that such practices amounted to a "basic 'commercialization of human relations,' where friends treat one another as advertising pawns, undercutting social trust."[95] BzzAgent actually started out similarly surreptitious before embracing disclosure as an official policy: "The first site we had, I think it said like, 'Shhh! Don't tell anyone you're here! You're about to become part of this secret thing,'" says Balter.[96] He adds that—contrary to my sentiments—as agents would disclose their status and affiliation with the company, the effectiveness of the buzz was not diminished.[97] Because people talk all the time about products and services anyway—one estimate puts it at 20 percent of all conversations—he asks, "Does the fact that [during Bzz campaigns] they're consciously helping the company through the sharing of their honest opinion make them untrustworthy?"[98] Not untrustworthy per se, but requiring disclosure nonetheless seems to introduce an element of awkwardness—a stilted sponsorship caveat—into everyday interaction.

Moreover, try as BzzAgent might—and there is no shortage of verbiage stressing the importance of honesty and disclosure in their participant training—they can ultimately only verify that transparency through the self-reporting of agents (who may well find it plainly awkward): "When Bzzing others, you must first let them know you're involved with BzzAgent, and that we've supplied you with the opportunity to experience a product or service," their website declares. It tracks claims of agents' disclosure (or absence thereof) by dutifully monitoring reports and flagging those who fail to meet their standards, though Balter acknowledges that, "It's just so authentic and natural to talk about brands everyday anyway that someone forgets to quote-unquote 'disclose'" sometimes.[99]

Yet is it "authentic and natural" to inaugurate a chat with friends on, say, the appeal of Starbucks Pike Place Roast (one of the campaigns BzzAgent ran during my participant-observation) with a "brought to you by" forewarning? What exactly does "being genuine" even mean in the context of these new social exercises precipitated by and coordinated through marketing institutions? And, even if disclosure is a genuine priority for buzz firms—which would still seem odd, given that the practice is often hyped precisely because it *doesn't* appear like the advertising that audiences otherwise want to avoid—the inherently outsourced structure of the marketing message makes disclosure impossible to definitively police. Thus, when WOMMA's ethics guidelines were released (stipulating transparency), some marketers seemed dubious: "*The whole idea of marketing is not to make it look like marketing,*" reasoned Jonathan Bond, co-author of *Under the Radar* and co-founder of Kirshenbaum Bond & Partners, which has run its own stealth campaigns using covert actors.[100]

Indeed, self-effacement has been highlighted in this book as philosophically essential to the project of the cool sell; disclosure undermines the guerrilla achievement of "invisibility" that this nontraditional approach affords. Just like BzzAgent's early days, other word-of-mouth firms seem to have actively encouraged the clandestine image in their marketing materials. For example, when General Mills launched a buzz unit in fall 2008, garnering 100,000 volunteers within its first month, it named that network "Pssst"—evoking shadowy practices and trench-coated participants.[101] Introducing itself on its website, A.D.D. Marketing quotes an apparently favorable *Washington Post* description of the guerrilla firm: "A.D.D. is kind of like the guys on the TV series *Mission: Impossible.* . . . They take the tough jobs and you don't ask too many questions about how they get it done." According to *Brandweek*, marketers tend to be "very hush-hush about their word-of-mouth campaigns," with one buzz marketing executive confiding that "clients employ euphemisms like 'Can you get [high school] campus attention for this?' instead of simply asking outright for a word-of-mouth campaign" and "[make] such requests over the phone [because] e-mail leaves a paper trail."[102]

And consider Girls Intelligence Agency or GIA (a not-irrelevant moniker evoking Langley spooks), with its 40,000 "Influencer" female "secret agents" as young as eight who host slumber parties convened for product seeding. It bills its services in language worthy of military espionage: "Behind *enemy lines*, GIA gets you into girls' bedrooms. . . . Obtain immediate, candid data *from the trenches . . .*"[103] The company's training guide reportedly advocates that agents "'gotta be sneaky' in promoting GIA."[104] Part buzz marketing shop, part ethnographic cool hunting boutique, GIA's CEO Laura Groppe flaunts that access: "Our clients feel like we're invited into the bedroom; it's a totally intimate setting with a girl and her best friends and that trust would take years and years to try and buy."[105]

GIA thus offers the latest incarnation of curiously gendered dynamics when it comes to buzz marketing, an industry constructed on feminized terms. The "labor" that is conscripted here is, fundamentally, sharing and socialization—practices stereotypically more associated with women's networks than men's. Moreover, as seen in the business rhetoric buttressing Avon and Tupperware's strengths, the hard sell of traditional advertising evokes a "masculine" aggressiveness: Recall the oft-cited bullying huckster whose talking points espoused a product's so-called rational benefits. Such a direct approach, in contrast to the circumlocution of word-of-mouth sales strategy, might perhaps map onto wider linguistic patterns when it comes to men's and women's differing interpersonal communication styles: the former approaching interaction (and especially persuasion) more loudly, hierarchically, and competitively (i.e., hot sell); the latter with more whispering, listening, emotional disclosure, and emphasis on connection (cool sell).[106]

Indeed, buzz marketing's pursuit of rapport—and guerrilla marketing's accent on "engagement," more broadly—is the gendered antithesis of purely impression-seeking TV and radio commercials.

This is not to claim, however, that buzz need only apply to women marketers and consumers. There are certainly plenty of examples of word-of-mouth tactics targeting a strictly female population beyond Avon and Tupperware: Vocalpoint's "community" of mom's orchestrated by Proctor & Gamble, GIA's girls-only network, and even the products pushed during my brief BzzAgent tenure seemed more oriented for female demographics. Yet one of the first PR campaigns to dabble in these methods was in fact the "Four-Minute *Men*" of World War I, and in more recent years buzz has been bought equally for both male and female consumers. Moreover, the vast majority of interviewees for this project were, in fact, men (though this might well be the product of organizational inequity at the executive level). If buzz is considered "feminized" and buzz is also so often touted as "authentic" (particularly for youth audiences), then by extension we might conclude a feminized approach is more authentic in reaching young people. At a moment of identity development when a sense of self-autonomy is still embryonic, perhaps the "light touch" is just the right touch of governance for that youth subject.

## The Entrepreneurial Ethos of Social Capital(ism)

This chapter has demonstrated the long trajectory of social capital being employed by retailers—from Avon and Tupperware in the early part of the 20th century through to BzzAgent and other contemporary word-of-mouth firms. Then as now, these firms have had an enduring program of governance they hope to execute—the conduct of consumers' conduct—and recognize, first in women's interpersonal networks and later in other demographic niches like pop music fan communities, a guerrilla marketing occasion to embed the cause. Critics like Commercial Alert or the Campaign for a Commercial-Free Childhood protest that word-of-mouth marketing represents a social perversion and commercialized betrayal of communal trust—even that which embraces disclosure as a policy model—a practice that is at its most dangerous when it involves the fragile identities of youth, so vulnerable (and valuably so) to peer-pressured consumer influence. They charge that this is one more step in the corporate colonization of what had been a truly authentic space. They are not necessarily wrong in this, and yet this critique doesn't seem to explain why—if this practice is *voluntary*—the ranks of would-be buzz agents continue to swell. Our conversations may be conscripted upon joining, but we are not, after all, conscripted to join in the first place.

There must be, then, a wider culture of "social capitalism" needing critique that makes word-of-mouth marketing possible: an increasingly indistinguishable blur of personal lives and professional commerce. It hinges upon the participant bringing ambitious market logic to everyday interaction so as to commodify relationships and monetize social network followings. Buzz marketing treats the status of consumers as practicable capital—that "social capital," as Bourdieu termed it—a functional resource, which can be wielded through various "transactions" in the life-world. Social capital can be exchanged for economic capital—in the form of Avon salaries or BzzAgent samples—but it seems to be just as much a way of *re*-investing in and cultivating *further* social (as well as cultural) capital. In other words, participation by being "in-the-know" as part of a market vanguard set has the tautological effect of further burnishing those credentials of being "in-the-know." If word-of-mouth is, as Ressler sells it, "real life product placement," then I suggest that this is affording everyday people the conceit—however faint—that they, too, harbor the kind of social capital (which can also be called by its related name, "fame") that a brand might find worth co-opting. Buzz agents are, after all, theoretically venerated as "trendsetters," "influencers," those 10 percent of "thought-leaders" in society that Ed Keller, CEO of a buzz research firm, identifies as impacting the rest.[107] According to Balter, buzz marketing "leverages . . . 'the power of *wanting* to be trendsetter.'"[108] In an interview, he adds:

> There's this pride people have when, "Oh, yeah, everyone's paying attention." Same thing [with buzz]: the idea that your voice is being heard and is being respected and others find it of value—that is a huge, huge motivator. . . . We tell [agents], "This is a way to get your voice heard." . . . We make it very clear this is about their empowerment more than anything else.[109]

Similarly, one researcher suggests that buzz comes naturally to people as a self-aggrandizing ritual: "It gives us self-enhancement. . . . If we know about this interesting product . . . we're hip and cool."[110] It caters to a "psychological principle" that "when we tell others something new, we feel that 'we're in the know' and we're typically rewarded by their reaction."[111] Ted Murphy, head of Izea, adds, "I think that there's a sense of celebrity that goes along with that and stature—that the brand would think enough of you to compensate you to endorse or to speak about their product."[112] Therefore, word-of-mouth marketing perhaps indulges the narcissistic delusion, however subtle, of playing the role of "micro-celebrity" product endorser within one's social network. Such narcissism already betrays the platonic ideal of selfless friendship and capacitates the eventual "selling out" of that space for brand buzz.

Thus, we ought to understand the rise of word-of-mouth marketing in the context of a broader opportunistic social entrepreneurialism. Pursuant to this lifestyle in which the subject is always "on the job," market demands are embedded in interpersonal relations; social networks are sized up for value and advantageousness; and friendship becomes a raw commodity to be instrumentalized like any other resource. After all, networking—a tool in which conviviality is coldly cultivated as self-interested strategy, a tool familiar to workers seeking employment and proprietors seeking business leads—predates the rise of MySpace and Facebook. Yet this networking also illuminates how conversation has long been hollowed out for enterprise; how camaraderie can be drained of its selflessness and pressed into the service of capitalism (particularly for those who wish to make their livelihood in a postindustrial economy); how the neoliberal subject is now meant to think of himself in terms of that "Brand You," as certain management gurus rhapsodize. Identity and socialization are folded into the promotional imperative; one's profile, whether online or off, is to be sculpted as a branded media property; and we are encouraged to treat social output as a product of labor rather than a gift of fellowship. In short, such entrepreneurialism has already converted ritual into capital; buzz agents just make it a deliberate commercial exchange.

For marketers, the allure of this consumer governance is to be found in the power of that which seems grassroots: an artless, legitimate form of conducting others' conduct that seems to rise up organically rather than being imposed externally and artificially. Indeed, the problem of unmanageable subjects mistrusting those who seek to govern them is redressed here in a clever, decentralized, populist manner: it gets subjects to govern *each other.* That is, after all, how the grassroots function as a means of influence and disposition of power, and it is grassroots energy that public relations has long sought to engineer. Subjects with designs on social capital are all too willing to collude with that program of power—even as their agency is targeted and instrumentalized for its ostensible autonomy from it. Having shown how word-of-mouth marketers have conscripted the conversations of consumers on behalf of the brand, in chapter 5 I analyze how those same consumers are increasingly volunteering similarly productive labor for advertisers, especially in an online realm as part of momentous changes that are taking place in today's new social media ecology.

5

## Crowd-Sourced Marketing and the Freedom to Labor

One does not so much give orders or shape actions according to a given norm, as much as one works from below, by providing an ambience in which freedom is likely to evolve in particular ways. One works with and through the freedom of the subject.
—Adam Arvidsson[1]

The arguments for citizen ads encompass every current marketing cliché. A company invites consumers to submit ads to its Web site, which means said consumers spend much time thinking about the product (marketing cliché alert: engagement, interacting with the brand). These ads are shown online to let the public chatter and vote on which is the best (cliché alert: community). That the ads come from the vox-pop ensures they are (cliché alert) authentic. With luck, what consumers submit is good enough to stand out from the omnipresent marketing noise (cliché alert: breaking through the clutter). And good enough so people come back to the site for more. Also, lest we forget: Letting consumers do the work is cheap.
—Jon Fine, *BusinessWeek* columnist[2]

Over the past decade, as broadcasting has increasingly given way to the network as the organizing principle of contemporary media ecology, interactivity has simultaneously emerged as a key component of how media work, and advertising more specifically, might be accomplished. Such a transition gives rise to "new kinds of ambiences, goals, and procedures for consumer interaction, participation, and productivity," presupposing two familiar themes: first, a subjective flexibility in terms of how the brand-text is conceptualized (i.e., that operability of an "open work"); second, a collaborative interpellation of amateur roles (i.e., that operability of "open labor").[3] Both developments provide opportunities and challenges that herald a potential dematerialization of not just advertising but the culture industries at large.

Interactivity, like advergaming in chapter 2, is, by design, a calibration of "a more or less open field of possibilities" in which "the behavior of acting subjects is able to inscribe itself."[4] Whether that manifests itself in viral and social media strategies, online self-publishing, consumer-generated video contests, or alternate-reality marketing scenarios, such advertisers "code" participation as central to the logic of their governance—both literally in the sense of the digital programming often required to stage these campaigns and figuratively as part of an abiding myth of brand "democratization" (which is itself an extension of the earlier hype around "dialogue"). The ongoing negotiation between structure and agency that has been centrally theorized throughout is specifically mapped here in the context of professional versus amateur content flows.

Theoretically, the "amateur" participant who is centrally situated within practices of networked interactivity—like the way the "viewer" was the locus of and target for broadcasting work—plays much the same role (and serves much the same purpose) as the grassroots did in chapter 4: She operates as a decentralized, flexible, organic, and therefore disinterested node of power. Her autonomy from professional media practice is what purportedly substantiates her authenticity as a content creator, and that authenticity is what these advertisers perhaps covet most. At a transformative moment in the media ecosystem when major corporate content providers from NBC to Paramount to the *New York Times* to J. Walter Thompson are facing the unpredictable "citizen media" practices of the crowd—when hierarchical concentrations of information flow are negotiating and being complemented by heterarchical patterns of co-production and co-distribution—it is *through* the amateur that structure is seeking to catch up to agency by embedding top-down exigencies in bottom-up digital freedoms.[5]

## The Uses of (New Media) Literacy

It is important to foreground the celebratory, populist ethos that has been assigned to Web 2.0 in both academic literature and popular sentiment—not because it is necessarily warranted or unwarranted, but for what it *warrants* of professional media work. In other words, amateur participation, through networked technologies, serves as an opportunity for marketers to construct more sophisticated schemes of governance in which that independent agency might be inscribed. Like buzz agency, this mode of governance, in outsourcing the instruments of engagement, seeks more power by wielding less control. The amateur is targeted as a "client" of power—an egalitarian means to embed and achieve structurally necessary ends.

Recall Henry Jenkins's portrait of that "newly empowered" media consumer as "active," "migratory," "socially connected," and "noisy and public."[6] It seems pivotal to snapshots, such as these, that those who populate "grassroots fan communities" at the vanguard of amateur co-creation (again, millennials come to the forefront here) are presumed to represent capillaries of power whose remove from centralized media institutions theoretically authenticates their role and resolve.[7] Amateurs are, in other words, artless, autonomous models of a kind of folk culture for the digital era; corporations, on the other hand, contrive, are vested, and represent a distant structure seeking to impose commercial interests on consumer audiences.

It is probably not surprising, then, that advertisers would find in amateurs, much like buzz agents before them, an appealing opportunity to digitally "vernacularize" their designs on power—to crowd-source promotional machinations through local, disinterested channels: a Facebook user, a basement blogger, a YouTube cineaste. By programming textual contingency and relying on collaborative (and often free) labor, this form of consumer management is as much organic governance as it is invisible and has the effect of shrouding structural ambitions beneath independent improvisations.

Christina Spurgeon frames the ascendance of interactivity and the increasing centrality of the network as a shift from—or, more aptly, overlay of—transmission media to conversationally inspired media (or "conviviality," as she puts it).[8] A system based upon transmission, structurally, has no real need for agency in executing its goals; fundamentally in its design audiences are but receptacles, and their agency is, at best, an incidental byproduct of semiotic "decoding," as Stuart Hall demonstrated in his rejoinder to transmission theory, rather than something written (by digitally strategic omission) into the message.[9] Conviviality, however, *depends* on agency: "New media audiences cannot be conceived of as passive consumers of [advertising and marketing] services. Indeed, their active participation, especially as content creators, is a crucial ingredient of commercial success."[10] Here, we find that adland seems to be taking to heart decades-old cultural studies' principles about "active" audiences, with new technology facilitating post-transmission theory campaign design. As Mark Deuze gleans:

> Advertising, marketing and PR are increasingly expected to be produced across different media platforms (with multiple tie-ins), while professionals in these industries additionally find themselves having to partly outsource their control over the advertising message to consumers

online via viral, word-of-mouth, "buzz" and other types of interactive marketing techniques. This kind of interconnectivity—between different media, between media makers and media users, and between consumers among each other—tends to be seen as a direct exponent of the potential of new media.[11]

Witnessing the self-publishing of consumers exhibited across a range of platforms characteristic of Web 2.0—Blogger, Twitter, YouTube, Wikipedia, MySpace, Facebook, and so on—brand managers today are endeavoring to make use of such abundant productivity (especially that which is endemic to millennials): acknowledging agency, channeling creativity, and framing freedom in ways that are functional to the brand. This interactive collaboration invites—and, at times, necessitates—the kind of "immaterial" or "free" labor that increasingly characterizes the postindustrial economies of advanced capitalism.

Maurizio Lazzarato defines this "immaterial labor" as "the labor that produces the informational and cultural content of the commodity"—a set of skills and activities not normally considered "work" like "defining and fixing cultural and artistic standards, fashions, tastes, consumer norms, and, more strategically, public opinion."[12] Advertising, Lazzarato recognizes, represents a classic form of such immaterial production, and the independent, self-organizing, and fundamentally "precarious" labor ethos emblematic of word-of-mouth and crowd-sourced advertising seems to extend these patterns further: "The cycle of production comes into operation only when it is required. . . . [O]nce the job has been done, the cycle dissolves back into the network and flows that make possible the reproduction and enrichment of its productive capacities."[13] Tiziana Terranova builds upon Lazzarato in critiquing the knowledge-based digital economy's overreliance on "free labor"— work that is "simultaneously voluntarily given and unwaged, enjoyed and exploited."[14] This term tracks, perhaps even more closely, to patterns of brand evangelism.

More recent research has empirically examined the complexities of blurring that which had been a more "fixed distinction between production and consumption, labor and culture" when it comes to interactive entertainment.[15] Mark Andrejevic, for example, explores online fan commentary for television programming: On one hand, fans are offered the "celebratory promise" of "shared control" over content while they simultaneously perform "value-enhancing labor" for cultural producers by way of off-loaded market research and self-motivated engagement with texts. Andrejevic fruitfully concludes that because "the interactivity of viewers *doubles* as a form of labor . . . in the interactive era, the binary opposition between complicit passivity and subversive participation needs to be revisited and revised."[16] And Brooke Duffy similarly threads the analytic space between empowerment and exploitation in her work on Dove's consumer-generated advertising campaign. She finds that while some participants bought into the "dominant [textual] meaning" intended for participation (i.e., hyping the contest as emblematic of the "empowered" consumer and a feminist agenda), many recognized the limitations of their empowerment within the program.[17]

Detlev Zwick, Samuel Bonsu, and Aron Darmody usefully outline how this "collective embrace of the idea of a newly empowered, entrepreneurial, and liberated consumer subject" portends certain strategic opportunities and advantages.[18] They add:

> Customer management, then, as the exertion of political power to produce particular forms of life, clearly does not mean domination because marketers presuppose, and in fact expect, the consumer subject to act, innovate, tinker and run free. The marketing challenge posed by the co-creation model rests, of course, with establishing ambiences that program consumer freedom to evolve in ways that permit the harnessing of consumers' newly liberated, productive capabilities. . . . Co-creation . . . aspires to build ambiences that foster contingency, experimentation, and playfulness among consumers.[19]

Working with and through these consumer freedoms, brand management can now outsource obligations that had once been circumscribed within its domain and, in turn, the ROI–validating metrics that tend to get cited for these crowd-sourced practices are as often how many people have *reached out* with contributions of their own to the brand (i.e., concrete engagement) as how many people may have been *reached by* exposure to it (i.e., estimated impressions). Amateur creativity and crowd-sourced labor—much in evidence authentically across the Web 2.0 landscape—are thus models for embedding an advertising message in seemingly egalitarian, ostensibly organic social and cultural flows, which don't really *feel* like advertising in the traditional, heavy-handed, top-down, "hot sell" sense. This is true not only in the fact that marketers utilizing the consumer-generated model construct the brand as more of an "open text" than advertising has traditionally allowed (inviting, even obliging, somehow "democratic" closure), but also in that, once closed, the circulation enlisted is from peer-to-peer as much as broadcaster-to-receiver (implying somehow "spontaneous" distribution because it is decentralized: many-to-many rather than one-to-many).

Strategies that proceed from a crowd-sourced premise concede both the flexibility of the brand-text as a contingent enterprise as well as the wayward nature of those feisty "new consumers" that Jenkins posits, even as it seeks to cultivate their momentum. Indeed, given consumers' presumed "unmanageability," especially as it is demonstrated in online spaces—where restiveness with professional content is apparent in the objections frequently lodged on comment boards, through blog postings, and in the mash-up bricolage rife across the Web—consumer-generated marketing might, too, be understood as a kind of guerrilla recourse to achieving engagement. It represents a way of anticipating and allowing for "the consumer subject to act, innovate, tinker, and run free" by delimiting a wider context in which the now-"prosumer" is encouraged to position herself by furnishing the raw digital materials to satisfy those co-creative needs. It is, then, not far removed from the same "jujitsu" principles that animate *Adbusters* and the Truth anti-smoking campaigns described earlier: working *with* the momentum and productivity of youth "audiences" online—fostering, optimizing, and marshaling it as a productive resource, rather than trying to stifle or contain it as an existential threat. The mash-up culture of Web 2.0 might, in fact, be considered the digitally "subversive" analogue to culture jamming.[20]

By inducing such digital labor (co-creation and co-circulation) from individuals present in our social networks—not to mention the hordes of amateur-creators we encounter online but don't know personally—these marketers are also arranging for commercial serendipity, because it is production from a disinterested source and distribution funneled through independent flows. When control is acceded to agency in this manner, the advertiser seeks to stage discovery rather than impose learning; this is partly what cues much rhetoric in the trade press about "brand democratization" (e.g., "Advertising of, by, and for the people," as one headline hypes it).[21]

Programming Power through Contingency

Rather than thinking of the content as a defined, unchangeable unit, it should be considered an *opera aperta*—or "open work of art"—the Latin term used by Umberto Eco to describe how literary texts, which leave room for individual interpretation and demand a higher level of reader involvement, will ultimately be more rewarding and engaging.[22]

As changes in the structure of the media environment have come to privilege interactivity, the notion of "going viral"—"today's electronic equivalent of old fashioned word of mouth"—has increasingly become a buzzword aspiration for content creators, be they amateur or professional.[23] This objective seeks to achieve the self-replicating dissemination of its bio-hazard namesake, and the growth of culture formatted for the Internet, wherein digital memes can be effortlessly diffused through e-mail, links, and self-publishing, lends itself particularly well to such an undertaking. Notoriety, in the decentralized viral model—where those memes trickle up to mainstream coverage from the blogosphere underground—is again portrayed as somehow more democratic than the mass media flows of old, where a more limited number of gatekeeping publishers and broadcasters determined a one-to-many circulation of content. With this so-called democracy, so, too, flows a perception of credibility and marketers eager to insinuate themselves into that authenticated context.

Viral is an appealing ideal for two main reasons: first, outsourcing circulation of the message to the crowd can often reduce overhead spent on buying conventional media space or time; second, by embedding the brand in peer-to-peer flows and attaining popularity through hit counts and web traffic analytics, such marketing is thought to skirt the problem of consumer cynicism that plagues those traditional advertising venues.[24] Viral content is, in short, opt-in, *chosen by*—discovered—in contrast with advertising in those traditional venues (e.g., a TV commercial interruption) where the message feels *chosen for* the audience. Here, a word or two more is in order on content—namely, advertising content, which is increasingly produced as the kind of *opera aperta* that Denmark-based GoViral CEO Jimmy Maymann describes.

To do this, I return to Mark Deuze, who theorizes a continuum of media content as it is produced today in terms of the degree to which it can be described as inherently "open" or "closed": "[These] refer to the extent to which a given media company shares some or all of its modes of operation with its target audiences . . . [gives] customers more control over their user experience" and "how its mode of production interpellates publics as either (individual) consumers or (co-) creators of content."[25] This offers a fruitful starting point for thinking through how and why "media work" gets done in a variety of industries ranging from journalism to film and television to video games to, indeed, advertising.[26] And it also nicely dovetails with the notion of the cool sell, where—drawing again upon my reformulation of Marshall McLuhan's typology—media that are less defined, more open (and therefore *cooler*) "interpellate" audience participation in ways more commercially useful than the passive presumptions that accompanied the hot/hard sell of old.

Textual flexibility therefore presumes the pleasures of interpretive involvement. And while cutting-edge technology and digital platforms ease that engagement opportunity, the *logic* of such governance rests upon some 2,000 years of rhetorical precedence—stretching back to Aristotle who defined an "enthymeme" as a "syllogism with part or parts missing," which enables "the persuader and persuadee to co-create reasoning by dialectically coming to a conclusion," requiring "the audience mentally to fill in parts of the reasoning process, thus stimulating involvement."[27] The enthymematic device is, therefore, a close (albeit ancient) precursor to the cool sell; that "interactive reasoning" is now strategized through the interactive co-creation that Web 2.0 affords. Semiotically, "unfinished" is meant to be read as "unforced"—an attempt at power that assumes agency.

Recall the instructions of brand consultant Alex Wipperfurth in chapter 3: "The hijacked brand manager's key job is to keep the brand neutral—a blank canvas, so to speak—so that the market can fill it in with meaning and enrich it with folklore."[28] This imperative to devise a brand tabula rasa—to program textual contingency, to propose ambiguity so as to ensnare appropriation—is closely tied to changes in the structure of today's media environment, notions about creative leisure, and management practices of outsourced labor. In an interview, Jimmy Maymann, head of a "viral distribution agency," offers a tidy summation of the Foucauldian philosophy fortifying this strategic turnabout. Note here how power is re-conceptualized as partnership rather than management amid digital "counter-conducts"[29]:

> For fifty years with broadcasting, [clients] have full control. . . . They've been wanting to have the same kind of control in this new channel and it's just not going to fly. . . . If they're putting something out online, it can be changed—it can morph, people can play with it—they can create, you know, something that [clients] want or that they don't want their brand to be. But even if [clients are] not putting anything out online, [people] can still take stuff that goes on TV and put it out online and actually play with it, right? . . . Some [clients] don't realize that they have lost control, whether they want it or not. And that's why we're saying: It's a consumer-to-consumer republic. They're in control, actually, and we need to play with them rather than trying to protect the stuff.[30]

Consumer-generated labor as such can range from simple interactivity and viral collusion (e.g., entering information into a website or forwarding an e-mail) to protracted self-publishing and video creation as well as labyrinthine transmedia mystery quests. One of the most hailed viral case studies of the last decade required only modest input from participants and—as one of the more bizarre advertising enterprises in that time—demonstrates both the "playfulness" that Maymann counsels as well as the notion that intrigue, coupled with interactivity, can breed involvement when it comes to "cool selling" through Internet-based initiatives. In 2004, as part of a promotion for Burger King's TenderCrisp chicken sandwich, the fast food chain's agency, Crispin Porter + Bogusky, hired digital shop The Barbarian Group to create a website that came to be known as "The Subservient Chicken." The project was said to be part of a broader effort by CP+B to re-brand Burger King from "boring, irrelevant, and unimaginative" to something "more edgy and cool."

By filming hundreds of video clips of a man in chicken suit and writing code for a database of terms that would respond to keyword commands for the Chicken to perform those videotaped actions, Barbarian concocted something that was, in its own words, "so creepy, weird and well-executed that many people who visited . . . thought they were actually controlling this person in a chicken suit in real life." Moreover, by "[toying] with the dirty underworld of transgressive webcam culture," Rick Webb, Barbarian's co-founder, also boasted that it was the "most gloriously subversive thing we have ever done."[31] As the site garnered a half-billion hits and 20 million unique visitors, the agency won two Cannes Lion trophies; the Chicken itself earned its own Wikipedia page, Snopes debunking, "tributes, imitators, rip-offs and homages," and a Webby nod as one of the most influential web videos of all time; and the chain reported "double-digit" growth in product awareness and "significantly increased" sales.[32] In an interview, Benjamin Palmer, Barbarian's CEO, adds that, like Truth and PBR, the project was chasing after that most resistant of subjects—teenagers and young adults—and sought a new approach to consumer governance that never disclosed its intentions to overtly "conduct conduct":

> You have to understand Burger King at the time—like, all the ads were like a picture of a cheeseburger and the price of the cheeseburger next to it. They hadn't done anything interesting at all. . . . Like, our brief—sort of our "playground"—was college kids, you know, who, like, get high and have to choose between McDonald's and Burger King and kids who look for weird stuff on the Internet. So we had been told by the agency that the stranger we made it, the better. And so we really wanted to make it, like, we tried to make it kind of perverse and it was going to be something that got a lot of attention. The nature of the project itself—I don't think anyone understood what we were doing until we sort of finished it. . . . It was sort of [about] flying under the radar.[33]

The project sits at the nexus of user-generated content—the Chicken as a contingent brand entity and digital enthymeme interpellating the site visitor to enter commands and "close the loop" of performance to communicate an (admittedly opaque) message—and crowd-sourced virality—its renown spread initially via decentralized digital channels. And it proved, according to Barbarian, "that you can utilize relationships—electronic and personal—between people and groups to spread ideas and messages, and it can still work *even if the message is, at its core, commercial in nature.*"[34]

This is an important point to draw out: Barbarian was able to utilize this social media labor of fans to co-create and spread an ad message for Burger King, because the message *didn't* feel "commercial in nature." Upon logging onto the Subservient Chicken site, there is no sense of a product being deliberately pitched to visitors; no obvious, pushy, vested salesperson waiting in the wings; no "picture of a cheeseburger with the price of the cheeseburger next to it," in Palmer's own words. There are, in short, no visible seams of governance and therefore no apparent project of conducting conduct; the interactive experience somehow seems, not unlike the advertisement from chapter 2, "disinterested" and therefore autonomous from the "ooze" of commercial intent.[35] It manages to self-efface any trace of managerial ambition—to casualize any semblance of persuasive force vis-à-vis transgressive ambiguity and enthymematic collaboration. One guerrilla agency CEO spells out this underlying logic of viral's "governance without governing":

> Do you understand the idea of social currency? So, if I'm trying to disseminate an idea about a new product that's coming out or create some type of excitement and I feel like you are part of a group that might take this idea as social currency and spread it—if I tell you I'm giving it to you as social currency and that I'm really trying to get you to spread it, then you might not want to do that, right? So, the same thing, if you find a funny video online, as an example, and there's no commercial aspect that you can discern easily, you might send that to ten, fifteen of your friends. But at the end of it, if there's a Honda logo or something else, you might send it to a couple of people, but you're probably not going to send it to as many people, because you're feeling like, "Ugh, I don't want to be used by Honda—I'm not doing their work."[36]

Yet the premise of viral marketing—and of the user-generated and word-of-mouth techniques of brand evangelism more broadly—is that you *are*, in fact, doing the work of Honda, Burger King, or any other brand. Thus, a viral campaign must apparently understate its intentions, misdirect its ambitions, and, if necessary, obfuscate its sponsor, for the core tension here is between accommodating an authentic sense of agency and making the participant feel "used" for his or her labor. To achieve that idealized "social currency" status, the brand must endow the value of its content with something more than mere commercial machinations (which is, not coincidentally, the same imperative weighing upon advertainment).

Put differently, this vision of the cool sell promises that the more low-profile the logo on, say, a piece of online video, the farther it has a chance of traveling through e-mail inboxes. A brand that wants to communicate through a viral message must thus embed itself for discovery rather than announce itself as patron. As the industry comes to privilege "engagement" more and more, a site like this—where the first 15 million visitors spent an average of seven minutes per session with the Chicken—seems likely to remain a lauded case study.[37] Jeff Hicks, CEO of CP+B, framed the success in the context of that decade-long shift from "push" to "pull" media: "Interruption or disruption as the fundamental premise of marketing no longer works. . . . You have to create content that is interesting, useful or entertaining enough to invite (the consumer). Viral is the ultimate invitation."[38] And invitation, rather than imposition, is the epitome of the philosophy that animates power in this regime of marketing engagement.

### The "Populist" Governance of Viral Culture

Part of the appeal of viral strategy, like so many other tactics of guerrilla marketing, rests on a pretense of populism—a means of commercial structure working "from below," through (and hence on) consumer audiences it can't seem to manage through the traditional institutions of authority. Unlike the intrusiveness of "interruption" advertising—where those audiences seem eager to avoid commercial messages—viral trades on the premise of participants *opting in* to the promotional project, oftentimes complimenting the campaign with their own contribution (anything from a photo submission to a short-film production), and then ratifying it through pass-along to members of their social network. Thus, in that shift from "push" to "pull" media, viral exudes a democratic affect—a "youocracy," even, as one interviewee spins it: "The epicenter of effective user-driven marketing campaigns [with] 'you' [the user] and the media landscape the advertiser faces is a 'media youocracy' with empowered users who can make or break any product or brand."[39]

Supposedly egalitarian features suffuse: amateurs, not professionals, are creating the content; decentralized not dictatorial channels circulate it; mash-up productivity that once drew cease-and-desist letters from corporations' copyright counsel is now being encouraged by many of those same companies; and all the while, CMOs enthuse about "dialogue," in contrast to the more tightly controlled, one-way monologue that once wholly comprised brand narratives. Even "citizen marketing," the oft-used synonym for the more clunky "consumer-generated marketing," is redolent of democratic affect.

Yet the notion that viral is somehow an organic tally of *authentically* achieved popularity assumes that advertisers aren't trying to game the blogosphere just as much as real-life politicians employ a variety of strategies (of varying ethical fidelity) to win elections and thus stretching the populist plausibility of online buzz metrics. Corporations increasingly desire assurances that viral campaigns will garner a set level of exposure, consequently "seeding links on video-sharing sites and blogs, even trying to manipulate YouTube rankings to gain visibility."[40] Fundamentally, advertisers still need scale—and clients still need a "mass" of consumers to buy their products and remain competitive—but viral content is thought to achieve that scale more organically through grassroots networked flows rather than broadcast transmission. Viral content, moreover, represents the digital manifestation of Sarah Thornton's "subcultural capital": it operates in a kind of "underground" online field, removed from the appearance of hierarchical power structures, and trickling up to become massified at a certain tipping point rather than being disseminated in a widespread fashion from the start.[41]

GoViral is one such firm offering its services to achieve those assurances of mass success; because it does not create any content of its own but rather plants others', it might be termed a kind of "media buyer" for the Web 2.0 space. Forged in response to the woeful click-through rates of banner advertisements (the web banner being a fitting, if ungainly symbol of old media persuasion and governance—the billboard specifically—plunked down in a new media environment), GoViral tries to strategize online marketing in more subtle, seemingly democratic ways. Early in the decade, the company tried to manually drum up buzz by "whispering in certain blog environments and forums" about client content, but, more recently, their work has evolved toward a more structured long-tail approach with systematic categories and channels assembled for digital seeding.[42] In an interview, Maymann discusses a viral campaign for a new Nissan car, which involved targeting young influencers "in a non-intrusive manner." One can hear chords of planted populism—of the grassroots gamed—in the cool sell ethos informing this project:

> By using numerous channels, as opposed to a central micro-site and letting the story unfold and progress in sequences, the [Nissan] campaign gains a certain air of underground activity. This does not mean that it won't be clear to people that this is a commercial message launched as branded entertainment, but it gives the users the opportunity to engage

with the brand in a different way. . . . [This] can be likened to a boutique hotel rather than a Hilton. By not being ubiquitous and flashy, it's a campaign designed to make users investigate and engage with it, by appearing at well-chosen locations which it takes a [connoisseur] to seek out. It is about ongoing storytelling, rather than quick delivery, letting the story evolve instead of the classic linear format which is more closed. To sum up, the strategy of the campaign is to leave as many doors open as possible, and maintain exclusivity by staying off the mainstream channels.[43]

That "exclusivity," so characteristic of Thornton's subcultural capital, informs promotion that unfolds in a context sensitive to (and indeed predicated on) the structure of contemporary media ecology. Avoiding a "central micro-site" here is the online equivalent of Cole & Weber slotting their Rainier beer show at 1 a.m. or Interference planting *Aqua Teen* light boards inconspicuously among the urban landscape: It is promotional content meant to be "stumbled upon" (serendipitous discovery) rather than "foisted upon" (intrusive interruption). Indeed, Maymann's delicate phrasing about a campaign that fundamentally wants to seem noncommercial but that would apparently still "be clear to people that this is a commercial message" once more runs aground of the difficulties of and dilemmas over disclosure. For example, GM drew criticism in 2006 when it planted three seemingly "member-generated" clips on video-sharing websites. The brand's agency defended the move in familiar language: "The decision to put [them] out and let people discover it on their own seemed like the natural, organic way to do it. . . . When you start promoting these things too heavily, people get annoyed that it is a promotion rather than something interesting."[44] As Maymann further suggests:

> One of the reasons that brands find it hard to influence social media is because the flaw of classic marketing tells us to complete our communication, brand value, and experiences, before we launch the product. . . . Social media can be defined as the democratization of information. . . . The illusion of control needs to be replaced by an understanding of the need to provide flexible scenarios of perception. For a better outcome, give your audience credit for their intelligence, invite them in, and let them use you in their identity project.[45]

The notion of advertising letting audiences "use you [the marketer] in their identity project" is predicated upon that operability of an open work. Such branded applications of self-expression—whereby the brand is positioned as a "cultural resource" available for use within an "identity project"—include:

CP+B's SimpsonizeMe.com promoting *The Simpsons Movie* in which users were invited to submit a photo that would be rendered à la Matt Groening's cartoon characters; MadMenYourself.com where fans could project themselves as an animated avatar in the 1960s fashion style of the AMC TV show; and, as part of an OfficeMax holiday campaign, an "Elf Yourself" micro-site that enabled participants to upload headshots that landed atop high-pitched, singing-and-dancing elf bodies. Presuming "prosumption" or "produsage" as the first stage in the marketing co-creation process, these campaigns then encouraged users to spread the branded content via e-mail and social network profiles.[46] Tactics like these try to get participants to see themselves, quite literally, *in* the brand-text—to embed and reroute identity through the digital circuits of these media properties, which, rendered newly lithe compared to the "closed" controls of traditional advertising, can accommodate that interactive agency and co-creation.

## Buzz Agency 2.0

Amateurs are not only being productively employed in anchoring a new media enthymeme like Subservient Chicken or MadMenYourself.com, they are being handed more ostensibly professional duties in the form of sponsored blogs and tweets, which represent, probably most acutely, the word-of-mouth analogue for the digital realm. As this portion of the advertising industry continues to grow (it is expected to top $3 billion in revenues by 2013), it holds the potential to reshape and reorganize the role played by marketers: from "top-down communicators, in control of what information is released, to whom and when, as well as the channels of communication themselves" to social and digital *facilitators*—cooperating and collaborating as partners rather than authoring and administering as supervisors.[47]

The operability of the advertisement as an *opera aperta*—agile and contingent as a tool for exerting governance and interpellating agency from the consumer subjects it courts—is as relevant here as it has been theorized throughout. For example, as became apparent in conversations with several social media marketing firms, if a promotional message is written out in full by an advertiser to be inserted into an amateur's online publishing stream (be it blog or tweet), the less authentic it sounds and, hence, the less "naturalized" that effort at exercising power. But by presenting the brand or product to digital interlocutors as an open work, hype is thought to emerge more organically as part of the process of agents discovering the features rather than having them drilled into memory through an explicit hot sell. Promotion, as such, is meant to blend in, guerrilla style, with the (nonpromotional) communication flow. Or, more abstractly, the legitimacy that freedom licenses when seeking to conduct subjects obliges vernacularization, not ventriloquism.

In an interview, Ted Murphy, CEO of Izea, which paid its 400,000 social media content creators for their "sponsored conversations" or "sponsored tweets," explains how less is more for advertisers who opt to allow participants to tailor the ad message to their individual online voices rather than cut and paste a pre-set sponsored message into their blog or tweet-stream:

> The most successful advertisers actually provide the least amount of information. And so, me saying, you know, "Here's our laptop, here's a couple of facts about it, we want to know what you think"—those advertisers are going to be a lot more effective than an advertiser that says, "Here are all the value propositions of our product and here's why we think it is better than our competition." Because you want people to approach it in their own way and kind of—whether you want them to directly repeat that information or not—the more you fill someone's head with information— kind of the less creative they get to form their own opinion.[48]

A similar logic emerged in conversation with Phoebe Jamieson, vice president of marketing for Magpie, a German firm that had 15 million agents among its ranks, which sprang up in recent years to capitalize on the phenomenon of micro-blogging (and has since been acquired by Izea). According to Jamieson, when agents rephrase a given advertisement placed in their Twitter stream (as opposed to just rehashing canned ad-speak), it results in a 32 percent higher click-through rate of engagement: "[Followers] are used to hearing a certain tone, a certain style. . . . By allowing that Twitterer to really contemplate the offering and think about it from 'what . . . my followers are going to find interesting,' it . . . hooks a lot more [of them]."[49] The logic here again is that the ad message should shroud itself—camouflaged, guerrilla-style—with the native vernacular of that particular digital space, rather than protrude outward as an obvious commercial interloper. For this reason, Magpie advocates to prospective clients: "Join the conversation, don't try to buy it. . . . By running more variations of ads, you will be able to generate an advertising campaign that comes across in a more natural and conversational manner. Better yet, allow the Twitterer to put your ad in their own words. . . . Keep your message conversational. Twitter is not the forum for 'hard sell.'"

That "hard sell" (or "hot sell," as I've tweaked it throughout) is a program of Taylorist discipline more suited to transmission ecology: a program more suited to a media world in which interactive agency was less feasible, much less preferable. But an environment where heterarchical patterns of information flow exist alongside (and are mobilized within) hierarchical structures—an environment that might be characterized as the "new media of mass conversation" or "mass self-communication"—flexibility in the service of populist decentralization is the promotional order of the day.[50] Murphy's Izea interlocutor is *expected* to "act, innovate, tinker, and run free" because it is that independent expression that authenticates her entreaty on the marketer's behalf; it is that digitally rendered sovereign agency that legitimizes the project of power in the service of commerce.[51]

To provide some brief background on the organizational process (as noted for BzzAgent in chapter 4), take the work of Matchstick, a Canadian social media firm, which unfolds in three parts: (1) a recruitment phase where they mine for and solicit interest from "online influencers" who are popular and prolific in the blogosphere, on Twitter, and through social networks; (2) an activation phase where those participants (from fifty to several hundred for a given campaign) receive a client's product and are expected to "talk about or write about or photograph or videotape their experience" with that product (lasting three to six months); and (3) a measurement phase where they follow up with survey questions and monitor the online buzz that is generated and spread. Perhaps the biggest challenge for Matchstick, over a decade of work, has been to wean clients away from that sense of authority they are typically accustomed to holding in a campaign: "Slowly, they start to take the steps in terms of engaging consumers, listening to consumers. . . . You can't do social media marketing or word-of-mouth marketing without giving up some control," acknowledges Matchstick's co-founder Matthew Stradiotto.[52]

Although buzz firms operating in the Web 2.0 space seem to be trading on the credibility of those social media influencers that they enlist, disclosure is no less a contested issue for these agencies than their offline cousins (see chap. 4). Earlier in the decade, for example, Murphy's Izea shop allowed bloggers to decide for themselves whether to disclose that some content was sponsored; now, like most other firms running online buzz campaigns, the agency mandates disclosure via, for example, a "#spon" hash-tag affixed to any particular paid tweet.[53] Nonetheless, several instances of deliberate corporate chicanery have cropped up over the years in the form of supposedly "user-generated" digital content: a site ("Wal-Marting Across America") purporting to be the cross-country chronicle of a couple who parked their RV each night in a Wal-Mart parking lot turned out to be a sponsored blog, put out by the retailer's PR agency; around the same time, Coke and Sony attempted to launch Coke Zero and PSP, respectively, by deploying their own quirky "flogs," or fake blogs; and a few years later, the electronics company

Belkin admitted to paying for good reviews on Amazon.[54] More recently, a group of businesses filed a class-action lawsuit against Yelp.com, alleging that the company lured advertisers with the promise of higher placement of positive reviews and lower placement of negative reviews. As the *Washington Post* reported of the suit, "What appears to be a spin-free, grass-roots marketplace of opinions is rapidly turning into a hotly contested battleground where public relations firms and a new breed of imagemakers help businesses counter negative online comments and manage their online reputations."[55]

By planting that which seems organic and simulating that which seems autonomous, this might represent the darker art of online buzz: astroturfing 2.0, if you will. In fall 2009, in response to some of those abuses of trust that have taken place in a digital context—like creating such vested blogs while purporting to objectivity, paying for favorable online reviews and comments, and posting information online under fictitious guises—the FTC laid out a series of guidelines clarifying what had long been law anyway: that disclosure of affiliation takes place and that only truthful claims are made.[56] The push, which was accompanied by a threat of $11,000 in fines for each infraction, was an attempt to promote greater transparency through blogging, social networking, and other Internet platforms; as one social media expert advised companies on the guidelines, "The enforcement environment has changed entirely. What you may have been able to get away with in the World Wide Web's Wild West era will no longer work."[57]

## Contesting the Advertisement

The consumer-generated advertising contest represents another recent example of marketer governance that seeks to marshal the productivity of the crowd and "shepherd" it to useful ends. In particular, the 2009 Ford Fiesta launch offers an archetypal case study in this regard for the way in which it sought to harness the momentum of "disinterested" digital interlocutors so as to embed hype in their social media flows and outputs—insinuating the structure of commercial objectives into the self-directed autonomy of amateur participation. The very name itself given to this program (the Fiesta "Movement") is evocative of public relations–worthy aspirations in terms of mobilizing and conducting the conduct of otherwise independent clients. Sam de la Garza, the Fiesta brand manager, states:

> The real reason why "grassroots" fits with this specific situation is because we're not selling this car [yet]. . . . What we're asking people to do is to fall in love with the car, fall in love with the movement, and start following the

movement and really hoping that that groundswell of activity and action can keep people interested and engaged. . . . We had a long list of different names that we considered and thought about and really started batting around. But at the end of the day, Fiesta "Movement" just conveyed a message of actual action. And it really worked in terms of the people that we were looking for . . . these initial agents for creating this change and creating this movement.[58]

Note here several of the themes that have been woven prominently throughout: the effacement of the sales component; the pursuit of grassroots authenticity for a program of structural contrivance (commerce); and the use of actual action from "change agents" as a resource to be fostered toward a particular end. The story of the Ford Fiesta campaign fittingly begins as something of an anxious response to demographic and institutional circumstances—and, once more, we find it centers on youth as the guerrilla target. According to de la Garza, Ford had been hemorrhaging market share annually for millennials at an "incredible rate," and the Fiesta was an attempt to woo that increasingly central (if, as seen here, generally assumed intractable) age cohort.

Experimenting with a decidedly social media-heavy approach and foregoing much of the initial mass media buy, the automaker financed a contest that gave one hundred young, web-savvy winners free gas, insurance, and six months behind the wheel of the new subcompact. In exchange, participants were expected to complete one "mission" each month with the car (based around a common theme, e.g., "travel," "technology," "social activism," "adventure") and post their impressions via YouTube, Flickr, MySpace, Facebook, blogs, and the like. Applicants for the program were scored based on their "social vibrancy" ("how much they were followed online and across how many platforms") and their creative and technical proficiency with the Web video medium.[59] By deploying popular, productive social media butterflies on behalf of the company, Ford hitched itself to the credibility of amateurs and concealed connotations of authority through guerrilla means—burying the project of consumer governance beneath the "guilelessness" of branded content borne of independent brand evangelists:

It's one thing when you go to ask somebody, "Hey, Mike, how many followers do you have on Twitter and how many friends do you have on Facebook?" And we jot down the numbers and go, "Oh, wow, you've got 1,000 friends on Facebook, you must be powerful!" The cool thing about making them actually execute a video was that (a) we learned how they told the story and could you tell a story through YouTube? But most importantly, it was: Now show me or demonstrate to me, demonstrate to the Ford Motor Company that of the content that you've developed, do people really listen? Do people watch that? So what it became was a really powerful tool to verify what they were telling us. . . . It's like, wow, this is proof now that these people can go out and generate an audience.[60]

This is, after all, what advertising has long specialized in (creating content and assembling audiences), yet when the industry conceives of its role as facilitator of bottom-up communication as much as administrator of information disseminated from the top down, audiences are being shepherded by commercial surrogates. Not only were these young amateur content creators meant to authenticate product enthusiasm to their social network followings in the form of Web 2.0 productivity, but they also themselves provided, for Ford, a ready resource (and an outsourced story source) when de la Garza was plying reporters for favorable coverage: "It made the message more personal. It didn't make the message [from us]: 'Ford Motor Company is selecting this person because they have all these characteristics.' It was more all of the questions coming from reporters [to participants], like, 'Why did you even want to apply for this Ford Motor Company thing?'"

This is, in a double sense, "circuitous power"—it operates through digital contexts and also it takes a tortuous approach to conducting conduct, à la public relations. It does this by obfuscating corporate authorship and channeling the ad message through more "authentic" intermediaries (be they Fiesta evangelists or the journalists writing about those evangelists) so as to corral disinterested parties and flows to do the work of marketers who are, by definition, not neutral and, therefore, trustworthy about the hype. To be certain, participants were ceded what appeared to be genuine autonomy in constructing their video installments; de la Garza, for instance, reported "major concern" about and subsequent "war-game . . . ideas" for potentially unflattering content that might get posted. The challenge was in achieving a modicum of panoptic awareness: "The thing that worried me the most was: Were we, as a team, going to be able to listen enough? . . . We're not staffed to read a million tweets every day—I can't physically read everything the agents are writing. The only thing I can do is probably read 5–10 percent of everything and hope that I'm listening enough."

This represents a significant reversal of roles that bespeaks contingency and instability: "The centralized model is essentially inside out. You create all the messages and you send them out," says one open-source marketing expert. "The new model is outside in: What you want to do is to receive all the information you can from the outside and incorporate them in the processes

of the company."[61] This again functions as not just outsourced proselytizing but self-sustaining reconnaissance, as crowd-sourced content acts like a
"real world" focus group finding, providing "naturalized" insight from consumers about the product—a digital Rorschach test, if you will, for collective
brand perceptions. And this is, moreover, one of the main critiques that Mark
Andrejevic levels at the "premature" celebration of interactivity as democratic
and empowering: The oft-hyped dialogue with the brand is actually but an
"invitation to submit to the monitoring gaze of market researchers" and the
"egocasting" emblematic of social networks and user-generated content "gives
marketers the most direct window into our psyche and buying habits they've
ever had."[62] Or, put differently, "To draw persuasive messages from the very
audience that one is trying to persuade is [the] ultimate form of marketing
research. In theory, customers know what they want, and . . . crowd-sourced
advertising . . . [gets] customers to produce it in the first place."[63]

To that end, the industry has developed a number of listening practices
in recent years—the magnanimous euphemism for the more cold and calculating "surveillance," but which has, like surveillance, control as its eventual
endgame. For instance, agencies like Omnicomm's Rapp and WPP's Wun-
derman are testing out "text mining" tools like "Digital Anthropology" and
"Listening Platform," respectively, that can sift through "the conversations
taking place on blogs, Twitter, or other social-media sites to identify the
emotional aspects and reasons behind consumer behavior." One Rapp client,
7-Eleven, champions the validity of such a data-gathering process: "It's not in
a focus-group setting so we were getting explicit and authentic data."[64]

Doritos represents another major company that has toyed with crowd-
sourced advertising. In 2006, the snack label launched their "Crash the
Super Bowl" contest, which offered fans the chance to craft a commercial
that, following a "public" vote, could air during the big game. A press release
hyped attendant projects in which "the brand *put the consumer in control,*"
like the "Fight for the Flavor" program, "which *invited* Doritos fans to determine which of two new flavors survived on store shelves and which one was
pulled": the "X-13D Flavor Experiment, where consumers *had a chance* to
name a mysterious new flavor of Doritos"; and the "Unlock Xbox" competition, "which *empowered* fans to design the first-ever consumer-created" Xbox
game (italics added). And, yet, as open and collaborative as these efforts are
meant to portray Doritos, just two clicks over to the FAQ part of the same
website hosting that press release,[65] a legal disclaimer disabuses the aspiring
consumer-creator of any illusions that might be harbored about the parity
of roles: "We are unable to accept ideas and suggestions from outside the
company. The policy not to accept unsolicited ideas was adopted to preserve

good relations with the public. We genuinely appreciate your interest, but do not want to foster false expectations as to the origin of any idea."

Co-creation, then, has its limits and even those imperatives do not always take. Whether the brand genuinely believes in ceding full control to the consumer as the "democratization" marketing myth holds—or has, in reality, a more limited view of that participatory space, as Doritos' legalese betrays above—the fact remains that by opening itself to "citizen" media contests, the brand is, potentially, opening itself up to wayward uses by new audiences of convergence culture.

General Motors learned this lesson well in 2006 when it became the poster child for consumer-generated advertising gone awry.[66] As part of a promotional initiative for its Tahoe SUV model, Chevy supplied audio and visual material online, and encouraged consumers to mash-up and submit a finished commercial from the raw media pieces. However, when culture jammers crashed the contest and populated Chevy's website with "endless iterations of one idea: that the gas-guzzling Tahoe was a grotesque offense against a green earth," it became more known for the subversive satire than the straitlaced participation.[67]

Nike learned a similar lesson when promoting its Nike iD website, which allowed consumers to customize their own shoes with a personalized message; as one company executive audaciously declared, "The Internet allows the brand to adjust or adapt to fit the individual, not the other way around." One activist's prank—attempting to apply "sweatshop" to his individualized sneaker pair—resulted in an amusing and highly publicized back-and-forth with the company that revealed "the limit to Nike's version of self-expression."[68] The British conglomerate Virgin Group halted its own consumer-generated advertising contest when members of an online community solicited to create commercials submitted insubordinate content featuring Virgin's founder, Richard Branson, in reportedly "compromising situations."[69] And Skittles' brief experiment enabling social media participation in the extreme—whereby the brand's homepage included a prominent "chatter" section that hosted a continuous stream of unfiltered tweets hash-tagging the brand—ended when "pranksters began posting inappropriate messages to appear on the site."[70]

Such transgression illustrates the challenge for those marketers that abdicate traditional message controls and allocate narrative responsibility to the crowd: "It's not all going to be rosy content," admitted a Chevy spokesperson, which, to its credit, continued to host the dissident creations for the duration of its Tahoe competition.[71] Going forward, observers would be well served to watch for how such contests frame amateur co-creative freedom within more or less stringent parameters and delimit a "safe playground" for digital participation and the mash-up of meaning. In positioning the brand as a *contingent* new media enthymeme (that is, eliciting closure from Web 2.0 participants), marketers will surely develop *contingency* measures just in case the loop of meaning is closed in unflattering ways. At a juncture when audiences (and youth audiences, most of all) appear emboldened to involve themselves in the mediation process—via tweets, blogs, homemade videos, and profile pages—the task for brand managers is to shape a semblance of empowering yet manageable conditions. "The challenge of [this] new marketing 'governmentality' is," as Zwick, Bonsu, and Darmody correctly conclude, "to ensure that consumer freedom evolves in the 'right' way."[72]

## The Immersive Interactivity of Alternate Realities

Jordan Weisman, the game designer and co-founder of 42 Entertainment, summarized for me the underlying philosophy here:

> If indeed we've developed all these defenses of [advertising] stuff being blared at us with neon, then let's flip it around and give the implication that you're not supposed to see any of this stuff, because we love to see stuff that we're not supposed to see—we all love the voyeuristic perspective. You know—looking under a rock and finding out what's going on there and so the idea is if we can incite curiosity, then what gets discovered is much more satiating than what's being put in my face. And to me it's all about: What's the appropriate amount of work to make someone put their eye to the keyhole? . . . Traditional advertising is pure exhibitionist: I'm putting it in your face and you can't get away from it. And this kind of marketing is much more voyeuristic: I'm going to entice you to give you a little peek and as a result it's more titillating.[73]

By programming choice and contingency into a campaign, interactive advertising signals the possibility of producing sprawling worlds rather than mere messages and even cultivating an alternate social universe altogether. But such strategy requires a uniquely expansive perspective when it comes to thinking about the use of "space" for a marketing endeavor—namely, that such space be intertextual, platform-agnostic, and, of course, interactive both in terms of advertiser-to-consumer and consumer-to-consumer communication flows. By laying out a cross-platform puzzle, it might cater to the "epistemophilial" pleasures assumed to be endemic to life in contemporary networked society.[74]

When *The Blair Witch Project* debuted in summer 1999—chronologically on the precipice of a momentous and tumultuous period in the advertising industry—it foretold the rise of precisely this kind of promotional platform, the alternate-reality game, which has since appeared with regularity. Interweaving elements of advertisement, alternative outdoor, buzz agency, and crowd-sourced marketing, these elaborate, even labyrinthine, predominantly digital ad-worlds have been variously called "live interactive theater," "immersive entertainment," and "'fractured narrative' campaigns."[75] *Advertising Age* most aptly dubbed them "alternate reality marketing," "a cross-media format that involves a combination of Web sites, fictional characters, and a puzzle that often links consumers to live, real-world elements (staged events, phone calls, classified ads) and to each other in pursuit of an elusive goal."[76]

Perhaps fittingly, Wikipedia offers a useful, concise summation of the main facets of this approach. These include, among others: real life as a medium; collaborative storytelling and hive mind design; storytelling as archaeology (that is, "instead of presenting a chronologically unified, coherent narrative, the designers scattered pieces of the story across the Internet and other media, allowing players to reassemble it, supply connective tissue and determine what it meant"); "the 'this is not a game' aesthetic" ("the game itself did not acknowledge that it was a game"); and, perhaps most evocative of the under-the-radar, cool sell mentality of guerrilla marketing, the notion that "a whisper is sometimes louder than a shout."

As Mike Monello, a co-producer of *Blair Witch* and co-founder of Campfire, one of the more prolific agencies in this space, says, "My internal manifesto for Campfire and my work in advertising is that: I want everything I do in advertising to not really be seen as advertising."[77] (Here, again, note that persistent self-effacement about persuasive intent and the commercial component in favor of something thought more culturally "pure.") Such work aims to "draw consumers into a brand-centric story in which they participate rather than pushing a one-way message via traditional media."[78] When asked to define the philosophy of alternate-reality marketing, Monello replies,

> We create a framework and experiences and content that captures people's imagination through the story and allows *them* to tell the story to each other. The philosophy for us generally is that we're not really the storytellers—we're creating experiences, whether they're digital, physical, or even through a billboard—but we're creating experiences that give *people* a story to tell. . . . [And] we adjust the framework based upon the story that the audiences are telling.[79]

Monello further advises: "You have to start from the narrative, and let the broadcast, print, and everything else come from the narrative, rather than the other way around."[80] Such an imperative could reshuffle historically siloed media departments within the traditional agency structure, as "discovery"—the conceptual model that has underpinned so much of the guerrilla work discussed to this point—reaches its apotheosis here.

As the pseudo-documentary horror story of the disappearance of three young filmmakers who set out to investigate a local ghost legend in the Maryland woods, *Blair Witch* achieved unprecedented box-office success. Some claim it represents the start of the "viral advertising" category as we know it, and others point to it as the "progenitor of the [alternate-reality] genre"; its innovative marketing tactics led to the *Guinness Book* world record for the "highest ever profit-to-cost ratio" with nearly $250 million in worldwide gross on a shoestring budget.[81] Moreover, as the symbol of a fully integrated guerrilla campaign that scattered its "web of information" across both digital and real world touch-points and subsequently relied on its youth fan subculture to piece the puzzle together, it provides an apt entry point into notions of paratextuality and brand community.

Co-directors Daniel Myrick and Eduardo Sanchez began by seeding the rumor of a real "Blair Witch" curse in an eight-minute segment of footage on a cable program; when that show's message board forums erupted with intrigue, Myrick and Sanchez launched a website that contained other "evidence" of the story, including police interviews and characters' journals. The film had been shot in an improvisational style based on a "mythology bible," which the creators had supplied the actors and, as raw footage was pared down, cutting room material became supplementary content for the website.

What is unique here is that the promotional materials were treated as *part* of the brand-text reality rather than external to it. Jonathan Gray dubs these add-ons "paratexts" (e.g., movie trailers, action figures, video game tie-ins, and other forms of media peripherals) and argues that "they create texts, they manage them, and they fill them in with many of the meanings that we associate with them."[82] Although now more commonplace, especially with the standard inclusion of bonus material on film websites and as DVD features, the strategic use of paratexts in 1999 to complement and corroborate the *Blair Witch* story was innovative for its time. While Gray initiates a "textual cartography" of these promotional story-worlds, he advocates more attention to the production context. For like many of the alternate-reality marketing programs that followed in its wake, *Blair Witch* was unique in decentering the mythology—and, with it, the promotion—outside the confines of traditional advertising space: "There was little thought to the idea that the website was marketing and the movie was the product. We didn't have that differentiation," says Monello. "At the end of the day, we were storytellers and when the website started, there was nothing to sell."[83] Much like advertainment, the self-effacing promotion was not just inseparable from, it was, in fact, concentric with the content itself.

The *Blair Witch* website was thus one of the first media properties to treat its online marketing space in this way—as a textual and multimedia extension of the reality traditionally encased between the opening and closing credits. To this digital augmentation, the producers added out-of-home, alternative ambient elements like "missing persons" fliers for the film's cast (not unlike the "micro-media" in chap. 3) and sent intern "community trend-setters" to high school and college hangouts to drum up buzz there (not unlike the grassroots scheming in chap. 4). The head of marketing at Artisan Entertainment, the studio that purchased and distributed *Blair Witch*, described their efforts fittingly: "We did commercial things, we just executed them in a non-commercial way."[84] This once more encapsulates the cool sell commercial ethos—to market without selling—and fan participation was uniquely critical to achieving that "non-commercial" status:

> We had long gaps where we weren't adding anything to [the website], because we were busy making the film, and the audience started to kind of speculate and create and fill in that gap. And we started kind of promoting that, because we saw that the audience was, in a way, telling the story to each other and threading that out. And to us that was of great value, because they were coming up with interesting theories and so we encouraged that. And even to the point where we would get some pieces of material sometimes—and it started as we just didn't have time to put it up on our website, so we would e-mail it to some of the fans who were building up fan sites and give them exclusive content. . . . We realized the fans were building better sites to tell the *Blair Witch* story than we had built. So instead of competing, why not play along and give them material that's unique for them? And this was actually pretty radical, because at the time Paramount was sending cease-and-desist letters to *Star Trek* fan sites.[85]

What this interactivity equally demands is a brand-text (here an entertainment product, a narrative flow) conceived as contingent with the "hive mind" in mind. It suggests a break from the time when media companies— and all brands, for that matter—retained a firmer grip over the use of their intellectual property and franchise icons to an era of more fluid negotiation with the subcultures that venerate them. The digital infrastructure of web-based storytelling largely enables that flexibility that encourages these "brand communities" to flourish.

Albert Muniz and Thomas O'Guinn developed this concept, which they define as "a specialized, non-geographically bound community, based on a structured set of social relations among admirers of a brand."[86] Similarly, Alex Wipperfurth recommends that advertisers try to cultivate a "brand tribe"—"a group of people who share their interest in a specific brand and create *a parallel social universe* ripe with its own values, rituals, vocabulary, and hierarchy."[87] And the veteran marketing executive Douglas Atkin further proposes that "cult" is precisely the level of loyalty that a brand should be striving for, as he challenges advertisers to generate, among consumers, the same magnetism of attraction to brands that *cults* have long harbored from their followers.[88] Nowhere is the notion of a branded "social universe" more apparent than in the alternate-reality marketing arena. Certain campaigns like "The Purification" (McKee Wallwork Cleveland's work for Taos Ski Valley) have even courted palpably cultish illusions of simulating an "underground movement." A creative director there recalls the cultural logic at play in brainstorming the project:

> If you were so fanatical about something, so passionate about something, it's your religion so to speak, how would you act? And we started thinking about the idea that it was: There is a secret movement. We did think of it that way. What if there was a secret movement to restore the pure skiing sport to where it came from—its soul?[89]

Their goal for "The Purification" was to be entirely "social network created," a hallmark, in fact, of authentic grassroots movements as well as artificial commercial ones. With an air of sectarian allegiance, their thematic catchphrase—"purification"—was part of a cryptic, encoded website teaser launch that contained no trace of the ski resort that was to be the eventual "product" pitched. To that, they added a "seeding" component, which included "littering public places" around the country with napkins, sticky notes, and playing cards featuring the opaque logo—a diamond-square-circle symbol meant to be cracked.[90] Bumper stickers were disseminated with the symbol, which, the creative director explains, "was like, 'I'm in the club and if you don't know what this means, then you're not going to be in this club.' So there was this whole psychological thing we were trying to seed."[91]

In the years since *Blair Witch* initiated this alternate-reality marketing format, a host of other firms have attempted to stage their own enigmatic efforts. By one estimate from a leading game designer and researcher, there were seventeen of these transmedia mystery-marketing programs in the first half of the last decade alone.[92] The phenomenon has become more "common," more "organized," and more "professionalized," and it is showing up both within the United States and internationally.[93] Volvo, for example, launched a new luxury S40 series with an elaborate "mockumentary" campaign (featuring faux websites) about a Swedish town of S40 obsessives.[94] Similarly, BMW released a half-hour mockumentary of branded content about a small Bavarian town's efforts to catapult a car from Germany to the United States (setting up fake websites for the town and its residents), while officially denying it had any hand in the hoax: "People were saying it was real. People were saying it was a marketing campaign. . . . We and the company wanted to stay in character and let them have fun with that discussion," remarked the campaign's art director.[95] In Malaysia, a BBDO affiliate ran an alternate-reality campaign to launch a MINI car model featuring a mysterious protagonist trying to reveal the truth about a secret plane cargo, including mass e-mails, video messages, curious packages, and online sites. "[T]his guerrilla campaign," the firm proudly and fittingly boasted, "did not produce a single piece of advertising.[96] And in the Dominican Republic, aiming for a "youth movement, not a new beer," the leading brewery there launched the "One Movement" campaign, which combined illegal guerrilla stickers, viral videos, faux protests, fines and arrests, social media engagement, and scarce product—all in "the language of rebellious youths who live both online and underground and like to feel they are discovering things for themselves."[97]

One of the most prolific companies has been 42 Entertainment, which developed one of the earliest promotional "alternate-reality games" ("The Beast" for the 2001 film *A.I. Artificial Intelligence*) as well as some of the most popular ("I Love Bees," for the 2004 release of *Halo 2*, claimed 3 million participants).[98] From start to finish, "The Beast" interpellated communal energy as it "required players to work together, seeking out friends, tapping Web communities, drawing in anyone you could find."[99] When an alternate-reality project is designed with gaps needing to be filled in like this, the labor of the participant curiously becomes the content of the advertising performance, as Susan Bonds, president and CEO of 42 Entertainment, makes clear: "In some ways we are the architects but [we are] also the observers of the story, because it plays out in ways that can't always be predicted. And the audience has a million little personal stories that are uniquely theirs—*they are a part of putting on this show*, so to speak."[100]

Take, for example, "Why So Serious?" 42 Entertainment's sophisticated and interactive teaser campaign, which helped launch the 2008 film *The Dark Knight*, and activated a reported 10 million unique participants,

750,000 of whom took part in live events and out-of-home activities around the world.[101] Around major American cities, 42 placed—and then subsequently defaced with graffiti ("graffadi")—an assortment of stickers and fly-posters for Harvey Dent, a character running for district attorney in the film. To unlock the "Why So Serious?" website, fans were tasked with sending in e-mails, each one enabling the removal of a single pixel of what would eventually reveal Heath Ledger's Joker character (a clever cover for creating e-mail datasets). Dozens of other covert and overt websites digitally fleshed out the contours of Gotham City. Participants who submitted photos and videotapes of themselves in Joker make-up at tourist landmarks worldwide received bonus materials and supplementary clues to the mystery unfolding (a user-generated content solicitation); other participants who rallied in urban public spaces on behalf of Harvey Dent (street spectacle) received voice mails and text messages from the candidate. In sum, "Warner Brothers positioned the audience not simply as consumers of advertisements, but as interactive partners in the advertising campaign itself," as GoViral's CEO Jimmy Maymann observes: "Allowing the controlled release of information to customize and reward a user's experience, based on their level of interaction, has allowed them to educate themselves about the movie. Empowering a dedicated, select fan base creates a powerful and loyal audience without having to push information at them."[102]

Clearly, the verbs here ("allow," "empower") once again bespeak the branding ethos emblematic of the regime of engagement, wherein the advertiser—not unlike a game designer—orchestrates an alternate reality and obliges participation from the consumer target by pulling rather than pushing a promotional message. Yet "message," and perhaps for that matter "campaign," is really the wrong context to frame the alternate-reality project within, because the alternate-reality marketer is more world-builder than message-sender and must arrange for an interactive architecture that can accommodate multiple tiers of audiences, from casual browser to die-hard loyalist.

According to Jordan Weisman, co-founder of 42 Entertainment, this leads to marketing explicitly designed in a "pyramid" structure, which can satisfy both those hard-core and occasional participants: "You're looking to that early advocator group—as we call them, 'the kindling'—that is going to be the spark to what you're putting out there initially and then, you know, you're going to use their enthusiasm, their excitement and their accomplishments to bring in successive larger circles of audience members."[103] "Kindling" is an instructive way of framing the function of intensely committed loyalists in this guerrilla marketing project, for without their engagement—both in terms of solving puzzles that unlock more of the mystery game and

in terms of proselytizing about the pleasure of participation to their network of friends—the media franchise will not catch fire. Moreover, "their
enthusiasm, their excitement, and their accomplishments" authenticate a
promotional energy more genuine than a conventional advertisement can
muster. This strategy leads to a relationship between labor and spectacle
identified thus: "The *content created by a small audience* in reaction to pri-
mary-producer content has actually become *the main product of consumption for mass audiences*."[104]

*Blair Witch* stumbled onto the utility of this collaboration during those
fallow narrative moments in the promotion process when fans would close
the loop of meaning and respond to the new media enthymeme by filling
in the gap of storytelling on the film's website. Now that outsourcing is not
only deliberate, it is *essential* to the progress of an alternate-reality campaign.
Again, as with so many cool sell case studies, less is ever more: The new
media enthymeme structures agency, stages discovery, and whispers rather
than shouts. In a campaign like "Why So Serious?" the *crowd*—that brand
community and social universe constructed in relation to the commercial-
text—serves as the authority for promoting *Dark Knight* rather than the studio or agency that stands to profit from it; it is yet another way of authenticating buzz by outsourcing hype through disinterested intermediaries
hooked into a game, which baits them both intellectually and socially. One
designer explains the "realism aesthetic" native to this approach: "[These] are
games with an identity crisis: 'IT doesn't know it's a game.'"[105] These are just
as much *advertising campaigns* with an identity crisis: IT doesn't know it's an
advertising campaign.

The Future of Net-Work?

These assorted examples of crowd-sourced marketing hold the potential to
reshape the role and self-conceit of the industry as it "dematerializes" the
media work conducted. Fittingly, this accords with other patterns of immaterial labor visible across the digital landscape right now. The more that
amateurs are invited into the production process and the more advertising
views its product as an *opera aperta*, the more it demolishes the myth of (and
therefore monopoly on) a "special" creative class that generates content from
an elevated professional perch—and the more it could augur change in what
those professionals in *all* media industries are expected to do.

Unilever, for one, fired Lowe, the agency responsible for its Peperami
account, a British snack brand, in favor of crowd-sourcing ad ideas through a
South African firm called Idea Bounty—a testament to both the institutional

flexibility that Web 2.0 hath wrought as well as the global flow of creative labor opportunities in that context. Rather than getting the ideation input from "two or four creatives" at Lowe, as it alleged, Unilever opened the advertising challenge up more widely, offering a $10,000 prize for the winning submission and, along the way, earning Idea Bounty "quite a lot of negative" feedback: "People get sensitive and think we are threatening the creative industry," the agency's marketing director confided.[106] Because creativity has long "been subject to mystification and thus relegated to the clutches of a small, elite group," as one observer puts it, such "democratization" is bound to "puncture" the "creative ego," which Daniel Neville, Idea Bounty's brand coordinator, acknowledged in an interview.[107]

Neville counters that while his company is, admittedly, in the business of *dis*-integrating a core competency of agencies, implementation still requires the creative skill sets of professionals. This is, however, cold comfort; if the past ten years are any indication, traditional barriers to creative entry into the media industries, like hardware cost and software proficiency, are likely to continue to erode. In other words, cultural production is no longer in the hands of just the professionals—as any web-cam cineaste, basement blogger, or bedroom DJ knows. Ideation *and* implementation are already both very much crowd-sourceable.

Ironically enough, Unilever was actually hoping to "pitch" the contest less to the general public and more to other "professionals in creative businesses." According to Neville, nearly half of the participants in Idea Bounty's previous ideation challenges came from *within* the advertising industry—copywriters, art designers, directors, strategy guys, and the like—a phenomenon that would seem to be corroborated in other competitions as well. One finalist in the Doritos Super Bowl contest was a location scout for commercials who took time off from work to create the video submission in the hopes of landing her creative content on a high-profile stage; another finalist claimed that he was "'doing whatever it takes to get some recognition' with [similar aspirations] of 'being signed by a production company' as a result of the exposure."[108]

It is interesting to note that it is not only amateur actors, musicians, and filmmakers who are often eager to take advantage of these "corporate canvases" but also those hoping to reach the higher creative rungs of the advertising industry itself. Even as advertising organizes the competitions illustrated here as a way of harnessing the collective productivity of the amateur media-makers, within that competition participants are vying to stand out in the crowd-source. This raises the question of how porous that designation of "amateur" versus "professional" may one day become, and whether, because of that blur, the former may increasingly lose its claims to authenticity that it has held over the latter. In sum, the crowd-sourced trend suggests a more flexible, stripped-down model of content creation that erodes former lines between the client, the agency, the production company, and the public; it even portends, as Axel Bruns has proposed, a "'casual collapse' of the traditional content and copyright industries. . . charged with the accumulation and dissemination of information, knowledge, and creative works."[109]

In this chapter we have seen how the enthymemes of new media provide a productive, enticing template for advertisers *if* they are willing to concede flexibility for the brand-text and furnish a digital toolkit to co-creative millennial audiences. Yet the *opera aperta* of "cool media" is appropriate for and applicable to more than mere marketing ends; I would, in fact, submit that *all* media industries might gradually remodel themselves with an eye toward this collaborative elasticity. Such a changing structure anticipates the audience's role differently and turns out a more versatile product—materializing cultural production that is, in a sense, *less* material than ever before.

Journalists who once authored a more definitive, independent article in print now volunteer more provisional, interactive blog posts in cyberspace. Pop music artists once accustomed to cutting a tangible, permanent, analog record on vinyl now know that their MP3 source material is forever incomplete—putty in the hands of a remixing mash-up alchemist somewhere down the line. For cultural producers of all stripes, their textual work goes "from being etched in stone to being written on a dry-erase board."[110] Media "content" is thus rendered more temporary, conditional, and synergetic: a forever-unfinished "final" product. And as the media ecosystem continues to evolve this will impact *how* advertisers and other media professionals do what they do and *whom* they believe they are doing it for. For the free labor of audiences is not just provisioned in the regime of engagement; it contributes necessary and expected productivity to the interactive project.

To be fair, though, for most amateur content creators, this "freedom to labor" is typically a labor of love. It is often unremunerated, yes, but it is also unrequired—gratuitous in the broadest sense. Why, then, do those interpellated by an *opera aperta* voluntarily submit to the part-time work? Is it the pursuit of a "networked reputation" that drives this voluntary media-making—an extension of the entrepreneurial self earlier elucidated?[111] This is certainly possible—although we cannot, of course, know from this research, since I have studied marketers, not audiences. Yet for those aspiring to Hollywood on YouTube, the *New York Times* in the blogosphere, and EMI on

MySpace Music, that "networked reputation" is perhaps assumed to be a down payment toward hopes of long-term financial stability as a member of the creative class in those cultural industries. At a time when advertising is going through a seismic reshuffle of its own traditional relationship with those mass media institutions, eager and cheap talent is, no doubt, a welcome development. One might wonder, though, if this profusion of voluntary labor might eventually erode and devalue the compensation structure that supports those professionals who have already made it in the culture industries.

# 6

## Managing Agency in the Regime of Engagement

When it comes to governing human beings, to govern is to presuppose the freedom of the governed. To govern humans is not to crush their capacity to act, but to acknowledge it and utilize it for one's objectives.
—Nikolas Rose[1]

In 2002, scholars convened a focus group of high-level advertising practitioners and industry experts to rechristen their business. They noted that, throughout history, with each epoch of technological change, so too did the definition of advertising change and the techniques thought to be ideally applicable.[2] Yet the focus group concluded by generating a new definition ("a paid, mediated form of communication from an identifiable source, designed to persuade the receiver to take some action, now or in the future") that still fails to encompass the scope of recent guerrilla marketing trends, primarily because what was once "identifiable" is increasingly elided or obscured as that "persuasion" act is itself designed to be obfuscated or denied.[3]

This book has peered into the logics and practices of power as located in those strategies of the past ten years. Simply stated, I have revealed how *subjects* are increasingly positioned and managed, commercially, as *agents*: how the "conduct of conducts and . . . management of possibilities" utilize freedom toward a particular set of objectives.[4] The consumer subject, in this scheme of governance, needs to act—that is, after all, how advertising effectiveness must ultimately be judged—but this consumer subject is strategically engaged to act *without the sense of being acted upon* in any way. This makes the program of exercising authority a complex, delicate, and even, at times, invisible task.

Just as those who run schools, businesses, and prisons face the challenge of controlling individuals while concurrently recognizing and reconciling those individuals' need to feel they are "not slaves, but free," as Nikolas Rose puts it, so too is the marketer confronted with the conundrum of compelling consumer behavior while self-effacing that contrivance by appearing in variously disinterested, anti-establishment, flexible, and autonomous guises.[5] Freedom is, foremost, the fulcrum for this negotiation of governance, for consumers are obviously not automaton slaves lacking agency in the marketplace (just ask Edsel or New Coke), so invisibility is the way power tries to pull the strings behind the scenes to manage that freedom. Of course, there are no guarantees when it comes to youth subjects so often bemoaned as unmanageable. Invisibility is, then, a means of legitimizing power, because it foregrounds surrogate forces—ambiences, resistances, grassroots, and amateurs—in place of its own obvious, vested, disciplinary intentions and impositions. "To govern is to recognize that capacity for action and to adjust oneself to it," Rose argues. "This entails trying to understand what mobilizes the domains or entities to be governed: to govern one must act upon these forces, instrumentalize them, in order to shape actions, processes and outcomes in a desired direction."[6]

Although advertising is, fundamentally, in the business of "conducting conduct," the industrial discourse (both trade press articles and interviews with professional practitioners) apparently prefers not to speak in such terms. This is because the project of contemporary consumer management— this "regime of engagement" that is informed by the participatory logic of the cool sell and executed through guerrilla media placement—is a project that tries to structure agency and elicit attentiveness through happenstance discovery; it accommodates a façade of content objectivity and disinterested space while self-effacing its own authority and intent; it democratizes and collaborates with subject autonomy and more populist communicative flows; and it opens up the brand as a more flexible, contingent textual form. It is, in short, persuasion without the heavy hand: *governance that tries not to seem like governance.*

The marketers I spoke with will likely disagree with this conclusion and disavow the implication that their work is in any way deceptive. To be clear, I'm not asserting that these guerrilla tactics are somehow "brainwashing," "subliminal," or even necessarily "deceitful" à la *Hidden Persuaders.*

Moreover, this is not meant to be read as a critique of "false consciousness" in new clothes. And certainly it's understandable if the advertising community declined to acknowledge any characterization of product placement or word-of-mouth as even "sly" on some level, for both ethical and legal reasons. Yet the logic of guerrilla strategy articulated by this community betrays a necessary recourse to slyness: Young consumers aren't being "tricked" here in a superficial sense, but because they are assumed, by these advertisers, to be cynical about or seeking to avoid advertising, one must naturally begin to produce a *different* kind of advertising. This different kind of advertising is not just about finding new spaces from which to address that consumer, but philosophically it is about finding a different disposition through which that consumer might be addressed—a disposition that comes across as more understated in seeking to achieve its goal.

Guerrilla marketing therefore functions as camouflage on two levels: It shrouds the advertising message in those unexpected media spaces while also shrouding the fundamental project of consumer discipline that is, ultimately, the eventual and necessary purview of advertising. If that agentic subject is to be used, her freedom cannot be perceived as simply a means to an external end: If the hot sell told her what to buy, the cool sell "lets" her figure it out for herself. Such an approach is, once again, not about interrupting the consumer but engaging her; and by not interrupting but instead "embedding" that message into nontraditional communication flows (a viral meme, sidewalk graffadi, a video game, etc.), some critics will charge "deceit" while many advertisers will rebut they're merely being subtle. How one perceives and evaluates that self-effacement of the persuasion project says much about how one judges audiences and consumers in general: as vulnerable and needing protection or empowered and capable of resisting appeals.

More broadly still, in our networked world of contemporary social ecology, agency is increasingly coded into structure. We, as audiences, are entering into a period of profound change and disruption in terms of how the media tries to govern culture and how advertising tries to govern consumption: "Push" media sought to govern us one way; "pull" media seeks to govern us in quite another. The former imperiously presumed and took for granted a more docile, fixed subject; the latter more deliberately accords and complies with the interactive choice that ensues. I have sought throughout this book to uncover and map the institutional discourse, cultural logic, and technological context underpinning that circuitry of attempted rule when it comes to advertisers toying with guerrilla methods. By situating this diverse set of tactics and strategies in sharp focus, we can begin to make out that broader philosophy of governance that animates them; it is a philosophy wherein the power over the consumer subject is softer, more subtle, and more sophisticated than ever before—where programs of determination are, paradoxically, dependent upon practices of freedom.

Power through Freedom

"Discovery," as heard so often invoked by name and in principle, represents a way of framing that attempt at power as something *em*powering for the subject it is visited upon. It is a way for macro-level machinations to work through the agency and fundamental sovereignty of that subject by setting out the parameters of governance rather than persisting overtly and restrictively—structuring that "possible field of action" in order to instrumentalize influence that emerges from "below" rather than being obtruded from "above." Indeed, discovery, as opposed to persuasion, in some ways mirrors the semantic difference between power and domination that Foucault identified: the former, unlike the latter, presupposes more of a self-determining subject and makes possible a means of embedding the objectives of the ruler in the free choice moment of the ruled.[7] Guerrilla marketers structure the project of agency by attempting to precipitate consumption without really forcing it—"casualizing" the imposition as much as possible. Domination would simply seek to make consumers buy, which it, of course, cannot do; power, on the other hand, seeks to "make consumers *willing*," as pithily summarized from an *Adweek* line in chapter 1.[8]

We saw this repeatedly: from the epigrammatic formulation in Cole & Weber's mission statement ("let them say yes") to the consultant-speak catchphrase Alex Wipperfurth coined to explain Pabst Blue Ribbon's improbable ascendance among young hipsterati (the "brand hijack"). "Let" has so often been the operative verb in the execution of this governance, because "let" allocates a sense of sovereignty rather than stripping those addressed by power of their experience of autonomy. Advertisement *lets* us discover the promotional message amid disinterested cultural content; alternative outdoor *lets* us discover it in the anti-establishment appropriation of public space; buzz agency *lets* us discover it through casual conversation with friends and family; and crowd-sourced marketing *lets* us discover it through new media flows.

When we arrive at the terminus of action under this mode of governance—that is, making a purchase—it must feel "chosen by" more than "chosen for" us, such that we discover rather than are told the commercial directive. Framed starkly, albeit simplistically, one might say that traditional advertising seeks to convince the consumer as a dictator might (interrupting and imposing), while the cool sell cultivates the consumer as a democrat might (being solicited and proposing). The technological conditions empowering audiences largely oblige this staging of and opportunity for agency. Yet agency as a means to obedience might also be contextualized within an even broader strand of neoliberal patterns: The marketing "regime of engagement" is perhaps but a microcosm of a much larger socio-political regime whose long march toward deregulation, open markets, privatized services, and the dismantling of the welfare state can be summarized through much the same unshakeable faith in and emphasis on free choice and personal liberty.[9]

"You've got a generation that doesn't want to be talked to; they want to be included and they're going to make their own decisions," one CEO explains of his firm's consumer-generated approach to reach that young adult demographic.[10] He continues, "The best way to get this demographic on your side is to empower them and give them responsibility, choice, and freedom to help shape your direction." Indeed, young people today represent the ideal neoliberal subject for reasons both timeless and historically specific. On one hand, chronologically, such a demographic is naturally positioned at a fruitful moment of embryonic liberty and identity development, and hence potential commercial attachment. Growing out of puberty and early adolescence, lifestyle choices are being offered and made for the first time and, yet, limitations still linger—all those "'dos' and 'don'ts' and rules" that teens' and even young adults' lives seem filled with. In that context, marketers believe they have to be especially careful about appearing to impinge upon those budding consumer freedoms. In other words, choices have been made *for* the youth subject all her life; advertising must therefore tantalize, above all, with the prospect for choices to be made *by* that subject. And because that identity project is still in motion, authenticity is so critical as cultural "cover" for the purchases made by—not for—the subject. Again, decisions "for" would betray external imposition, which is the basic experience of growing up; decisions "by" suggests autonomous self-direction, which is constitutive of adulthood. This is why your average fourteen-year-old likely cares more about the specter of "selling out" than your average forty-year-old who has likely gotten over such binaries of commercialism-set-against-authenticity. Authenticity, that is, accounts for the experience of the active subject whose (consumer) conduct does not feel conducted as such by marketers. For brands to serve as "cultural resources" to be used in the production of the self—especially a young person whose self is most acutely in flux—"brands must be *disinterested*; they must be perceived as invented and disseminated by parties without an instrumental economic agenda, by people who are intrinsically motivated by their inherent value."[11]

On the other hand, there is something more topical than timeless about these imperatives, and not simply because today's millennial subject faces more advertising and allegedly responds with more instinctive cynicism and jaded resistance than did previous generations. The architects of neoliberal policy and economics might well recognize this ethos and language of governance as related to a shift in political consciousness from collectivity to individualism. Just as citizens have been trained to loathe the "nanny" state in this regime of consciousness, so too are consumers now thought to loathe the "nanny" marketer. Self-reliance—that neoliberal creed of honor—is, after all, a strategy of governance whereby the individual "discovers" what works best for her rather than having it imposed or chosen by an external authority. The irony here, of course, is that while the neoliberal state has slowly dismantled and outsourced its supportive apparatus for citizen governance in the name of freedom—delegating responsibility to the individual wherever it can—these technologies and articulations of *consumer* governance that also accentuate freedom ultimately seek to make the consumer *more* dependent on the marketer. This is also deeply reflective of the changing structure of the media industries: "Impressions," the marketing metric of Fordist communication, presumed a more passive subject; "engagement," the metric of an interactive era, not only acknowledges but obliges the subject's participation.

This suggests a further irony and contradiction to be plumbed in marketers' conceptualizations of their consumer targets. They readily concede audience agency—acknowledging frustrations about ad-zapping, clutter, and cynicism; shrugging off any pretense of wielding manipulative power; and repeating the mantra that "the consumer is in control" nowadays. Yet institutionally, marketers cannot really fully embrace that, for it is their job to be able to regard audiences as subjects to be governed. Certainly in pitches with clients, I highly doubt they're throwing up their hands and announcing an impotence to affect sales. Quite the contrary: What the advertiser sells to the client is the message that she can control and deliver the consumer. In truth, then, the reality of power likely lies somewhere in between marketer manipulation and marketer impotence—and, likewise, the reality of agency lies somewhere in between consumers mindlessly duped and consumers utterly impervious to that entreaty—which, of course, is what has made Foucault's nuanced theorization of governance so useful for this work. Because audiences *do* have genuine agency (and, today, technological forces augment and exhibit it so palpably), marketers have to take that agency into account more than ever. Think here of all the ways chronicled throughout that "the subject-effects implied or aimed for by programmes of [advertiser] rule" could not be assumed in practice: the failure that was Bud.TV's online micro-channels, the powerlessness inherent in needing a "TVH" database of cool, the wily "flock" of consumers that confounds Ressler, and the wayward ad-contest submissions that bedeviled Chevy, Nike, Virgin, and Skittles.[12] An advertisement that decrees, "You must," is interpellating a dupe of a subject; a guerrilla advertisement that suggests, "You may," takes that autonomy, unpredictability, and heterarchicality of that subject far more seriously.

## Self-Effacing Designs

Appearing to abdicate a traditional position of more didactic authority when negotiating consumer behavior is essential when strategizing this governance. It registered every time an advertiser made a fussy show of self-effacing his or her real objectives (i.e., to induce a purchase) and points, once more, to public relations as the intellectual precursor to guerrilla marketing practice. Because selling is ultimately an exercise in power and because youth consumers are thought to be increasingly skeptical of and inclined to filter out those overtures, especially when they can be recognized in familiar contexts, there is a persistent effort to expunge any semblance of behavioral diktat; the anti-authority ethos of the guerrilla approach is a project of minimizing, even obfuscating the role of persuasive force.

This explains why Scott Goodson eschewed the calculating context endemic to the 30-spot ("it's manipulated content that's supposed to persuade you to buy something"); the reverse-psychology engineering of the Truth campaign ("[if we] tell the consumer not to smoke, that's going to be falling on deaf ears"); the articulation of the presumed mentality of the consumer target for BMW's *The Hire* ("its: 'Don't sell me. Like, let me make a decision for myself'"); and Mike Monello's "internal manifesto" for Campfire's alternate-reality marketing campaigns ("I want everything I do in advertising to not really be seen as advertising"). This again educes that central paradox: to act upon an acting subject without that subject feeling as though they've been acted upon.

In fact, the decision to utilize guerrilla media is, from the very start, a deliberate choice to self-efface persuasive intent because these "under-the-radar" contexts tend to lack the conspicuously commercial connotation that might accompany a billboard or 30-spot. Marketers assume that audiences are more drawn to the objective and credible sheen associated with entertainment programming, graffiti and street art, interpersonal relationships, social networks, and amateur and viral content. Recalling the warfare metaphor, these spaces do not look like a "battle" is taking place there to win over consumers' hearts, minds, and pocketbooks quite like the assault they experience amid conventional advertising fields. These are contexts that intrinsically obfuscate the machinations of power embedded within them, which is what makes them so appealing as vehicles for conducting the conduct of audiences so often decried these days as regrettably unmanageable.

For centuries, "Those seeking to exercise power have sought to rationalize their authority."[13] Antonio Gramsci formulated his own summation of this when he wrote, "The attempt is always made to ensure that force will appear to be based on the consent of the majority."[14] And just as Edward Bernays first engaged these principles in the service of PR, the best way of achieving the rationalization of that authority is *to attempt to deny that any such power or authority even exists.*[15] This provides a rationale for the not-uncommon recourse by the interviewees to frame their work here as "education" as much as marketing (and this, too, is a legacy of PR and branding): By skirting the very acknowledgement of one's role as advertiser, one might deactivate the filter that the consumer employs when encountering an advertising message. It naturalizes the agenda of governance. The fact that those in charge of campaigns drawn from so many different contexts often evaded acknowledging their fundamental task of managing desire and moving product also testifies to some unspoken sense of that task, selling, being somehow sullied—at least relative to the more noble and welcomed aspirations officially espoused for the work performed (i.e., culture, community, identity, etc.). Such work, like the "raising awareness" campaigns for pharmaceutical drugs or the commercially unadorned YouTube video that gets forwarded along, aims to shuttle the audience through supposedly neutral content so as to engineer serendipitous encounters with the brand.

The advertainment approach illustrated in chapter 2 is clear evidence of this use of "disinterested" space, but so is the simulated subversion seen in the tactics on display in chapter 3: By embedding a persuasive message in unauthorized, even illicit communicative flows, an anti-establishment (and, thereby, anti-authority) ethos might be cultivated. Micro-media, trading on its claims to authenticity and integrity, governs persuasion differently than broadcast channels do: less imposingly, more casually. It suggests rather than interrupts; whispers rather than shouts. An inconspicuous piece of corporate street art like that of *Aqua Teen* or unexpected branded flash mob by T-Mobile functions transgressively not only in terms of the legality of how noncommercial urban public space is appropriated—because communication, much less corporation communication, is not usually permitted in this way—but also in terms of effacing its own fundamental commercial intent.

## Authenticating through Autonomy

Self-effacement and the creation of a disinterested space are not the only tactics through which authority can obscure its position of power in the process of guerrilla persuasion; embedding the brand in autonomous social and
creative flows is equally a way of outsourcing hype and, hence, concealing
the intent of governance. This is the appeal—and the challenge—of executing something "grassroots," for it is through grassroots flows that choice and
behavior can ostensibly rise up from the people rather than seem imposed
upon them. As the manifestation of a spontaneous, populist (even guerrilla)
uprising, this grassroots energy can function as power because it operates
through independent agents, communities, and networks—that is, those farthest from the appearance of the dominant interests served by it. Public relations is, once again, well versed in this logic of power, particularly "astroturfing," that clandestine approach to simulating political campaigns and social
movements intended to seem impromptu and authentic while actually being
coordinated by a behind-the-scenes organization. As buzz and viral increasingly become a hallowed metric and crucible for success, campaigns for consumer products may increasingly resemble these tactics more traditionally
associated with politics.

This kind of strategy thus bespeaks an attempt to flatten the hierarchy of
relations between authority and subject: a shift in self-conceit from management to facilitation, from administrator to collaborator, from top-down to
bottom-up. Yet in arranging to stage the conditions of governance through
freedom, the marketer *is*, in fact, relinquishing certain patterns of control,
while still aiming for management through collaboration. At a time when
audiences—especially online "prosumer" audiences—seem noisier and more
socially productive than ever as consumer subjects, the logic of such practice
makes it sensible for corporate and political power to work *with* this momentum rather than trying, likely fruitlessly, to stifle or contain it.

Adapting to that socially productive amateur momentum—those blogs,
those tweets, those status updates, that sprawling "public" conversation—is
yet another way of disguising authority; for by furnishing the raw digital
materials meant to satisfy audiences' co-creative needs, the marketer hopes
to frame freedom and channel creativity. Thus, this line of governance is how
employment gets induced through a guise of empowerment; the latter serves
as a strategic rhetorical cover for the former, as consumers co-create value
for the brand and their free labor is appropriated to constructive and dis-
tributive ends. It is a way of putting participation to good use, especially at a
time when self-publishers eagerly populate the Internet with amateur media

making. Indeed, this "ethical surplus" in relation to brands is often in excess of what marketers often want or can even deal with—think here of the angry and empowered consumer behind such viral phenomena as 2007's comcast-mustdie.com or the "United [Airlines] Breaks Guitars" song viewed 11 million times since its 2009 debut on YouTube.

Working through the labor of the crowd—and, more specifically, their social and cultural capital—is a populist approach to exerting authority. After all, what better way to instantiate power and govern subjects than through democracy, which uses the will of the people as consent to and a rationale for force wielded in a particular way? Hence, the abundant industry hype about "brand democratization," which is a fulcrum for both the instrumentalization of agency in the governed and the abdication of traditional authority by the governing in exercising that power. Both "dialogue" and "virality" are pitched as magnanimous gestures in this regime of engagement in much the same way; they imply and, at times, explicitly spell out a strategy for ostensibly "splitting" such power as part of a profound and allegedly egalitarian shift from being spoken *at* by brands to speaking *with* them.

This shift must again be placed equally in the context of technological change, for the move from brand "autocracy" to brand "democracy" is made possible by an evolution in media ecology from one-way broadcasting transmission to two-way networked interaction. Because dialogue is also a useful way for corporations to elicit personal information and refine their strategies for selling goods, it is also valuable, in and of itself, as an extraction measure independent of its democratic façade. Similarly, viral memes enabled by that environmental transformation can be cast as somehow more organic, populist, and therefore credible than such formerly so-called tyrannical broadcaster flows; being content that is opt-in, *chosen by*—discovered, supposedly, from the bottom-up—in and through decentralized social networks, viral advertising contrasts with mass media advertising that feels more *chosen for* audiences.

## Staging Participation

Even if brand democracy is as much contrived hype as substantiated egalitarianism, advertisers *do* seem to be relaxing what had been greater control and precision over the message by strategizing consumer governance in this fashion. After all, buzz agency conscripts rather than scripts dialogue; consumer-generated advertising similarly presupposes a more autonomous contribution from the sometimes unwieldy amateurs in the crowd. In both cases, the audiences for that message (i.e., friends exposed to word-of-mouth marketing, Twitter users who are fed a sponsored tweet) are encountering a brand-text, which is conceived as more of a semiotic open work than at perhaps any time in the past.

In order to allocate a sense of agency in this regime, the brand *has* to be conceived as a more contingent, unfinished work-in-progress; to govern through freedom, there must be an opportunity for participation. The nature of the openness of the advertising work can vary. Advertainment "opens" the brand up through flexible use by artistic interlocutors in long-form storytelling; alternative outdoor through dissident yet ambiguous out-of-home display; buzz agency through social improvisation; and crowd-sourcing through digital toolsets. Because ambiguity invites interpretation (recall the principles of the cool sell here), a denotatively flexible, albeit materially obdurate form like the *Aqua Teen* light board or the *House* graffadi is thought to elicit inquisition from passersby by withholding its status as commercial communication: a coy visual code whose definition is meant to be cracked. Conceptually, PBR's tabula rasa brand image operates along much the same lines by inviting engagement from the "anti-brand" loyalists who took to its cause and inscribed it with meaning. Even more obviously, the creation of an online enthymeme à la Subservient Chicken or MadMenYourself addresses audiences as co-creators, and obliges closure and subsequent circulation of what is, ultimately, a promotional message. And the immersive interactivity of alternate reality marketing schemes like those of *Blair Witch* or *Dark Knight* extends the openness of this project in full.

Yet for marketers, the recourse to dialogue and open work as a relinquishment of control and propagation of freedom needs to be understood not just as an enthusiastic, newfound affirmation of the subject's agency but equally as a surrender to an escalating sense of audience unmanageability, and thus a failure of Taylorist aspirations of disciplining want and need on command. This represents a paradoxical gamble in terms of governance: Force needs to be lithe, and power is actually found in accommodating flexibility. What is lost by way of careful supervision is thought to be gained by expanding the space in which more casual, improvisational influence can take place and, more importantly, in situating that influence in what is thought to be a more credible, less disciplinarian, noncommercial reach into those spaces (i.e., by outsourcing the authority of governance through "disinterested" storytellers, street artists, buzz agents, and amateur videographers who can conceal the exercise of power).

The new media enthymeme that ensues is, therefore, not just a template for consumer governance available to marketers but a model for how all media companies—in film and television, in popular music, in journalism, and so on—might increasingly structure and orient themselves to their audiences. The free, co-creative labor of social gadflies and amateur producers is "assumed" here—both in the sense of *presupposed* as integral to textual engagement and completion, and also *appropriated* as a useful resource. By expanding the definition of media, these developments and themes also call into question the very notion of what we mean by creative industry. "Industry" perhaps still retains its 19th-century connotations of, say, coal and steel production: a set of economic practices involving more or less fixed producers, goods, distributors, and consumers. Guerrilla marketing, on the other hand, portends a fundamental fluidity in that system, reflective of the aforementioned patterns of participation, populism, heterarchicality, decentralization, and freedom.

Still, these guerrilla tactics represent but a fraction of the hundreds of billions of dollars spent on global advertising annually; it is a format trained more exclusively on millennial consumers and far from the dominant outlay when it comes to advertising budgets as compared to TV upfronts, for example. But it is a fraction that is growing amid marketer insecurity—a time when traditionally dominant placement venues like newspapers, magazines, terrestrial radio, and network television would be eager to staunch the scattering of audiences and the bleeding of revenues. That said, the structure of those creative industries is also perhaps being dematerialized, and the more that clients shift funding toward the unconventional channels illuminated here, the more that reallocation could further destabilize how the media environment is underwritten and heighten the uncertainty already facing legacy cultural producers who depend on that sponsorship. As a bitter irony, these cultural producers will be asked to do more to feed that assumed participatory need of their consumers while depending on fewer financial resources to achieve it; journalists, to take one example from the creative class, have learned this paradox all too grimly in the past decade: needing to blog more and more with less and less workforce available.

Truth in Advertising?

> According to . . . Anthony Giddens, we now are threatened by a number of "dilemmas of the self," like uncertainty, powerlessness, and commodification. We are lost, struggling with a "looming threat of personal meaninglessness." And that's where our consumer culture fits in. Brands provide an answer to our identity crisis by giving us meaning. They help us construct our social world. In other words, in our search for place and purpose in

life, consumer culture is replacing tradition. . . . No longer is history or government or the church at the center of our culture. It is instead the products of our marketing-driven economy that now create the greatest common bond between us.[16]

So goes the explanation of one brand manager—opining, in a self-aggrandizing diagnosis, that the fruit of his labor represents but the last tie that binds, the only surviving institution that offers social glue to a culture existentially adrift. Certainly some caveat is needed here, for even if commercial culture alone didn't cause that "looming threat of personal meaningless" (industrialization, urbanization, secularization, and migration, among others, are equally apt historical suspects), it surely perpetuates the emptiness as much as it satiates it—not least due to the fact that the meanings and values attached to branded products are *made* to be ephemeral and disposable. It is, after all, a Sisyphean quest to definitively fulfill identity through consumption, because the capitalist marketplace will always need to get us to buy more and therefore renders goods deliberately and inevitably obsolete (and also, hence, the social selves and connections predicated upon them as written into advertising). Moreover, the problems with consumer culture are rife and well documented: its divisive inclinations toward status envy; its "nonproductive" additive costs (e.g., the $100 Nike sneaker made for a mere pittance); its complicity in obfuscating labor conditions and promoting unrealistic female body ideals; and its apparent drive for thoughtless, even addictive, shopping behaviors with little recompense for the environmental consequences.

Yet the inadequacy of consumer culture to permanently satisfy existential needs neither makes us mindless dupes (as critics from Adorno to Lasn have prosecuted) nor does it invalidate the ways—albeit insecure and transitory—in which this culture can still be socially productive. For better or worse, commercial objects *do* play a meaningful role in people's lives, and they *do* seem to act as communicative tools. Brands, like faith or polity in prior epochs, provide for some sense of the social order—a communion that James Carey might well have recognized among Mac fanatics and Harley riders.[17] Like cults, brands—as one marketing consultant rather provocatively argues—help "you become more you."[18] Ideally, religion, political affinity, family ties, folk culture, or geographic anchoring should play this role, but, sadly, postmodern life no longer affords such guarantees. We take what we can get from what we can afford—and, again, this is not to be blind to nor untroubled by the fact that "the 1 percent" can afford more than ever, even as consumer life grows more precarious and less sustainable for the middle class or the working poor. Nor is this to exonerate (much less celebrate) advertising's aforementioned often-dubious values and shallow excesses.

Functions once given over to traditional institutions in representing the social world, locating our place in it, and satisfying the need for the experience of a common culture are now somewhat accurately, if lamentably, seen as the province of marketers. But this is also because our faith in those other institutions is ever dwindling to new-historic lows; a crisis of institutions is, simultaneously, a crisis of identity and a crisis of community. The marketplace and the advertising that buttresses it is as much responding to those frayed social moorings (family, religion, politics, locality, etc.) as it is supplanting healthy incarnations of them per se. To be sure, this kind of "ethical surplus" (e.g., relations, rituals, etc.) that is generated from the bottom up contributes to the brand equity of a corporation's bottom line; it is not interested in that ethical surplus for altruistic reasons alone. Quite the contrary: It is in the interest of marketers to stage the conditions that will contribute to the formation of such communities, and marketing programs and brand management initiatives outlined here are increasingly being explored to that end. If, in the past, traditional advertising remained stuck on a "transmission" model for its operations—a linear sequence of simply relaying fixed messages, mechanistically, to what it presumed to be comparatively passive receptacles—the evidence here suggests a model closer to Carey's emphasis on "sharing, participation, association, fellowship, and the possession of a common faith" as the fabric and function of commercial communication.[19]

Indeed, part of the reason for the transition away from the rational, utility-oriented, product appeals of a century ago to the cultural ambitions spotlighted here is directly related to that crisis of faith in traditional social institutions; in that, contemporary advertising apparently seeks to fill that vacuum of external resources necessary for one's identity project. This, then, seems to be its "socially productive" aspirations: not simply to push product within the limited confines of a 30-second spot or billboard frame but to avail itself of a wider humanistic purpose in our lives. There is something unsettling and hollow about that aim—and it does fail to allow participation for those who can't afford it—but we can't write off its utility as brainwashing if it fulfills, albeit incompletely and temporarily. Human beings need symbols; we need stories; we need ways to connect. Advertising might well lie to us about its facts—that *this* cell phone will make you popular or *that* pair of jeans will make you cool—but it does get those larger truths right.

This identity project brings us to the second meaning of the title of this chapter. "Managing agency in the regime of engagement" refers to, primarily, the strategies of consumer governance that obfuscate authority, discipline through discovery, and exercise power through freedom. But managing agency also has a second implication that can be read from the perspective of the subject rather than the ruler in this regime: "managing" in the sense of eking out, surviving through, or getting by on the experience of that self-determination and the satisfaction that accompanies choice, however imperfect. In light of these contemporary dilemmas of the self and the existential anxiety that accompanies Giddens's "looming threat of personal meaninglessness," managing a bit of agency and meaning through a logo (and the lifestyle for which it stands) might not come at too steep a cost to make it utterly worthless to the subject in this regime, despite critics' understandable angst that brands now seem to define us as much as traditional, ascribed, ideally more dependable identity markers. The term "subject" has, in itself, a relevant double meaning: dependence under the authority of another *and* self-knowledge. In considering and critiquing how brands execute the former, we should not overlook or condescend to the simultaneous value to be found in the latter.

In closing, I return to a caveat that opened this book in order to articulate where research might go from here: This has not been a study of audiences and consumers directly, yet discussion of audiences and consumers, both theoretically and empirically, has figured prominently throughout. This has been a second-order study of those audiences and consumers—particularly youth and young adults—through the lens of those tasked with reaching and selling to them. Having mapped out that first moment of "encoding" in the commercial communication process here, future scholarship might well take up its counterpart on the "decoding" side of Stuart Hall's famous equation. We should inquire about the reception of guerrilla marketing—and not simply through a narrowly quantitative effects perspective on success-or-failure that clients demand but, more broadly, whether that "looming threat of personal meaningless" is more cured or exacerbated through the postmodern marketplace as it takes shape in these ways. This would also further mediate, empirically, whether we ought to judge the audiences and consumers for guerrilla marketing as more vulnerable or empowered—and, in turn, whether official disclosure and state regulation of such practices should be necessary. At the very least, more media literacy about these guerrilla efforts can't hurt, and this project has hopefully contributed to those educational goals—to encourage us, as both consumers and scholars of consumer culture, to *think* more deeply about that which advertisers would prefer to self-efface; to pause before buying what they're selling. Personal debt levels certainly demand it.

One of my favorite film noir crime dramas ends on this haunting note: "The greatest trick the devil ever pulled was convincing the world he didn't exist."[20] I am reminded of this in weighing final judgment on the regime of engagement as a mode of consumer governance—not because advertisers are necessarily evil but because it succinctly articulates their project of *obfuscating influence*. Advertising is slowly receding from view even as it, paradoxically, becomes more ubiquitous than ever. It markets without selling and shows without telling; it is governance *sotto voce*. Perhaps the greatest trick the guerrilla marketer ever pulled was convincing the consumer that she didn't exist. This project has illustrated a technology of self-effacement by a source of power we would do well to keep our eyes on.

# APPENDIX

The excellent works of Thomas Lindlof, Pertti Alasuutari, and Martyn Hammersley and Paul Atkinson, among others, inform my methodological training.[1] I have approached this research with the exploratory, inductive posture they advocate: collecting bits and pieces of observation—whether found in press coverage or heard in interviews—and comparing, contrasting, and connecting to "funnel" an emerging mass of raw data into an integrated understanding of the phenomena at hand while achieving abstracted answers to my primary research questions. As I reviewed press coverage and prepared semi-structured interview schedules, these works have served as my compass points via "many iterations of tacking between the cases and the general cultural theories that informed this research to search for patterns."[2]

The popular and trade press served as an overview entry point for the project—offering coverage of the phenomena of guerrilla marketing that provided examples (which I then pursued further through interviews) as well as necessary background for getting a sense of public discourse about the practice. Whereas articles on guerrilla advertising in the popular press naturally speak to a wider audience and explain the work in nonspecialist terms, coverage in the trade press offers greater depth for the industry community in addition to more substantive insight and potential contacts for my purposes. I used the Factiva online database to generate a corpus of articles on guerrilla marketing, limiting the database search to the past ten years. My rationale for choosing the first decade of the 21st century as the time frame for analysis was deliberate in that by 2000, Internet usage had spread to almost half of the United States; prophecies of traditional advertising's "death" had grown louder in scholarly journals and trade texts while "interactive" panaceas began to be heralded with similar volume; older media institutions like newspapers, magazines, terrestrial radio, and broadcast television stood on the precipice of a tumultuous era; and advertising dollars began sloshing into newer venues at a greater pace. At a moment when these and other relevant trends were in motion, the start of a new century provided a convenient moment to consider guerrilla marketing practices and prospects. Moreover, the close of 2009 brought its own useful flurry of decade-in-retrospective coverage in the press from which I could amass avenues for further inquiry.

From the trade press, I searched from *Advertising Age, Adweek, Brand Republic* (UK), *Brand Strategy, Brandweek, Campaign* (UK), *Creativity, Marketing* (UK), *Marketing Magazine* (Canada), *Marketing News, Marketing Week* (UK) *Mediaweek,* and *Promo Magazine.* From the popular press I drew from daily newspapers (*Boston Globe, Los Angeles Times, New York Times, USA Today, Wall Street Journal, Washington Post*), weekly newsmagazines (*Newsweek, Time*), and business magazines (*BusinessWeek, Forbes, Fortune*). My primary search from those publication sources was for articles with at least two mentions of "guerilla" or "guerrilla" (it can be spelled either way) and "advertising" or "marketing"; this yielded a collection of 344 documents to be analyzed.

I also conducted a second search with a more expansive set of keywords so as to cast a wider net into the universe of popular and trade reporting on a phenomena whose label is often as shifty as its modus operandi—indeed only a fraction of the tactics I'm considering "guerrilla" have been usually labeled as such (and most of those that do are analyzed in chapter 3). I searched from those same publication sources using nine other terms in combination with "advertising" or "marketing": "ambient" (producing 1,225 documents), "branded entertainment" (1,322), "buzz" (9,342), "consumer-generated" (433), "experiential" (1,734), "interactive" (23,107), "stealth" (814), "undercover"(658), and "viral" (4,544). These search trawls yielded a document load obviously beyond the scope of these efforts (or efficiency of interest); I therefore looked at the twenty-five most relevant articles for each search term, as ranked by Factiva's filtering mechanism, which is based on keywords appearing. To wit, this textual analysis of 569 articles considered how these press accounts could provide insights and answers to the primary research questions as well as offer a starting point for contacts to interview and examples to include. Yet even that figure grossly underrepresents by several hundred the actual number of press documents consulted for this research; for many of the examples I chose to examine, I combed through Factiva using these sources (with, for example, "BzzAgent" as a search term) in order to gather background information in preparation for productive interviews.

The bulk of my data for this book came from that stage in the process: one-on-one, semi-structured, in-depth interviews by phone (with one in-person exception) with prominent practitioners, creatives, and executives involved in the guerrilla campaigns of note. The vast majority of interviewees were linked to or involved in the production of campaign examples that make up my case studies, and I engaged in detailed conversations with them about these as well as contextualizing them against the state of advertising more generally. Additionally, I spoke with brand consultants like Lucian James and

Noah Brier; trade journalists like Becky Ebenkamp, who regularly covered guerrilla marketing for *Brandweek*, and Scott Donaton, the former editor of *Advertising Age*; and storytellers and content creators like the author Karin Slaughter, the film producer Mike Monello, and the game designer Jordan Weisman—all of whom brought to bear their own particular lens on guerrilla advertising.

Between the fall of 2008 and the spring of 2010, I carried out some forty-six interviews with forty-eight interviewees (out of ninety-three attempted contacts)—some as short as twenty minutes, some as long as more than an hour, but generally lasting about forty minutes each (a list with descriptions of the name, job title, and date of the interview follows). While longer interviews might certainly have been preferable, given the busy schedules of my interviewees (more than a handful were company CEOs), I appreciated any opportunity to speak with them; moreover, for many, we had pretty well exhausted the topic by the time their availability ran out. I had initially hoped to use a snowball sample as much as possible—"cold calling" interviewees by phone or through e-mail when necessary but also relying on early contacts to put me in touch with more informants. As it turned out, the bulk of contacts were in fact made through that cold-calling approach, as few interviewees provided much in the way of suggestion of other contacts, the product, I suspect, of my asking about what are, in effect, industry competitors.

Although research often understandably anonymizes participants out of habit, I have—unless requested otherwise by interviewees (and none did so)—used their real names here. I had three reasons for doing that: First, any attempt at rendering them anonymous was, in reality, a flimsy measure of protection. These interviewees were being contacted because most are high-level creative decision-makers involved in very specific and prominent campaigns and more often than not I got their names from quotes in the popular and trade press (i.e., they are already in the public eye). To refer anonymously to, for example, "the creative director behind XYZ campaign" does not really offer much in the way of anonymity, when a simple Google search can fill in the blank where a proper name would go—and I needed to refer to their specific roles to lend credibility and significance to the thoughts they shared. Second, any attempt at rendering them anonymous runs somewhat counter-intuitive to the nature of an industry predicated on professional promotion. My research participants will no doubt be desirous of recognition for their creative production and will want to be credited publicly for the time and energy they generously invested in speaking with me. And, finally, the power differential (with a powerful researcher and vulnerable research participant presupposed) that is often of concern to institutional research boards and methodological ethics seminars was, in this instance, reversed: that is, high-level executives can hardly be characterized as "helpless" vis-à-vis a scholar's research project (who was, at the time, just a humble graduate student and remains but a humble media studies professor).

Aldhous, Chris. Founding director and creative partner, GOODPILOT. Phone interview, December 15, 2009.

Asche, Eric. Senior vice president of marketing, Legacy for Health. Phone interview, January 19, 2010.

Balter, Dave. Founder and CEO, BzzAgent. Phone interview, October 13, 2009.

Bologna, Anne. Partner, Toy. Phone interview, November 16, 2009.

Bonds, Susan. President and CEO, 42 Entertainment. Phone interview, December 17, 2009.

Brenner, Jake. Partner, Marathon Ventures. Phone interview, November 9, 2009.

Brier, Noah. Head of strategic planning, The Barbarian Group. Phone interview, January 12, 2010.

Cleveland, Bart. Creative director, McKee Wallwork Clevand. Phone interview, November 20, 2008.

De La Garza, Sam. Brand manager, Ford Fiesta. Phone interview, October 13, 2009.

Donaton, Scott. President and CEO, Ensemble. Phone interview, February 1, 2010.

Earley, Joe. Executive vice president of marketing and communications, Fox. Phone interview, January 14, 2010.

Ebenkamp, Becky. Journalist, *Brandweek*. Phone interview, January 8, 2010.

Eliason, James. Founder and CEO, Twittad. Phone interview, October 12, 2009.

Ellis, Gareth. Senior planner, Saatachi & Saatchi. Phone interview, January 13, 2010.

Ewen, Sam. Founder and CEO, Interference. Phone interview, November 5, 2008.

Gleason, David. Senior vice president of strategy director, Publicis New York. Phone interview, November 30, 2008.

Goodby, Jeff. Co-chairman, Goodby, Silverstein & Partners. Phone interview, March 9, 2010.

Goodfried, Greg. President and COO, EQAL. Phone interview, November 19, 2009.

Goodson, Scott. Founder and CEO, StrawberryFrog. Phone interview, January 11, 2010.

Grasse, Steven. Founder and CEO, GYRO/Quaker City Mercantile. In-person interview, September 28, 2009.

Groppe, Laura. CEO, Girls Intelligence Agency. Phone interview, January 8, 2010.

Hahn, Nate. Founder and president, Street Virus. Phone interview, October 6, 2009.

James, Lucian. Founder, Agenda. Phone interview, December 10, 2009.

Jamieson, Phoebe. Vice president of sales and marketing, Magpie. Phone interview, November 5, 2009.

Keller, Ed. CEO, Keller-Fay. Phone interview, January 22, 2010.

Leonard, Scott. President, A.D.D. Marketing. Phone interview, January 15, 2010.

Loos, Andrew. Managing director, Attack! Phone interview, January 4, 2010.

Maymann, Jimmy. CEO, GoViral. Phone interview, January 11, 2010.

Monello, Mike. Co-founder and executive creative director, Campfire. Phone interview, January 27, 2010.

Murphy, Ted. Founder and CEO, Izea. Phone interview, December 17, 2009.

Neville, Daniel. Brand coordinator and captain, Idea Bounty. Phone interview, November 10, 2009.

Palmer, Benjamin. CEO, The Barbarian Group. Phone interview, January 26, 2010.

Peterson, Britt. Partner and director of business development, Cole & Weber. Phone interview, January 28, 2010.

Ressler, Jonathan. CEO, Big Fat. Phone interview, November 7, 2008.

Salacuse, Adam. CEO, ALT TERRAIN. Phone interview, September 30, 2009.

Sjonell, Calle. Creative director, BBH. Phone interview, October 13, 2009.

Slaughter, Karin. Author, *Cold Cold Heart*. E-mail interview, December 7, 2009.

Steinman, Todd. COO, M80. Phone interview, December 4, 2009.

Stone, Rob. Founder, Cornerstone. Phone interview, February 5, 2010.

Stradiotto, Matthew. Co-founder, Matchstick. Phone interview, January 15, 2010.

Suter, Janice. Associate media director, GSD&M's Idea City. Phone interview, November 19, 2008.

Thoburn, Patrick. Co-founder, Matchstick. Phone interview, January 15, 2010.

Turner, Chad. President, Student Workforce. Phone interview, November 5, 2009.

Wardynski, Casey. Director, Army Office of Economic and Manpower Analysis. Phone interview, December 7, 2009.

Waterbury, Todd. Co-executive creative director, Wieden + Kennedy. Phone interview, December 16, 2009.

Wax, Steve. Co-founder and managing partner, Campfire. Phone interview, January 27, 2010.

Weisman, Jordan. Founder and CEO, Smith & Tinker. Phone interview, December 3, 2009.

# NOTES

NOTES TO CHAPTER 1

1. Kalle Lasn, *Culture Jam: The Uncooling of America* (New York: Eagle Brook, 1999), 113.
2. Michel Foucault, "The Subject and Power," in *The Essential Works of Foucault, 1954–1984: Power*, ed. James D. Faubion, trans. Robert Hurley (New York: New Press, 2000), 341.
3. The notion of a "mass" market was born alongside "mass" circulation periodicals in the late 19th century and "mass" audience radio programming in the 1930s. Following television's midcentury ascendance, the three major networks could still claim to reach 90 percent of the nation during primetime through the late 1970s. Yet even at television's supposedly monolithic height, Lizabeth Cohen charts postwar stirrings toward market segmentation, which included experimentation with "narrowcasting," or the targeting of niche demographics. Since then, the further explosion of media options and platforms inevitably prefigured boundless variety and thinning slices of the audience pie. In a decade when cable, after years of eroding network viewership, for the first time collectively outstripped network share, some of the most powerful figures in media, advertising, and consumer businesses are pointedly acknowledging this: "There is no 'mass' in mass media anymore," Proctor & Gamble's global marketing officer announced at a 2004 conference. Lizabeth Cohen, *A Consumer's Republic: The Politics of Mass Consumption in Postwar America* (New York: Vintage, 2003), 302; Henry Jenkins, *Convergence Culture: Where Old and New Media Collide* (New York: New York University Press, 2006), 60; Ed Keller, "In Search of True Marketplace Influencers: Influentials Inspire Buyer Confidence," *Advertising Age*, December 5, 2005, http://adage.com/article/viewpoint/search-true-marketplace-influencers-influentials-inspire-buyer-confidence/105452/
4. Jay Conrad Levinson, *Guerrilla Marketing: Secrets for Making Big Profits From Your Small Business* (Boston: Houghton Mifflin, 1984).
5. Matthew P. McAllister, *The Commercialization of American Culture: New Advertising, Control and Democracy* (Thousand Oaks, CA: Sage, 1996), 250.
6. Denis McQuail and Sven Windahl, *Communication Models: For the Study of Mass Communications*, 2nd ed. (London: Longman Publishing Group, 1993), 6.
7. Stuart Hall, "Encoding/Decoding," in *Culture, Media, Language: Working Papers in Cultural Studies, 1972–1979*, ed. Stuart Hall, Dorothy Hobson, Andrew Lowe, and Paul Willis (London: Hutchinson, 1980), 128–138; James W. Carey, *Communication as Culture: Essays on Media and Society* (New York: Routledge, 1992); Denis McQuail, *McQuail's Mass Communication Theory*, 4th ed. (New York: Sage, 2000), 47.
8. See, for example, Henry Jenkins, *Textual Poachers: Television Fans and Participatory Culture* (New York: Routledge, 1992); Janice A. Radway, *Reading the Romance: Women, Patriarchy, and Popular Literature.* (Chapel Hill, NC: University of North Carolina Press, 1984).
9. Gavin Lucas and Michael Dorian, *Guerrilla Advertising: Unconventional Brand Communication* (London: Lawrence King, 2006), 16.

10. Scott Donaton, "Cannes Fest Can Recognize Mad + Vine is Not Just a Fad," *Advertising Age*, June 16, 2003, http://adage.com/article/viewpoint/cannes-fest-recognize-mad-vine-a-fad/48792/

11. Don Slater, *Consumer Culture and Modernity* (Cambridge: Polity, 1997), 190.

12. Axel Bruns, *Blogs, Wikipedia, Second Life, and Beyond: From Production to Produsage* (New York: Peter Lang, 2008), 14.

13. Christina Spurgeon, *Advertising and New Media* (London: Routledge, 2008), 9.

14. Foucault, "The Subject and Power."

15. Jonathan Bond and Richard Kirshenbaum, *Under the Radar: Talking to Today's Cynical Consumer* (New York: John Wiley & Sons, 1998), 3 (italics original).

16. Upon closer inspection, marketing discourse turns out to be shot through with warfare as a conceptual analogy. Creative department leaders have variously described advertising as "poison gas" and recommend that a good campaign should be "militaristic" in its strategy. See William Leiss, Stephen Kline, and Sut Jhally, *Social Communication in Advertising: Persons, Products, and Images of Well-Being*, 2nd ed. (London: Routledge, 1997), 177. One agency CEO suggests that product placement on TV and in film is a kind of "invasion and assimilation" strategy. See David Verklin and Bernice Kanner, *Watch This, Listen Up, Click Here: Inside the 300 Billion Dollar Business Behind the Media You Constantly Consume* (New York: John Wiley & Sons, 2007), 110. Marketing scholars Andrew Kaikati and Jack Kaikati advocate "stealth" marketing (so named for the military aircraft) as a way of "catch[ing] people at their most vulnerable by identifying the weak spots in their defensive shields." See Andrew M. Kaikati and Jack G. Kaikati, "Stealth Marketing: How to Reach Consumers Surreptitiously," *California Management Review* 46, no. 4 (2004): 6. And Bond and Kirshenbaum, in perhaps the most elaborate use of the metaphor, maintain that it is the consumers' "mental *machine guns*" that torpedo an ad's potential as much as the remote control (4); that "there are only a handful of techniques today that are sophisticated enough to act as *stealth bombers*, dropping new messages [that escape] detection;" that "many launches of new products are planned in ways not unlike those used to plan the dropping of the *A-bomb* or the *Normandy invasion*" but that an effective "under-the-radar launch . . . is executed more along the lines of the *American Revolution*" (93); that "the closest thing to . . . insider market overviews can be found in the *military*," whereby "before *invading* a country, any good *army* will find out . . . the true, hidden infrastructure of communications, key people, and so on" (138, 140); and that "just like the designers of real *fighter planes*, we as marketers need to keep evolving our 'technology' so that it can stay one step ahead of the consumers' defenses" (163) (italics added throughout).

17. Bond and Kirshenbaum, *Under the Radar*, 93.

18. Ernesto Guevara, *Guerrilla Warfare* (Melbourne: Ocean Press, 2006), 54.

19. Tom Himpe, *Advertising is Dead: Long Live Advertising!* (New York: Thames & Hudson, 2006), 14 (italics added).

20. Rob Walker, *Buying In: The Secret Dialogue Between What We Buy and Who We Are* (New York: Random House, 2008), xvii.

21. George Ritzer, *Modern Sociological Theory*, 7th ed. (New York: McGraw-Hill, 2008); David Croteau, William Hoynes, and Stefania Milan, *Media/Society: Industries, Images, and Audiences*, 4th ed. (Los Angeles: Sage, 2012).

22. Antonio Gramsci, *Selections From the Prison Notebooks*, trans. Quintin Hoare and Geoffrey Nowell Smith (New York: International Publishers, 1971); Roger Simon, *Gramsci's Political Thought: An Introduction* (London: Lawrence and Wishart, 1982), 64.

23. Foucault, "The Subject and Power," 341.

24. Michel Foucault, "Governmentality," in *The Essential Works of Foucault, 1954–1984: Power*, ed. James D. Faubion, trans. Robert Hurley (New York: New Press, 2000), 201–222.

25. Michel Foucault, "Preface to The History of Sexuality, Volume Two," in Faubion and Hurley, *The Essential Works of Foucault, 1954–1984*, 203.

26. Foucault, "The Subject and Power," 341.

27. Claire O'Farrell, *Michel Foucault* (London: Sage, 2005), 101.

28. Foucault, "The Subject and Power," 340, 341 (italics added).

29. Michel Foucault, *Security, Territory, Population: Lectures at the Collège De France, 1977-78*, ed. Michel Senellart (Basingstoke, Hampshire: Palgrave Macmillan, 2007), 201; Michel Foucault, "Security, Territory, and Population," in Faubion and Hurley, *The Essential Works of Foucault, 1954–1984*, 292.

30. Foucault, "The Subject and Power," 342.

31. Tony Bennett, "Introduction: Popular Culture and the 'Turn to Gramsci,'" in *Popular Culture and Social Relations*, ed. Tony Bennett, Colin Mercer, and Janet Woollacott (Milton Keynes, England: Open University Press, 1986), xi–xix; Timothy Havens, Amanda D. Lotz, and Serra Tinic, "Critical Media Industry Studies: A Research Approach," *Communication, Culture & Critique* 2, no. 2 (2009): 234–253; Gramsci, *Selections From the Prison Notebooks*, 161.

32. John Storey, *Cultural Theory and Popular Culture: An Introduction*, 4th ed. (Athens: University of Georgia Press, 2006), 11, 106.

33. It is in his later lectures and interviews, working at the frontier of this new logic of governmentality, that Foucault appeared to clarify these nuances of "power relations" vis-à-vis the implication that emerges from, say, *Discipline and Punish*, in which (panoptic) power seems to dominate the (prisoner) subject absolutely. Indeed, the intellectual arc of Foucault's career might be mapped from a self-described change in "problematic" that proceeds from the analysis of more "passive, constrained" subjects like the ill or insane to a more "politically active," self-governing subject of power—a spectrum that corresponds with the increasing sophistication of agency charted here in which the subject, as audience member and consumer target, can be suitably located. Michel Foucault, "The Ethics of the Concern of the Self as a Practice of Freedom," in Faubion and Hurley, *The Essential Works of Foucault, 1954–1984*, 283, 292; Colin Gordon, "Governmental Rationality: An Introduction," in *The Foucault Effect: Studies in Governmentality*, ed. Graham Burchell, Colin Gordon, and Peter Miller (Chicago: University Of Chicago Press, 1991), 5; Foucault, "The Ethics of the Concern," 291; Paul Rabinow, "Introduction," in *The Foucault Reader*, ed. Paul Rabinow (New York: Pantheon Books, 1984), 11.

34. Mitchell Dean, *Governmentality: Power and Rule in Modern Society*, 2nd ed. (Los Angeles: Sage, 2010), 29; Mark Bevir, "The Construction of Governance," in *Governance, Consumers and Citizens: Agency and Resistance in Contemporary Politics*, ed. Mark Bevir and Frank Trentmann (New York: Palgrave-Macmillan, 2007), 40, 57; Janet Newmann, "Governance as Cultural Practice," in Bevir and Trentmann, *Governance, Consumers and Citizens*, 49–68.

35. Alice Malpass, Clive Barnett, Nick Clarke, and Paul Cloke, "Problematizing Choice: Consumers and Skeptical Citizens," in Bevir and Trentmann, *Governance, Consumers and Citizens*, 236.

36. Mark Bevir and Frank Trentmann, "Introduction: Consumption and Citizenship in the New Governance," in Bevir and Trentmann, *Governance, Consumers and Citizens*, 8.

37. Roland T. Rust and Richard W. Oliver, "The Death of Advertising," *Journal of Advertising* 23, no. 4 (1994), 74.

38. Joseph Turow, *Niche Envy: Marketing Discrimination in the Digital Age* (Cambridge, MA: MIT Press, 2006), 36.

39. Bob Garfield, *The Chaos Scenario* (New York: Stielstra Publishing, 2009), 44.

40. Turow, *Niche Envy*, 44.

41. Ibid., 22.

42. Joseph Jaffe, *Life After the 30-second Spot: Energize Your Brand with a Bold Mix of Alternatives to Traditional Advertising* (Hoboken, NJ: John Wiley & Sons, 2005), 171 (italics added).

43. McAllister, *The Commercialization of American Culture*, 7.

44. Foucault, *Security, Territory, Population: Lectures at the Collège De France, 1977–78*, 200.

45. Bevir and Trentmann, "Introduction," 8.

46. This binary is equally a nod to the classic "hard" versus "soft" sell distinction that has vacillated in and out of fashion throughout advertising history, with no clear or lasting agreement on the more effective strategy. Here, hard sell persuasion (straightforward and rational) aligns with the hot sell (explicit and obvious), while the cool sell (subtle and ambiguous) extends the idea of the soft sell (suggestive and creative).

47. Marshall McLuhan, *Understanding Media: The Extensions of Man* (Cambridge, MA: MIT Press, 1994).

48. Paul Levinson, *Digital McLuhan: A Guide to the Information Millennium* (London: Routledge, 2001), 9.

49. McLuhan, *Understanding Media*, 23.

50. Kaikati and Kaikati, "Stealth Marketing," 6.

51. David W. Stewart and Paul A. Pavlou, "The Effects of Media on Marketing Communications," in *Media Effects: Advances in Theory and Research*, ed. Jennings Bryant and Mary Beth Oliver, 3rd ed. (New York: Routledge, 2009), 362–401; Laura Petrecca, "Madison Avenue Wants You! (Or At Least Your Videos)," *USA Today*, June 21, 2007, http://www.usatoday.com/money/advertising/2007-06-20-cannes-cover-usat_N.htm

52. James B. Twitchell, *Adcult USA: The Triumph of Advertising in American Culture* (New York: Columbia University Press, 1997), 56.

53. See William Leiss, Stephen Kline, Sut Jhally, and Jacqueline Botterill for a review of the state of contemporary advertising clutter and its impact on effectiveness. William Leiss, Stephen Kline, Sut Jhally, and Jacqueline Botterill. *Social Communication in Advertising: Consumption in the Mediated Marketplace*. 3rd ed. (New York: Routledge, 2005), 352–356.

54. Micael Dahlén and Mats Edenius, "When is Advertising Advertising? Comparing Responses to Non-Traditional and Traditional Advertising Media," *Journal of Current Issues & Research in Advertising* 29, no. 1 (2007): 33.

55. Industry practitioners coin their own slang for this frustrating impediment: Bond and Kirshenbaum, for example, refer to it as the "impenetrable, mollusk-like shell that's hardened after years of ad abuse;" Jaffe calls it our "BS [blocker] to prioritize, sanction, and weed out the attention invaders from the welcome guests." See Bond and Kirshebaum, *Under the Radar*, ix; Jaffe, *Life After the 30-second Spot*, 47.

56. Dahlén and Edenius, "When Is Advertising Advertising?" 34.

57. Jens Nordfalt, "Track to the Future? A Study of Individual Selection Mechanisms Preceding Ad Recognition and their Consequences," *Journal of Current Issues & Research in Advertising* 27, no. 1 (2005): 19–29.

58. Robert Goldman and Stephen Papson, *Sign Wars: The Cluttered Landscape of Advertising* (New York: Guilford Press, 1996), 83.

59. Micael Dahlén, "The Medium as a Contextual Cue: Effects of Creative Media Choice," *Journal of Advertising* 34, no. 3 (2005): 89–98.

60. Dahlén and Edenius, "When is Advertising Advertising?"

61. Ibid., 35.

62. Walter J. Carl, "What's All the Buzz About? Everyday Communication and the Relational Basis of Word-of-Mouth and Buzz Marketing Practices," *Management Communication Quarterly* 19, no. 4 (2006): 603.

63. McAllister, The Commercialization of American Culture, 104–130.

64. Twitchell, *Adcult USA*, 16.

65. Michael Schudson, *Advertising, the Uneasy Persuasion: Its Dubious Impact on American Society* (New York: Basic Books, 1986), 101.

66. McAllister, *The Commercialization of American Culture*, 85.

67. Dan Hanover, "Guerrilla Your Dreams," *Promo* 14, no. 7, June 1, 2001, 91 (italics added).

68. Mae Anderson, "Tall Tales: Advertising Steps into Interactive Fiction, Where the Buzz is Real - Even When the Stories Aren't," *Adweek*, October 11, 2004 (italics added) http://business.highbeam.com/15/article-1G1-123323736/tall-tales-advertising-steps-into-interactive-fiction

69. Herbert Simon, "Designing Organizations for an Information-Rich World," in *Computers, Communications, and the Public Interest*, ed. Martin Greenberger (Baltimore, MD: The Johns Hopkins Press, 1971), 40–41.

70. Sarah Thornton, *Club Cultures: Music, Media, and Subcultural Capital* (Hanover, NH: University Press of New England, 1996), 11.

71. Pierre Bourdieu, "The Forms of Capital," in *The Sociology of Economic Life*, ed. Mark Granovetter and Richard Swedberg (Boulder, CO: Westview Press, 2001), 96–111; Thornton, *Club Cultures*, 3–4.

72. Edward L. Bernays, *Propaganda*, (New York: Horace Liveright, 1928); Stuart Ewen, *PR! A Social History of Spin* (New York: Basic Books, 1996), 15.

73. Ibid., 20, 75, 166.

74. Scott M. Cutlip, *The Unseen Power: Public Relations, a History* (Hillsdale, NJ: Lawrence Erlbaum Associates, 1994), 761.

75. Bernays, *Propaganda*, 54, 56.

76. Foucault, "The Subject and Power," 340, 341.

77. John C. Stauber and Sheldon Rampton, *Toxic Sludge is Good for You: Lies, Damn Lies, and the Public Relations Industry* (Monroe, ME: Common Courage Press, 1995), 193.

78. Al Ries and Laura Ries, *The Fall of Advertising and the Rise of PR* (New York: HarperBusiness, 2002), xi.

79. Siva K. Balasubramanian, "Beyond Advertising and Publicity: Hybrid Messages and Public Policy Issues," *Journal of Advertising* 23, no. 4 (December 1994): 30.

80. Joseph D. Rumbo, "Consumer Resistance in a World of Advertising Clutter: The Case of Adbusters," *Psychology and Marketing* 19, no. 2 (2002): 132.

81. Liz McFall, "Advertising, Persuasion and the Culture/Economy Dualism," in *Cultural Economy: Cultural Analysis and Commercial Life*, ed. Paul Du Gay and Michael Pryke (London: Sage Publications, 2002), 148–165.

82. Thomas Frank, *The Conquest of Cool: Business Culture, Counterculture, and the Rise of Hip Consumerism* (Chicago: University of Chicago Press, 1997), 126.

83. Michael Schudson, *Advertising, the Uneasy Persuasion.*

84. James Curtis, "Speed Branding," *Marketing*, November 20, 2003. http://www.marketing-magazine.co.uk/news/196087/

85. Garfield, *The Chaos Scenario*, 44, 46.

86. Verklin and Kanner, *Watch This, Listen Up, Click Here*, 7; Erik Sass, "Red Ink: Newspaper Revs Tumble," *MediaDailyNews*, April 15, 2010. http://www.mediapost.com/publications/article/126257/red-ink-newspaper-revs-tumble.html

87. Garfield, *The Chaos Scenario*, 44.

88. *Alternative media spending growth accelerates in 2007, hastening transition from traditional to alternative advertising & marketing strategies.* PQ Media, March 26, 2008. http://www.pqmedia.com/about-press-20080326-amf2008.html

89. Sandra Ward, "Glad Men," *Barron's*, September 14, 2009.

90. "Advertising by Medium," *Advertising Age*, December 19, 2011, 8.

91. Leiss, Kline, and Jhally, *Social Communication in Advertising*, 119 (italics added).

92. Mark Deuze, *Media Work* (Cambridge: Polity, 2007), 124.

93. See, among others, Yochai Benkler, *The Wealth of Networks: How Social Production Transforms Markets and Freedom* (New Haven, CT: Yale University Press, 2006); Bruns, *Blogs, Wikipedia*; Jean Burgess and Joshua Green, *YouTube: Online Video and Participatory Culture* (Cambridge: Polity, 2009); Deuze, *Media Work*; Jenkins, *Convergence Culture*; Clay Shirky, *Here Comes Everybody: The Power of Organizing Without Organizations* (New York: Penguin Press, 2008).

94. Manuel Castells, *The Rise of the Network Society*, 2nd ed. (Oxford: Blackwell Publishers, 2000), 500.

95. Mark Deuze "Convergence Culture in the Creative Industries," *International Journal of Cultural Studies* 10, no. 2 (2007): 245.

96. Manuel Castells, "Communication, Power and Counter-Power in the Network Society," *International Journal of Communication* no. 1 (2007): 238–266.

97. Ibid., 257, 258.

98. Ibid., 258. Moreover, Castells's refinement of this theory of power (as "primarily exercised by the construction of meaning in the human mind through processes of communication enacted in global/local multimedia networks of mass communication, including mass self-communication" and that "communication networks are fundamental networks of power-making in society") speaks to the advertiser's—and in particular the guerrilla advertiser's—challenge. Manuel Castells, *Communication Power* (Oxford: Oxford University Press, 2009), 416, 426.

99. Spurgeon, *Advertising and New Media*, 2, 17.

100. Deuze, "Convergence Culture," 256.

101. Castells, *The Rise of the Network Society*, 359.

102. Spurgeon, *Advertising and New Media*, 112.

103. Bruns, *Blogs, Wikipedia*, 1.

104. Jenkins, *Convergence Culture*, 18.

105. Ibid., 18–19.

106. Deuze, *Media Work*, 48.

107. Deuze, "Convergence Culture," 255 (italics added).

108. Deuze, *Media Work*, 128.

109. John D. Leckenby and Hairong Li, "From the Editors: Why We Need the Journal of Interactive Marketing," *Journal of Interactive Advertising* 1, no. 1 (2000): 1–3.

110. Roland T. Rust and Sajeev Varki, "Rising From the Ashes of Advertising," *Journal of Business Research* 37, no. 3 (1996): 173.

111. Deuze, *Media Work*, 126.
112. Bruns, *Blogs, Wikipedia*, 4.
113. Peter Dahlgren, "Media Logic in Cyberspace: Repositioning Journalism and its Publics," *Javnost/The Public* 3, no. 3 (1996): 63.
114. Deuze, *Media Work*, 234.
115. For a detailed review, see Richard A. Peterson and N. Anand, "The Production of Culture Perspective," *Annual Review of Sociology* 30 (2004): 311–334.
116. David Hesmondhalgh, *The Cultural Industries*, 2nd ed. (London: Sage Publications, 2007); see also Laura Grindstaff and Joseph Turow. "Video Cultures: Television Sociology in the 'New TV' age." *Annual Review of Sociology* 32, no. 1 (2006): 103–125.
117. Hesmondhalgh, *The Cultural Industries*, 37, 40 (italics original).
118. Ibid., 45 (italics original).
119. Jenkins claims that this kind of ecumenical "détente" between political economy and cultural studies is all the more necessary at a moment when production and consumption roles have blended more than ever. Henry Jenkins, "The Cultural Logic of Media Convergence," *International Journal of Cultural Studies* 7, no. 1 (2004): 36.
120. Todd Gitlin, *Inside Prime Time*, 2nd ed. (Berkeley, CA: University of California Press, 2000), xiv.
121. Notable exceptions include, among others, Arlene M. Dávila, *Latinos, Inc.: The Marketing and Making of a People* (Berkeley, CA: University of California Press, 2001); Timothy deWaal Malefyt and Brian Moeran, eds., *Advertising Cultures* (Oxford: Berg, 2003); Liz Moor, *The Rise of Brands* (Oxford: Berg, 2007); Sean Nixon, *Advertising Cultures: Gender, Commerce, Creativity* (London: Sage, 2003); Sean Nixon, "The Pursuit of Newness: Advertising, Creativity and the 'Narcissism of Minor Differences,'" *Cultural Studies* 20, no. 1 (2006): 89–106; Katherine Sender, *Business, Not Politics: The Making of the Gay Market* (New York: Columbia University Press, 2004).
122. Judith Williamson, *Decoding Advertisements: Ideology and Meaning in Advertising* (London: Marion Boyars, 1978). Liz McFall, calling for a more "empirical approach" to research on the business, adds that not enough work has been done to trace the changing methods of advertising and "gathering insight into the motivations behind its form." I take this as my point of departure. McFall, "Advertising, Persuasion," 149. For historical work, see Stuart Ewen, *Captains of Consciousness: Advertising and the Social Roots of the Consumer Culture*, 2nd ed. (New York: Basic Books, 2001); Jackson Lears, *Fables of Abundance: A Cultural History of Advertising in America* (New York: Basic Books, 1994); Roland Marchand, *Advertising the American Dream: Making Way for Modernity, 1920–1940* (Berkeley, CA: University of California Press, 1985); Daniel Pope, *The Making of Modern Advertising* (New York: Basic Books, 1983); Frank Presbrey, *The History and Development of Advertising*, (Garden City, NY: Doubleday, 1929).
123. Matthew Soar, "Encoding Advertisements: Ideology and Meaning in Advertising Production," *Mass Communication and Society* 3, no. 4 (2000): 419; Stuart Hall, "Encoding/Decoding."
124. Aidan Kelly, Katrina Lawlor, and Stephanie O' Donohoe, "Encoding Advertisements: The Creative Perspective," *Journal of Marketing Management* 21, no. 5 (2005): 505–528.
125. Don Slater, "Corridors of Power," in *The Politics of Field Research: Sociology Beyond Enlightenment*, ed. Jaber F. Gubrium and David Silverman (London: Sage, 1989), 121.
126. Soar, "Encoding Advertisements," 421.
127. Dean, *Governmentality*, 41.

128. Ibid., 48.
129. Clifford Geertz, *The Interpretation of Cultures: Selected Essays* (New York: Basic Books, 1973), 6.
130. Ibid., 5.
131. Havens, Lotz, and Tinic, "Critical Media Industry Studies," 247.
132. Ibid., 237, 246.
133. See appendix for more details on the method for this investigation.

NOTES TO CHAPTER 2

1. Scott Goodson, personal communication, January 11, 2010.
2. Emily Nussbaum, "What Tina Fey Would Do For a Soy Joy," *New York*, October 5, 2008, http://nymag.com/news/features/51014/
3. Alex Wipperfurth, *Brand Hijack: Marketing Without Marketing* (New York: Portfolio Trade, 2005), 119.
4. *New PQ Media Report Finds U.S. Branded Entertainment Spending on Consumer Events & Product Placements Dipped Only 1.3% to $24.63 Billion in 2009 & on Pace to Grow 5.3% in 2010, Exceeding Most Advertising & Marketing Segments.* PQ Media, June 29, 2010. htte://www.pqmedia.com/about-press-20100629-gbem2010.html
5. Lawrence A. Wenner, "On the Ethics of Product Placement in Media Entertainment," *Journal of Promotion Management* 10, no. 1 (2004): 107; Scott Donaton, *Madison & Vine: Why the Entertainment and Advertising Industries Must Converge to Survive* (New York: McGraw-Hill, 2004), 21.
6. Mark Andrejevic, *iSpy: Surveillance and Power in the Interactive Era* (Lawrence: University Press of Kansas, 2007), 12.
7. Jean-Marc Lehu, *Branded Entertainment: Product Placement & Brand Strategy in the Entertainment Business* (London: Kogan Page, 2007), 23; Douglas B. Holt, "Why Do Brands Cause Trouble? A Dialectical Theory of Consumer Culture and Branding," *Journal of Consumer Research* 29, no. 1 (2002): 83.
8. Lehu, *Branded Entertainment*, 224.
9. Andrew Wernick, *Promotional Culture: Advertising, Ideology, and Symbolic Expression* (London: Sage Publications, 1991).
10. Liz Moor, *The Rise of Brands*, 6.
11. Ibid., 143.
12. Celia Lury, *Brands: The Logos of the Global Economy* (London: Routledge, 2004), 1, 151.
13. Holt, "Why Do Brands Cause Trouble?" 80.
14. Ibid., 82.
15. Adam Arvidsson, "Brands: A Critical Perspective," *Journal of Consumer Culture* 5, no. 2 (2005): 244, 248 (italics original).
16. Ibid., 244–245 (italics original).
17. Ibid., 245 (italics original).
18. Foucault, "The Subject and Power," 341.
19. Holt, "Why Do Brands Cause Trouble?" 83, 87 (italics added).
20. George Yudice, *The Expediency of Culture: Uses of Culture in the Global Era* (Durham: Duke University Press, 2003), 9; Moor, *The Rise of Brands*, 77.
21. Otto Riewoldt, ed., *Brandscaping: Worlds of Experience in Retail Design* (Basel, Switzerland: Birkhäuser Basel, 2002), 10.
22. Jenkins, *Convergence Culture*, 61, 63.

23. Casey Wardynski, personal communication, December 7, 2009.

24. Foucault, "Governmentality," 211.

25. Ibid., 211.

26. Ewen, *PR!*, 91.

27. Ibid., 382, 384.

28. Adam Arvidsson, *Brands: Meaning and Value in Media Culture* (London: Routledge, 2006), 68 (italics added).

29. Jim Newell, Charles Salmon, and Susan Chang, "The Hidden History of Product Placement," *Journal of Broadcasting & Electronic Media* 50, no. 4 (2006): 575–594.

30. Kerry Segrave, *Product Placement in Hollywood Films: A History* (Jefferson, NC: McFarland & Company, 2004), 1, 94.

31. Newell, Salmon, and Chang, "The Hidden History," 576, 588.

32. Ibid., 576, 585.

33. Newell, Salmon, and Chang, "The Hidden History," 584; Kathleen J. Turner, "Insinuating the Product into the Message: An Historical Context for Product Placement," *Journal of Promotion Management* 10, no. 1 (2004): 9–14.

34. Segrave, *Product Placement in Hollywood Films*, 164.

35. Balasubramanian, "Beyond Advertising and Publicity," 34.

36. Lehu, *Branded Entertainment*, 38; Segrave, *Product Placement in Hollywood Films*, 208.

37. Lehu, *Branded Entertainment*, 3, 159. Reality TV, however, comes with its own unique set of challenges for product integration, given the ostensibly "unscripted" nature of the programming. Commenting on a partnership between Johnson & Johnson and a BET reality docudrama, the network's senior vice president for integrated marketing noted that cast members were canvassed about health and wellness habits to see if an allergy medicine could be woven into the "storyline": "You need to have those conversations far enough in advance so you understand where some of the natural, organic places for integration are, so things don't feel staged." "Natural" and "organic"—a sense that the ad message doesn't "feel staged"—cuts to the core of how advertainment seeks to obfuscate its intention to sell. The central question here is one of balance: a sponsor's interests, the audience's interests, and how, for content producers, the cool sell might adequately calibrate those. To that end, the executive added, "We don't necessarily have to showcase them gargling for 30 seconds to make sure you get the full effect, but [there are ways] you can get the sense that Listerine is part of their daily process." Briar Stelter, "Product Placements, Deftly Woven Into the Storyline," *New York Times*, March 1, 2009. http://www.nytimes.com/2009/03/02/business/media/02adco.html?_r=3&adxnnl=1&adxnnlx=1250100154-kMheUMUWrzpAssoFRn+4wQ

38. Wenner, "On the Ethics of Product Placement," 102.

39. Arvidsson, "Brands," 245.

40. Segrave, *Product Placement in Hollywood Films*, 96, 166.

41. Ibid., 184, 194.

42. Jonathan Hardy, *Cross-Media Promotion* (New York: Peter Lang, 2010), 233, 240.

43. T. L. Stanley, "That's Advertainment!" *Brandweek*, February 28, 2010. http://nyi-www.brandweek.com/bw/content_display/news-and-features/direct/e3i7f27204a864d83e7dd44fb9ff07414c1

44. Holt, "Why Do Brands Cause Trouble?" 82.

45. Segrave, *Product Placement in Hollywood Films*, 185.

46. Donaton, *Madison & Vine*, 152 (italics added).

47. Balasubramanian, "Beyond Advertising and Publicity," 32.

48. Stauber and Rampton, *Toxic Sludge*, 13.

49. Kaikati and Kaikati, "Stealth Marketing," 12.

50. Lauren Cox, "Top 7 Celebrity Drug Endorsements: Commercial or a Cause?" *ABC News*, April 1, 2009, http://abcnews.go.com/Health/CelebrityCafe/story?id=7209401&page=1

51. Jake Brenner, personal communication, November 9, 2009.

52. Wenner, "On the Ethics of Product Placement," 120.

53. Anne Bologna, personal communication, November 16, 2009.

54. Donaton, *Madison & Vine*, 98, 99.

55. Ibid., 99–100.

56. Ibid., 101.

57. Jaffe, *Life After the 30-Second Spot*, 189.

58. Ann-Christine Diaz, "Best Non-TV Campaigns," *Advertising Age*, December 14, 2009, http://adage.com/article/print-edition/book-tens-tv-campaigns-decade/141011/; Jaffe, *Life After the 30-Second Spot*, 188.

59. Britt Peterson, personal communication, January 28, 2010.

60. Alissa Quart, *Branded: The Buying and Selling of Teenagers* (Cambridge, MA: Perseus Publishing, 2003), 90.

61. Jeremy Mullman, "Anheuser-Busch Pulls the Plug on Bud.TV," *Advertising Age*, February 18, 2009, http://adage.com/article/madisonvine-news/anheuser-busch-pulls-plus-tv/134701/

62. Eric Newman, "With the Wind In His Sails: Sailor Jerry Spiced Rum," *Brandweek*, February 25, 2008. http://business.highbeam.com/137330/article-1G1-175875867/wind-his-sales-sailor-jerry-spiced-rum

63. Steven Grasse, personal communication, September 28, 2009.

64. Bethany Klein, *As Heard on TV: Popular Music in Advertising* (Farnham, UK: Ashgate, 2009).

65. Ibid., 77.

66. Balasubramanian, "Beyond Advertising and Publicity," 32 (italics original).

67. Holt, "Why Do Brands Cause Trouble?" 83.

68. Lehu, *Branded Entertainment*, 171, 172.

69. In 2003 alone, for instance, Mercedes racked up 112 mentions, followed by Lexus (48), Gucci (47), Cadillac (46), and Burberry (42). Kaikati and Kaikati, "Stealth Marketing," 15.

70. Lehu, *Branded Entertainment*, 174–175.

71. Ibid., 173.

72. Kaikati and Kaikati, "Stealth Marketing," 15.

73. Lucian James, personal communication, December 10, 2009.

74. Bourdieu "The Forms of Capital"; Thornton, *Club Cultures*.

75. Arvidsson, "Brands," 237 (italics original).

76. Arvidsson, *Brands: Meaning and Value*, 68; Holt, "Why Do Brands Cause Trouble?" 83.

77. In the case of "Stones"—as well as Radio Shack's "The Shack" and Pizza Hut's "The Hut" self-christening—that chumminess might come off a bit premature when it is cooked up at brand headquarters rather than vocalized "organically" by an artist writing lyrics or reflected in the authentic vernacular of a given subculture. Jeremy Mullman, "What's in a Nickname? In Spirits World, An Implied Warm-and-Fuzzy Felationship," *Advertising Age*, April 19, 2010, 4.

78. Lehu, *Branded Entertainment*, 176 (italics added).

79. Klein, *As Heard on TV*, 77.

80. Scott Donaton, personal communication, February 1, 2010.

81. Klein, *As Heard on TV*, 59.

82. Wipperfurth, *Brand Hijack*, 117; Andrew Hampp, "A Reprise for Jingles on Madison Avenue," *Advertising Age*, September 6, 2010, http://adage.com/article/madisonvine-news/a-reprise-jingles-madison-avenue/145744/

83. Ethan Smith and Julie Jargon, "Chew on This: Hit Song is a Gum Jingle," *Wall Street Journal*, July 28, 2008, http://online.wsj.com/article/SB121721123435289073.html

84. Helen Pidd, "Radio 1 Pulls 'Promotional' Track for Brand of Hair Gel," *Guardian*, May 8, 2007, http://www.guardian.co.uk/media/2007/may/05/advertising.bbc

85. Rob Stone, personal communication, February 5, 2010, italics added.

86. Suzanne Vranica, "Hellman's Targets Yahoo for Its Spread," *Wall Street Journal*, June 27, 2007, B4.

87. Newell, Salmon, and Chang, "The Hidden History," 578–579.

88. Lehu, *Branded Entertainment*, 167.

89. Richard Alan Nelson, "The Bulgari Connection: A Novel Form of Product Placement," *Journal of Promotion Management* 10, no. 1 (2004): 206, 207 (italics original).

90. Ibid., 207.

91. Ibid., 208.

92. Nate Hahn, personal communication, October 6, 2010.

93. Wenner, "On the Ethics of Product Placement," 103.

94. The "subtlety" of inclusion is perhaps in the eye of the shareholder: "In one of the 35- to 60-minute stories (timed for the length of typical commutes), the wife of a California real estate investor accuses him of loving his car more than he loves her. 'It's not a car,' he snaps. 'It's a BMW Z4.'" Verklin and Kanner, *Watch This, Listen Up, Click Here*, 114; Kate Nicholson, "Are BMW's Audio Books a Gimmick?" *Campaign*, February 17, 2006, http://www.campaignlive.co.uk/news/541812/Close-Up-Live-Issue—-BMWs-audio-books-gimmick/?DCMP=ILC-SEARCH

95. Karin Slaughter, personal communication, December 7, 2009 (italics added).

96. Arvidsson, *Brands: Meaning and Value*, 2.

97. Rob Stone, personal communication, February 5, 2010.

98. Lehu, *Branded Entertainment*, 199.

99. Benjamin R. Barber, *Consumed: How Markets Corrupt Children, Infantilize Adults, and Swallow Citizens Whole* (New York: W. W. Norton, 2007), 229.

100. Presbrey, *The History and Development of Advertising*.

101. Verklin and Kanner, *Watch This, Listen Up, Click Here*, 114; Quart, *Branded*, 12; Josh Levin, "Bill Simmons, Brought to You by Miller Lite," *Brow Beat*, September 11, 2009, http://www.slate.com/blogs/blogs/browbeat/archive/2009/09/11/bill-simmons-brought-to-you-by-miller-lite.aspx

102. Scott Donaton, personal communication, February 1, 2010.

103. Wenner, "On the Ethics of Product Placement," 107, 123.

104. Havens, Lotz, and Tinic, "Critical Media Industry Studies."

105. Karin Slaughter, personal communication, December 7, 2009.

106. Interestingly—if from differently aligned politics—the United Nations also put out its own advergame, *Food Force*, where gamers are charged with delivering food rations to a besieged, fictitious island nation; the game was downloaded more than 1 million times in its first six weeks from the World Food Program website hosting it. "U.N. humanitarian game is a hit," *MSNBC*, June 10, 2005, http://www.msnbc.msn.com/id/8173381/

107. Jenkins, *Convergence Culture*, 75.

108. Verklin and Kanner, *Watch This, Listen Up, Click Here*, 90.

109. Matt Quinn, "War (Video) Games." *Fast Company*, January 24, 2005. http://www.fastcompany.com/articles/2005/01/top-jobs-wardynski.html (italics added).
110. Jaffe, *Life after the 30-Second Spot*, 133, 136.
111. Quart, *Branded*, 100.
112. Strictly speaking, this is not entirely accurate. The army tracks a voluminous amount of data associated with players: "[W]hat roles did you assume; what training did you complete; what players you like to play with; how do you play; like, you know, are you a guy that breaks the rules or are you a guy that adheres to the rules." Some players do become real-life soldiers, who are then potentially subjected to post-hoc surveillance using game data from the past: "So, we get a lot of this broader information—now, when somebody enters the Army, we can ask them, 'Did you play the game?' And we do that here at West Point. . . . And if they want to, they can give us their game name and we can go off and see how long they played and so forth and we can see how they do in the Army." Casey Wardynski, personal communication, December 7, 2009.
113. Holt, "Why Do Brands Cause Trouble?" 87.
114. Lucian James, personal communication, December 10, 2009.
115. Donaton, *Madison & Vine*, 6.
116. Suzanne Vranica, "Marketing Business Rebrands as an Entertainment Provider," *Wall Street Journal*, July 12, 2006.
117. See McAllister, *The Commercialization of American Culture*, 11–36.
118. The Writers Guild and Screen Actors Guild, for example, recently complained about the intrusiveness of brand names into TV show plots. Stanley, "That's Advertainment!"
119. Wenner, "On the Ethics of Product Placement," 113, 114.
120. Scott Donaton, personal communication, February 1, 2010.

NOTES TO CHAPTER 3

1. Dick Hebdige, *Subculture: The Meaning of Style* (London: Methuen, 1979), 96.
2. Esteban Contreras, "Interview: Alex Bogusky Talks Ads, CP+B Culture, Fun, and Focus," *Social Nerdia*, May 27, 2009, http://socialnerdia.com/index.php/2009/05/interview-alex-bogusky-cpb
3. "Agencies of the Decade," *Advertising Age*, December 14, 2009. http://adage.com/article/print-edition/book-tens-agencies-decade/141055/
4. Foucault, "The Subject and Power," 342.
5. Foucault, *Security, Territory, Population*, 201.
6. Ibid., 199, 201.
7. Foucault, "The Subject and Power," 348.
8. Raymond Williams, *Marxism and Literature* (Oxford: Oxford University Press, 1977), 112.
9. Sandra Dolbow, "Landscape of the Giants," *Brandweek*, November 12, 2001.
10. Betsy Ebenkamp, "Guerrilla Marketing '06: A Brandweek Staff Report," *Brandweek*, November 20, 2006, http://business.highbeam.com/137330/article-1G1-155028857/guerrilla-marketing-06-brandweek-staff-report
11. Andrew Loos, personal communication, January 4, 2010.
12. Dolbow, "Landscape of the Giants" (italics added).
13. Toni Fitzgerald, "Big Driver Behind Out-of-Home: Digital," *Media Life*, August 14, 2009, http://www.medialifemagazine.com/artman2/publish/Alternative_media_43/Big_driver_behind_out-of-home_Digital.asp
14. Lasn, *Culture Jam*; Naomi Klein, *No Logo* (New York: Picador USA, 2000).

15. Lasn, *Culture Jam*, xvii, 103.
16. Ibid., 101.
17. Ibid., 18.
18. Ibid., 103, 128.
19. Gramsci, *Selections from the Prison Notebooks*, 641.
20. David Forgacs, ed., *The Antonio Gramsci Reader: Selected Writings, 1916–1935*, (New York: New York University Press, 2000), 421 (italics added).
21. Ibid., 323.
22. Ibid., 224.
23. Maria Hynes, Scott Sharpe, and Bob Fagan, "Laughing With the Yes Men: The Politics of Affirmation," *Continuum: Journal of Media & Cultural Studies* 21, no. 1 (2007): 109.
24. Vince Carducci, "Culture Jamming: A Sociological Perspective," *Journal of Consumer Culture* 6, no. 1 (2006): 122.
25. Klein, *No Logo*, 280.
26. Anne Elizabeth Moore, *Unmarketable: Brandalism, Copyfighting, Mocketing, and the Erosion of Integrity* (New York: New Press, 2007), 56–57.
27. Lasn shows a particular fondness for jujitsu as an explanatory metaphor for the mechanics of culture jamming: "In one simple deft move you slap the [brand] giant on its back [and . . . ] use the momentum of the enemy." This is meant to contrast with more traditional, straightforward, and earnest (read: boring) tactics of corporate confrontation like boycotts, street marches, and political petitioning—tactics which, oddly enough, came to define Occupy Wall Street's success. Carducci, "Culture Jamming," 132; Klein, *No Logo*, 281.
28. Carducci, "Culture Jamming," 127, 133–134 (italics added).
29. Moore, *Unmarketable*, 58, 83 (italics added).
30. Frank, *The Conquest of Cool*, 235.
31. Ibid., 94.
32. Andrew Loos, personal communication, January 4, 2010.
33. Leiss et al., *Social Communication in Advertising*, 273–274.
34. Walker, *Buying In*, 104; Wipperfurth, *Brand Hijack*, 156.
35. "Most Influential Players in Marketing," *Advertising Age*, December 12, 2011, 8.
36. Williams, *Marxism and Literature*, 113.
37. Peterson and N. Anand, "The Production of Culture Perspective," 325–326.
38. Brooke Capps, "The Reserved Ruler of In-Your-Face Marketing," *Advertising Age*, March 5, 2007, http://adage.com/article/print-edition/reserved-ruler-face-marketing/115372/
39. Lasn, *Culture Jam*, 133.
40. Moore, *Unmarketable*, 4.
41. Gyro's founder Steven Grasse—writing here under the nom de guerre Harriet Bernard-Levy, in a self-aggrandizing history of the company—actually cites Situationist lineage in brashly (and likely ironically) overstating the agency's genius: "*Détournement*, this practice of cultural collage, or 'remixing,' had been abandoned since the European Situationist International ended their prankster days in the late 1960s. Resurrected by Grasse . . . it would now be ripped off by everyone from DJ Spooky to the magazine *Adbusters* under the umbrella term 'culture jamming.' Few knew that this, like so many dominant subcultural trends of the late 1990s and early 2000s, was born as a campaign at 304 Walnut [Street]." Harriet Bernard-Levy, *Virus: The Outrageous History of Gyro Worldwide* (Regina, Saskatchewan: Gold Crown Press, 2008), 15, 33.
42. Goldman and Papson, *Sign Wars*, 142, 143.

43. Malcolm Gladwell, "The Coolhunt," *New Yorker*, March 17, 1997, http://www.gladwell. com/1997/1997_03_17_a_cool.htm

44. Janine Lopiano-Misdom and Joanne De Luca, *Street Trends: How Today's Alternative Youth Cultures are Creating Tomorrow's Mainstream Markets* (New York: HarperBusiness, 1997).

45. Thornton, *Club Cultures*, 3, 4, 11.

46. Leiss et al., *Social Communication in Advertising*, 318, 428.

47. Bond and Kirshenbaum, *Under the Radar*, 135.

48. Adam Salacuse, personal communication, September 30, 2009.

49. Hamilton Nolan, "Stop Calling Black People 'Urban,'" *Gawker*, March 21, 2012, http:// gawker.com/5895216/stop-calling-black-people-urban

50. Joseph Anthony, "Hip-Hop Culture Crosses into Brand Strategy," *Brand Channel*, September 12, 2005, http://www.brandchannel.com/brand_speak.asp?bs_id=120

51. Norman Mailer, "The White Negro," *Dissent*, Fall 1957, http://www.dissentmagazine.org/ online.php?id=26

52. Bernard-Levy, *Virus*, 25.

53. Goldman and Papson, *Sign Wars*, 8.

54. Michel Foucault, *Discipline and Punish: The Birth of the Prison*, trans. Alan Sheridan (New York: Vintage, 1977).

55. Ibid., 201, 207, 209.

56. Gordon, "Governmental Rationality," 3–4.

57. Foucault, *Discipline and Punish*, 204, 214.

58. Andrew Loos, personal communication, January 4, 2010.

59. Gladwell, "The Coolhunt," 78.

60. Moore, *Unmarketable*, 45.

61. Harold Adams Innis, *The Bias of Communication* (Toronto: University of Toronto Press, 1951).

62. Bond and Kirshenbaum, *Under the Radar*, 144–146.

63. Ibid., 161; Thornton, *Club Cultures*.

64. Adam Salacuse, personal communication, September 30, 2009.

65. Walter Benjamin, "The Work of Art in the Age of Mechanical Reproduction," in *Media and Cultural Studies: Keyworks*, ed. Meenakshi Gigi Durham and Douglas Kellner, 48–70 (Malden, MA: Blackwell Publishers, 2001).

66. Joe Earley, personal communication, January 14, 2010.

67. Walker, *Buying In*, 101.

68. Wipperfurth, *Brand Hijack*, 5.

69. Ibid., 23, 39, 43.

70. Ibid., 43 (italics added).

71. Leiss et al., *Social Communication in Advertising*, 493.

72. Wipperfurth, *Brand Hijack*, 6, 12 (italics added).

73. Ibid., 82.

74. Ibid., 35.

75. Eric Asche, personal communication, January 19, 2010.

76. Christine Harold, "Pranking Rhetoric: 'Culture Jamming' as Media Activism," *Critical Studies in Media Communication* 21, no. 3 (2004): 203.

77. Ibid., 206.

78. Eric Asche, personal communication, January 19, 2010.

79. Moreover, like Sender, I often found it difficult at times to move my conversations beyond the spin: "Marketing 'pitch' was an underlying frame for my research; it structured many interactions with my subjects. . . . 'The pitch' describes, most typically, the process whereby ad creatives introduce a new campaign to clients—selling ideas to sell products." Similarly, most of the interviewees I spoke with were invested in "promoting the idea" of their guerrilla marketing methods: whether that be for a branded entertainment partnership, a street art campaign, a word-of-mouth program, or a crowd-sourced contest. Just as they had sold clients on the efficacy of their practices, they were also selling me on the success of those implementations. Thus, like Sender, I got the impression that "many of my interviewees may have believed that both the discussion and the results of my project would feed back into their work . . . by raising their profile" and that "the interview itself [was . . . ] a marketing opportunity." Time will tell whether this proves the case. Sender, *Business, Not Politics*, 244, 245, 251.

80. Moore, *Unmarketable*, 119.

81. Deanna Zammit, "Steven Grasse on the Spot,"*Adweek*, October 20, 2004, http://www.adweek.com/news/advertising/steven-grasse-spot-74876

82. Bernard-Levy, *Virus*, 8.

83. Ibid., 16–17.

84. Ibid., 17.

85. Andrew Loos, personal communication, January 4, 2010.

86. Adam Salacuse, personal communication, September 30, 2009.

87. Andrew Loos, personal communication, January 4, 2010.

88. Iain Murray, "Guerrilla Tactics to Get Your Word on the Street," *Marketing Week*, July 8, 2004.

89. Given my earlier discussion of the linkages between guerrilla marketing and public relations, it is also perhaps noteworthy that Ewen, when asked to define the former volunteered the latter: "Guerrilla marketing is how a lot of people thought of marketing for, you know, over a hundred years. . . . In the earlier part of the 1900s, when you had people like Jim Moran or Edward Bernays who were these kind of PR guys but they understood that using public spectacles that got people's attention—got media's attention—was a very valuable thing to do. The 'Torches of Liberty' parade that Bernays did or even something like the Ivory Soap competition that he ran—what it did was touch people in ways that *they didn't know they were being marketed to and they didn't feel it was a brand trying to sell you something*. It was: 'How do I work to get my brand into what can be the generalized style and culture of how people behave?'" Invisible governance once more comes to the forefront of this scheme of power. Personal communication, November 5, 2008 (italics added).

90. Louise Story, "A Boston Marketing Stunt that Bombed, or Did It?" *New York Times*, February 2, 2007, http://www.nytimes.com/2007/02/02/business/media/02guerilla.html

91. The serendipitous discovery meant to be staged through the random location of the light boards' placement is equally part of the cool sell strategy (similar to Cole & Weber "planting" their Rainier beer show on late-night cable [see chap. 2] ). And like the *House, M.D.* "graffadi" analyzed earlier, because the ambiguous image is enigmatically untagged as a TV brand, withholding explanatory information, it foists the interpretation imperative on passersby, potentially better eliciting their engagement.

92. Andrew Hampp, "Lite-Brites, Big City and a Whole Load of Trouble," *Advertising Age*, February 5, 2007, http://adage.com/article/mediaworks/lite-brites-big-city-a-load-trouble/114752/.

93. Goldman and Papson, *Sign Wars*, 4, 58.
94. "Out From the Irony Gap," *Boston Globe*, February 3, 2007, http://www.boston.com/news/globe/editorial_opinion/editorials/articles/2007/02/03/out_from_the_irony_gap/
95. Nat Ives, "Guerrilla Campaigns Are Going to Extremes, but Will the Message Stick?" *New York Times*, June 24, 2004, http://www.nytimes.com/2004/06/24/business/media-business-advertising-guerrilla-campaigns-are-going-extremes-but-will.html?pagewanted=all&src=pm
96. Sam Ewen, personal communication, November 5, 2008 (italics added).
97. Hebdige, *Subculture*, 104.
98. Goldman and Papson, *Sign Wars*, 259, 260.
99. Karl Greenberg, "Marketers of the Next Generation: Nissan's John Cropper,"*Brandweek*, April 12, 2004, http://www.allbusiness.com/marketing-advertising/branding-brand-development/4687815-1.html
100. Ellen Gamerman, "The New Pranksters," *Wall Street Journal*, September 12, 2008, http://online.wsj.com/article/SB122119092302626987.html
101. Gareth Ellis, personal communication, January 13, 2010.
102. Doreen Carvajal, "Dancers in the Crowd Bring Back 'Thriller,'" *New York Times*, March 10, 2008, http://www.nytimes.com/2008/03/10/business/media/10adco.html; Gamerman, "The New Pranksters."
103. Frank, *The Conquest of Cool*, 19; Gladwell, "The Coolhunt."
104. Benjamin, "The Work of Art."
105. Joseph Heath and Andrew Potter, *Nation of Rebels: Why Counterculture Became Consumer Culture* (New York: HarperBusiness, 2004), 129.
106. Ibid., 217.
107. Ibid., 208.
108. Bill Wasik, *And Then There's This: How Stories Live and Die in Viral Culture* (New York: Viking, 2009).
109. Steven Grasse, personal communication, September 28, 2009.
110. Conrad Lodziak, *The Myth of Consumerism* (London: Pluto Press, 2002).
111. Ibid., 68.
112. Ibid., 69.
113. Ibid., 77, 135.

NOTES TO CHAPTER 4

1. Ed Keller and Jon Berry, "Word-of-Mouth: The Real Action is Offline," *Advertising Age*, December 4, 2006, http://adage.com/article/print-edition/word-mouth-real-action-offline/113584/
2. Jonathan Ressler, personal communication, November 7, 2008.
3. William M. Bulkeley, "Pass It On: Advertisers Discover They Have a Friend in 'Viral' Marketing," *Wall Street Journal*, January 14, 2002.
4. Goldman and Papson, *Sign Wars*.
5. Dave Balter and John Butman, *Grapevine: The New Art of Word-of-Mouth Marketing* (New York: Portfolio Hardcover, 2005), 161–162 (italics added).
6. Barbara B. Stern, "A Revised Communication Model for Advertising: Multiple Dimensions of the Source, the Message, and the Recipient," *Journal of Advertising* 23, no. 2 (1994): 7.
7. Garfield, *The Chaos Scenario*, 45.

8. Steve McClellan, "Word-of-Mouth Gains Volume," *Brandweek*, August 25, 2009, http://www.adweek.com/news/advertising-branding/word-mouth-gains-volume-106304

9. Verklin and Kanner, *Watch This, Listen Up, Click Here*, 84.

10. Alex Donohue, "Use of Buzz Marketing on the Increase," *Brand Republic*, July 3, 2006, http://www.brandrepublic.com/news/566537/Use-buzz-marketing-increase/

11. Ted Murphy, personal communication, December 17, 2009 (italics added).

12. Dave Balter, personal communication, October 13, 2009.

13. Matthew Creamer, "Foul Mouth: Stealth Marketers Flirt With the Law," *Advertising Age*, October 3, 2005, http://adage.com/article/news/foul-mouth-stealth-marketers-flirt-law/104763/; Suzanne Vranica, "Buzz Marketers Score Venture Dollars," *Wall Street Journal*, January 13, 2006.

14. Balter and Butman, *Grapevine*, 69; Tara Siegel Bernard, "Small Firms Turn to Marketing Buzz Agents," *Wall Street Journal*, December 27, 2005, http://online.wsj.com/article/SB113563963024831678.html

15. Moore, *Unmarketable*; Wasik, *And Then There's This*.

16. Dave Balter, personal communication, October 13, 2009.

17. Foucault, *Discipline and Punish*, 218.

18. Ibid., 214.

19. Turow, *Niche Envy*.

20. Moore, *Unmarketable*, 186, 187.

21. Balter and Butman, *Grapevine*, 113.

22. Cutlip, *The Unseen Power*, 106; Stuart Ewen, *PR!* 117.

23. Bernays, *Propaganda*, 34, 53; Cutlip, *The Unseen Power*, 196; Stauber and Rampton, *Toxic Sludge*, 23.

24. Stuart Ewen, *PR!* 119.

25. Stauber and Rampton, *Toxic Sludge*, 79.

26. Alternate-reality marketing scenarios like those that catapulted *The Blair Witch Project* to box-office success (see chap. 5) have their own roots in a kind of "commercial astroturfing." Stuart Ewen, *PR!* 29; Stauber and Rampton, *Toxic Sludge*, 81.

27. Stauber and Rampton, *Toxic Sludge*, 87.

28. Kaikati and Kaikati, "Stealth Marketing."

29. Quart, *Branded*, 38.

30. Elihu Katz and Paul Lazarsfeld, *Personal Influence: The Part Played by People in the Flow of Mass Communications*, 2nd ed. (New Brunswick, NJ: Transaction Publishers, 2006).

31. Susan Douglas, "Personal Influence and the Bracketing of Women's History," *ANNALS of the American Academy of Political and Social Science* 608 (2006): 41–50.

32. Alison J. Clarke, *Tupperware: The Promise of Plastic in 1950s America* (Washington, DC: Smithsonian Institution Press, 1999); Katina Manko, "'Now You are in Business for Yourself': The Independent Contractors of the California Perfume Company, 1886–1938," *Business and Economic History* 26, no. 1 (1997): 5–26.

33. Clarke, *Tupperware*, 92.

34. Manko, "'Now You are in Business for Yourself,'" 9, 10.

35. See Roland Marchand, *Creating the Corporate Soul: The Rise of Public Relations and Corporate Imagery in American Big Business* (Berkeley: University of California Press, 1998), 4, 25, 44, 69, 72.

36. Bourdieu, "The Forms of Capital"; Manko, "'Now You Are in Business for Yourself,'" 11.

37. Alison J. Clarke, "Tupperware: Suburbia, Sociality and Mass Consumption," in *Visions of Suburbia*, ed. Roger Silverstone (London: Routledge, 1997), 142.

38. Clarke, *Tupperware*, 83, 85.

39. Greg Metz Thomas, "Building the Buzz in the Hive Mind," *Journal of Consumer Behaviour* 4, no. 1 (2004): 65.

40. Todd Steinman, personal communication, December 4, 2009.

41. Thornton, *Club Cultures*.

42. Betsy Ebenkamp, "Guerrilla Marketer Sam Ewen Finally Speaks About What Happened in Boston," *Brandweek*, February 19, 2007.

43. Thornton, *Club Cultures*, 6.

44. Barak Goodman, "The Merchants of Cool,"*Frontline*, PBS, February 27, 2001, http://www.pbs.org/wgbh/pages/frontline/shows/cool/.

45. Thornton, *Club Cultures*, 138.

46. Moore, *Unmarketable*, 42.

47. Todd Steinman, personal communication, December 4, 2009.

48. Rebecca Gardyn, "Internet Trustbusters," *Creativity*, November 1, 2009.

49. Will Brooker and Deborah Jermyn, eds., *The Audience Studies Reader* (London: Routledge, 2003); Lisa A Lewis, ed., *The Adoring Audience: Fan Culture and Popular Media* (London: Routledge, 1992).

50. Todd Steinman, personal communication, December 4, 2009.

51. Nate Hahn, personal communication, October 6, 2009 (italics added).

52. Jonathan Ressler, personal communication, November 7, 2008.

53. Emanuel Rosen, *The Anatomy of Buzz: How to Create Word-of-Mouth Marketing* (New York: Doubleday/Currency, 2000), 15.

54. Dave Balter explains: "If we were to try and start [BzzAgent] in, let's say, the '80s, it would have required us mailing hundreds of thousands of people every few days; a lot of cost of postage; communications would have taken five times as long; there would have been less channels for people to communicate through—it just wouldn't have worked. The cost structure wouldn't have worked. Because of the Internet, we can aggregate a large audience at a low cost; we can communicate with them easily and simply without difficulty; and, ultimately, you know, people were able to rally around, you know, the sort of online tools that allowed them to have better communication with others." Personal communication, October 13, 2009.

55. Ed Keller, personal communication, January 22, 2010.

56. Dean, *Governmentality*, 23 (italics original).

57. Bruns, *Blogs, Wikipedia*.

58. Bourdieu, "The Forms of Capital," 103.

59. Foucault, "Security, Territory, and Population," 68.

60. Spurgeon, *Advertising and New Media*.

61. See, for example, chap. 2 of Vincent Mosco, *The Digital Sublime: Myth, Power, and Cyberspace* (Cambridge: MIT Press, 2005).

62. Dave Balter, personal communication, October 13, 2009.

63. Wipperfurth, *Brand Hijack*, 82 (italics original).

64. Ibid., 6.

65. Kaikati and Kaikati, "Stealth Marketing," 6.

66. Britt Peterson, personal communication, January 28, 2010 (italics added).

67. Ted Murphy, personal communication, December 17, 2009.

68. Detlev Zwick, Samuel K. Bonsu, and Aron Darmody, "Putting Consumers to Work: 'Co-Creation' and New Marketing Govern-Mentality," *Journal of Consumer Culture* 8, no. 2 (2008): 167.

69. Robert Goldman and Stephen Papson, "Advertising in the Age of Hypersignification," *Theory Culture Society* 11, no. 3 (1994): 26.

70. Foucault, "The Subject and Power," 341.

71. Jonathan Ressler, personal communication, November 7, 2008.

72. Foucault, "The Ethics of the Concern."

73. Gordon, "Governmental Rationality," 5.

74. Arvidsson, *Brands: Meaning and Value*, 8 (italics original).

75. Scott Goodson, personal communication, January 11, 2010.

76. Though he is hardly alone in exaggerating this—recall how the *Journal of Advertising* once puffed, "In advertising's prime, producers held virtually all of the power in the marketplace." Rust and Oliver, "The Death of Advertising," 74.

77. Elizabeth Rose McFall, *Advertising: A Cultural Economy* (London: Sage Publications, 2004).

78. Ted Murphy, personal communication, December 17, 2009.

79. Dave Balter, personal communication, October 13, 2009.

80. Keller and Berry, "Word-of-Mouth."

81. Sam Ewen, "Lose Control: It's Good for Your Brand." *Brandweek*, November 26, 2007, http://www.brandweek.com/bw/magazine/features/article_display.jsp?vnu_content_id=1003676853

82. Rosen, *The Anatomy of Buzz*, 57.

83. Garfield, *The Chaos Scenario*, 14–15.

84. Ibid., 74–75.

85. Suzanne Vranica, "That Guy Showing Off His Hot New Phone May Be a Shill," *Wall Street Journal*, July 31, 2002.

86. Capps, "The Reserved Ruler."

87. Sam Ewen, personal communication, November 5, 2008.

88. Other examples of stealth initiatives like this have been outed over the years: Vespa promoted its product by hiring biker gangs of attractive models to rove major U.S. cities and hand out phone numbers to solicitous bar-goers that reached not them but local dealerships; similarly, ABC sent their own models onto New York City transit to flirt with commuters and oblige interested parties with handwritten e-mail addresses (that eventually directed them to the website); and Word of Net employees "spend hours voyeuristically 'lurking' online in search of potential consumer hangouts for their clients" to then "infiltrate the online exchanges, posting (or 'seeding') carefully crafted commercial messages." Gerry Khermouch and Jeff Green, "Buzz Marketing," *BusinessWeek*, July 30, 2001, http://www.businessweek.com/magazine/content/01_31/b3743001.htm; Betsy Spethmann, "Bracing for Backlash," *Promo*, November 1, 2006, http://promomagazine.com/mag/marketing_bracing_backlash/; Gardyn, "Internet Trustbusters."

89. Hanover, "Guerrilla Your Dreams."

90. Daniel Eisenberg, "It's an Ad, Ad, Ad, Ad World," *Time*, September 2, 2002, http://www.time.com/time/magazine/article/0,9171,1003158,00.html

91. Jonathan Ressler, personal communication, November 7, 2008.

92. Betsy Spethmann, "Brand Illusions," *Promo*, February 1, 2002, http://promomagazine.com/mag/marketing_brand_illusions/

93. Turow, *Niche Envy*, 77 (italics added).

94. Walker, *Buying In*, 168; Todd Wasserman, "What's the Buzz? One Organization Says 'Fraud,'" *Brandweek*, October 18, 2005, http://www.billboard.com/news/ask-billboard-1001307628.story#/news/ask-billboard-1001307628.story

95. Robert Berner, "I Sold It through the Grapevine," *Business Week*, May 29, 2006, http://www.businessweek.com/magazine/content/06_22/b3986060.htm

96. Dave Balter, personal communication, October 13, 2009.

97. See, for example, Carl, "What's All the Buzz About?"

98. Balter and Butman, *Grapevine*, 176.

99. Dave Balter, personal communication, October 13, 2009.

100. Suzanne Vranica, "Getting Buzz Marketers to Fess Up," *Wall Street Journal*, February 9, 2005 (italics added).

101. Elaine Wong, "Pssst . . . CPG Cos. Love W-O-M," *Brandweek*, October 6, 2008.

102. Todd Wasserman, "Word Games," *Brandweek*, April 24, 2006.

103. Barbara F. Meltz, "Protecting Kids from Marketers' Clutches." *Boston Globe*, September 30, 2004, http://www.boston.com/yourlife/family/articles/2004/09/30/protecting_kids_from_marketers_clutches/?page=full

104. Juliet Schor, *Born to Buy: The Commercialized Child and the New Consumer Culture* (New York: Scribner, 2004), 77.

105. Laura Groppe, personal communication, January 8, 2010.

106. Deborah Tannen, *You Just Don't Understand: Women and Men in Conversation* (New York, Ballantine, 1990).

107. Ed Keller and Jon Berry, *The Influentials* (New York: Free Press, 2003).

108. Walker, *Buying In*, 180 (italics original).

109. Dave Balter, personal communication, October 13, 2009.

110. Drake Bennett, "Is This the Future of Advertising?" *Boston Globe*, September 24, 2006. http://www.boston.com/news/globe/ideas/articles/2006/09/24/is_this_the_future_of_advertising/

111. Rosen, *The Anatomy of Buzz*, 175.

112. Ted Murphy, personal communication, December 17, 2009.

## NOTES TO CHAPTER 5

1. Arvidsson, *Brands: Meaning and Value*, 74.

2. Jon Fine, "What Makes Citizen Ads' Work," *Business Week*, February 19, 2007, http://www.businessweek.com/magazine/content/07_08/b4022025.htm

3. Spurgeon, *Advertising and New Media*, 2.

4. Foucault, "The Subject and Power," 341.

5. Bruns, *Blogs, Wikipedia*; Jenkins, *Convergence Culture*; Shirky, *Here Comes Everybody*; Benkler, *The Wealth of Networks*.

6. Jenkins, *Convergence Culture*, 18, 19.

7. Ibid., 22.

8. Spurgeon, *Advertising and New Media*.

9. Hall, "Encoding/Decoding."

10. Spurgeon, *Advertising and New Media*, 4.

11. Deuze, *Media Work*, 126.

12. Maurizio Lazzarato, "Immaterial Labor," in *Radical Thought in Italy: A Potential Politics*, ed. Paolo Virno and Michael Hardt (Minneapolis: University of Minnesota Press, 1996), 133.

13. Ibid., 137.

14. Tiziana Terranova, "Producing Culture for the Digital Economy," *Social Text* 63, no. 18 (2000): 33.
15. Ibid., 35.
16. Mark Andrejevic, "Watching Television without Pity: The Productivity of Online Fans," *Television and New Media* 9, no. 1 (2008): 24, 37, 42–43.
17. Brooke Erin Duffy, "Empowerment through Endorsement? Polysemic Meaning in Dove's User-Generated Advertising," *Communication, Culture & Critique* 3, no. 1 (2010): 39, 40.
18. Zwick, Bonsu, and Darmody, "Putting Consumers to Work," 164.
19. Ibid., 165, 166.
20. Michael Serazio, "The Apolitical Irony of Generation Mash-Up: A Cultural Case Study in Popular Music," *Popular Music and Society* 31, no. 1 (2008): 79–94.
21. David Kiley, "Advertising of, by and for the People," *BusinessWeek*, July 25, 2005, http://www.businessweek.com/magazine/content/05_30/b3944097.htm
22. Jimmy Maymann, *The Social Metropolis*. 2008. http://www.goviral.com/book_2008.html
23. Theresa Howard, "'Viral' Advertising Spreads through Marketing Plans," *USA Today*, June 23, 2005, http://www.usatoday.com/money/advertising/2005-06-22-viral-usat_x.htm
24. Douglas Holt defines "viral branding" in a passage worth quoting in full: "[It] is a compendium of ideas rooted in the classic ideas about public influence—diffusion of information, word of mouth, and public relations—that responded to two major shifts in the 1990s: the increased cynicism toward mass marketing and the emergence of the internet. Viral branding assumes that consumers, and not firms, have the most influence in the creation of brands. Cynical consumers will no longer heed the missives of mass marketers, so instead must 'discover' brands on their own. The Internet provided a means to accelerate this discovery. . . . In addition, many experts today recommend below-the-radar marketing, which seeds the brand among the most influential people. The basic idea is that if the firm can convince these people to make the brand their own, and configure the brand, like a virus, to make it easy to talk about, these influencers will rapidly spread their interest in the brand to others through their social networks, just as a virus spreads. . . . In viral branding, a covert public relations mode becomes the core of the branding effort." Douglas Holt, *How Brands Become Icons: The Principles of Cultural Branding* (Boston: Harvard Business School Press, 2004), 28, 29.
25. Deuze, "Convergence Culture," 247, 251.
26. Deuze, *Media Work*.
27. Garth Jowett and Victoria O'Donnell, *Propaganda and Persuasion*, 4th ed. (Thousand Oaks, CA: Sage, 2006), 40.
28. Wipperfurth, *Brand Hijack*, 41.
29. Foucault, *Security, Territory, Population*, 201.
30. Jimmy Maymann, personal communication, January 11, 2010. Interestingly, the chief executive of the Interactive Advertising Bureau cautioned that not all marketers should subscribe to viral strategy for this same reason: "While youth and alternative brands have benefitted greatly from online viral marketing, it is not necessarily a formula open to all marketers. . . . Let's be clear—marketers cannot control what happens once a viral campaign is released. It's out there and the internet users are the ones in control." Jamie Hill, "We're Not Immune to Viral Advertising—Yet," *Marketing Week*, March 25, 2004, 15.
31. Rick Webb, "Happy 5th Birthday, Subservient Chicken," *Barbarian Blog*, April 6, 2009. http://www.barbariangroup.com/posts/1938-happy_5th_birthday_subservient_chicken
32. Ibid.
33. Benjamin Palmer, personal communication, January 26, 2010.

34. Webb, "Happy 5th Birthday, Subservient Chicken" (italics added).
35. Holt, "Why Do Brands Cause Trouble?" 83.
36. Scott Leonard, personal communication, January 15, 2010.
37. Jaffe, *Life After the 30-Second Spot*, 217.
38. Howard, "'Viral' Advertising Spreads."
39. Nathalie Kilby, "Viral: The Final Frontier," *Marketing Week*, August 30, 2007, 16.
40. Brian Morrissey, "Clients Try to Manipulate 'Unpredictable' Viral Buzz," *Adweek*, March 19, 2007, http://www.adweek.com/news/advertising/clients-try-manipulate-unpredictable-viral-buzz-88325
41. Thornton, *Club Cultures*.
42. Chris Anderson, *The Long Tail: Why the Future of Business is Selling Less of More* (New York: Hyperion, 2006).
43. Maymann, *The Social Metropolis*, 90.
44. Spethmann, "Bracing for Backlash."
45. Maymann, *The Social Metropolis*, 15.
46. Bruns, *Blogs, Wikipedia*.
47. Michael S. Rosenwald, "Reputations at Stake, Companies Try to Alter Word of Mouth Online," *Washington Post*, March 29, 2010, http://www.washingtonpost.com/wp-dyn/content/article/2010/03/28/AR2010032802905.html?nav=emailpage; Spurgeon, *Advertising and New Media*, 1.
48. Ted Murphy, personal communication, December 17, 2009. Unlike the procedures in place at BzzAgent, where no money changes hands and agents are free to cast their own judgment, Izea compensates its 400,000 social media content creators in cash paid out from some 35,000 participating advertisers for expressly favorable chatter such that buzz is, in this case, more scripted, not just conscripted.
49. Phoebe Jamison, personal communication, November 5, 2009.
50. Spurgeon, *Advertising and New Media*; Castells, "Communication, Power and Counter-Power."
51. Zwick, Bonsu, and Darmody, "Putting Consumers to Work," 165.
52. Michael Stradiotta, personal communication, January 15, 2010.
53. Brian Morrissey, "Izea: Trick or Tweet,"*Adweek*, June 5, 2009, http://www.adweek.com/news/technology/get-ready-pay-tweet-99491
54. Pallavi Gogoi, "Wal-Mart's Jim and Laura: The Real Story," *BusinessWeek Online*, October 9, 2006, http://www.businessweek.com/bwdaily/dnflash/content/oct2006/db20061009_579137.htm; Garfield, *The Chaos Scenario*, 105; Tamara Chuang, "Ouch! Belkin Admits Employee Paid for Fake Reviews on Amazon," *Orange County Register*, January 21, 2009, http://gadgetress.freedomblogging.com/2009/01/20/ouch-belkin-admits-employee-posted-fake-reviews/8876/
55. Rosenwald, "Reputations at Stake."
56. Alan Friel, "Navigating FTC's Guidance on Social Media Marketing," *Adweek*, November 30, 2009, http://www.adweek.com/news/advertising-branding/navigating-ftcs-guidance-social-media-marketing-100969
57. Dallas Lawrence, "Social Media and the FTC: What Businesses Need to Know," *Mashable*, December 16, 2009, http://mashable.com/2009/12/16/ftc-social-media/. Ann Taylor was the target of the first publicly announced investigation by the FTC into such "blogola." Although no action was taken against the women's clothing retailer, the federal agency nonetheless expressed concern about bloggers failing to disclose the receipt of gift cards

for their coverage of the company's summer preview. Natalie Zmuda, "Ann Taylor Probe Shows FTC Keeping a Close Eye on Blogging," *Advertising Age*, May 3, 2010, http://adage.com/article/news/ann-taylor-case-shows-ftc-keeping-close-eye-blogging/143567/

58. Sam de la Garza, personal communication, October 13, 2009.

59. Matthew Dolan, "Ford Takes Online Gamble with New Fiesta," *Wall Street Journal*, April 8, 2009, http://online.wsj.com/article/SB123915162156099499.html

60. Sam de la Garza, personal communication, October 13, 2009.

61. Garfield, *The Chaos Scenario*, 214–215.

62. Andrejevic, *iSpy*, 5, 27, 136.

63. Daren C. Brabham, "Crowdsourced Advertising: How We Outperform Madison Avenue," *FlowTV* 9, no. 10 (2009), http://flowtv.org/?p=3221

64. Michael Bush, "Text Mining Provides Marketers With the 'Why' Behind Demand," *Advertising Age*, July 27, 2009, http://adage.com/article/digital/marketing-text-mining-demand/138110/

65. Doritos FAQ, http://fritolay.com/about-us/most-common-questions.html#6

66. Sarah Banet-Weiser and Charlotte Lapsansky, "RED is the New Black: Brand Culture, Consumer Citizenship and Political Possibility," *International Journal of Communication* 2 (2008): 1248–1268.

67. Garfield, *The Chaos Scenario*, 149.

68. Andrejevic, *iSpy*, 23, 25.

69. Bobbie Johnson, "Virgin Ends Ad Campaign with Anarchic Site Over Images of Branson," *Guardian*, October 30, 2006, http://www.guardian.co.uk/technology/2006/oct/30/news.media

70. Brian Morrissey, "Skittles Site Ends Extreme Social Makeover," *Adweek*, February 4, 2010, http://www.brandweek.com/bw/content_display/news-and-features/digital/e3i9f46c57380aa314fd4a92055eb8b7d88

71. Petrecca, "Madison Avenue Wants You!"

72. Zwick, Bonsu, and Darmody, "Putting Consumers to Work," 184.

73. Jordan Weisman, personal communication, December 3, 2009.

74. Jenkins, *Convergence Culture*, 98.

75. Lucy Aitken, "Why Clients Are Waking Up to the Global Reach of Viral Work," *Campaign*, May 14, 2004, http://www.brandrepublic.com/news/210976/; Susan Bonds, personal communication, December 17, 2009; Noreen O'Leary, "Q & A: Robert Rasmussen," *Adweek*, June 30, 2008, http://www.adweek.com/news/technology/qa-robert-rasmussen-96247

76. Teressa Iezzi, "Marketers Tapping into the Magic of an Alternate Reality," *Advertising Age*, November 21, 2005. http://adage.com/article/viewpoint/marketers-tapping-magic-alternate-reality/105343/

77. Mike Monello, personal communication, January 27, 2010.

78. Lisa Sanders, "Stories Around the Campfire," *Advertising Age*, November 21, 2005, http://adage.com/article/news/stories-campfire/105360/

79. Mike Monello, personal communication, January 27, 2010.

80. Anderson, "Tall Tales."

81. Ibid."; Jimmy Maymann, personal communication, January 11, 2010; Maymann, *The Social Metropolis*, 68. Moreover, one branding consultant claims that *Blair Witch* "probably wreaked more havoc on the world of marketing than any case study since Bill Bernbach's groundbreaking advertising work for VW in the '60s" and cites a Proctor & Gamble executive who says the conglomerate used it as "the BIG case study" in their push for thinking about "seeding and unconventional approaches." Wipperfurth, *Brand Hijack*, 99.

82. Jonathan Gray, *Show Sold Separately: Promos, Spoilers, and Other Media Paratexts* (New York: New York University Press, 2010), 6.

83. Mike Monello, personal communication, January 27, 2010.

84. Nicholas Maiese, "'Blair Witch' Casts its Spell," *Advertising Age*, March 20, 2000, http://adage.com/article/news/blair-witch-casts-spell/58984/

85. Mike Monello, personal communication, January 27, 2010.

86. Albert M. Muniz, and Thomas C. O'Guinn, "Brand Community," *Journal of Consumer Research* 27, no. 4 (2001): 412.

87. Wipperfurth, *Brand Hijack*, 131 (italics added); see also Bernard Cova and Veronique Cova, "Tribal Marketing: The Tribalization of Society and its Impact on the Conduct of Marketing," *European Journal of Marketing* 36, no. 5 (2002): 595–620.

88. Douglas Atkin, *The Culting of Brands: When Customers Become True Believers* (New York: Portfolio Trade, 2005).

89. Bart Cleveland, personal communication, November 20, 2008.

90. Brooks Barnes, "It Seemed Like a Good Idea . . .," *Wall Street Journal*, April 30, 2007, R7.

91. Bart Cleveland, personal communication, November 20, 2008.

92. Jane Evelyn McGonigal, "This Might Be a Game: Ubiquitous Play and Performance at the Turn of the Twenty-First Century" (PhD diss., Berkeley: University of California, Berkeley, 2006), 277, http://avantgame.com/McGonigal_THIS_MIGHT_BE_A_GAME_sm.pdf

93. Henrik Ornebring, "Alternate Reality Gaming and Convergence Culture: The Case of Alias," *International Journal of Cultural Studies* 10, no. 4 (2007): 447.

94. Howard, "'Viral' Advertising Spreads."

95. Stephanie Kang, "BMW Ran Risk with Role in Mockumentary," *Wall Street Journal*, June 20, 2008, http://online.wsj.com/article/SB121391470578790089.html

96. "BBDO/Proximity Malaysia Wins Echo Silver!" *Adoi Magazine*, October 21, 2008, http://www.adoimagazine.com/index.php/news/130-breaking-news-2008/3354-bbdoproximity-malaysia-wins-echo-silver

97. Laurel Wentz, "Fines, Arrests, Beer: Here's One Guerrilla Effort That Has It All," *Advertising Age*, May 21, 2007, http://adage.com/article/print-edition/fines-arrests-beer-guerrilla-effort/116739/

98. Christy Dena, "Emerging Participatory Culture Practices: Player-Created Tiers in Alternate Reality Games," *Convergence* 14, no. 1 (2008): 41–57.

99. Jenkins, *Convergence Culture*, 125.

100. Susan Bonds, personal communication, December 17, 2009 (italics added).

101. Ibid.

102. Maymann, *The Social Metropolis*, 65, 68.

103. Jordan Weisman, personal communication, December 3, 2009.

104. Dena, "Emerging Participatory Culture Practices," 42 (italics original).

105. Ibid., 48.

106. Emma Hall, "Don't Look Now, But the Crowd Just Might Steal Your Ad Account," *Advertising Age*, September 14, 2009, http://adage.com/article/global-news/unilever-embraces-crowdsourcing-sacks-lowe-peperami-biz/138978/

107. Jaffe, *Life After the 30-Second Spot*, 221; personal communication, November 10, 2009. Indeed, the agencies of record on other Unilever accounts were no doubt eyeing this development with trepidation, as a managing director for the conglomerate went on record saying, "This could work for other brands. . . . We're looking at a long-term model to produce content and I'm keeping [Unilever CMO] Simon Clift involved." Hall, "Don't Look Now."

Outwardly, creative executives might scoff, as the director of one boutique agency remarked in a *BusinessWeek* piece on crowd-sourcing: "We are pros and although it looks easy to create advertising, it isn't. . . . User-generated content reminds me that there's a reason I have a job." Fine, "What Makes Citizen Ads' Work." Only time will tell whether this holds—and whether Lowe's fate on the Peperami account was anomaly or bellwether.

108. Petrecca, "Madison Avenue wants you!"; Brabham, "Crowdsourced Advertising."
109. Bruns, *Blogs, Wikipedia, Second Life, and Beyond*, 5.
110. Serazio, "The Apolitical Irony," 83.
111. Deuze, *Media Work*, 77.

## NOTES TO CHAPTER 6

1. Nikolas Rose, *Powers of Freedom: Reframing Political Thought* (Cambridge: Cambridge University Press, 1999), 4.
2. Jef Richards and Catherine Curran, "'Oracles on 'Advertising': Searching for a Definition," *Journal of Advertising* 31, no. 2 (2002): 63–77.
3. Ibid., 74.
4. Foucault, "The Subject and Power," 341.
5. Rose, *Powers of Freedom*, 67.
6. Ibid., 4.
7. Michel Foucault, "The Ethics of the Concern."
8. Anderson, "Tall Tales."
9. David Harvey, *A Brief History of Neoliberalism* (New York: Oxford University Press, 2005).
10. Michelle Halpern, "Uncapping Consumer Generated Content," *Marketing News*, July 17, 2006, http://www.marketingmag.ca/news/marketer-news/uncapping-consumer-generated-content-19721
11. Holt, "Why Do Brands Cause Trouble?" 83 (italics added).
12. Malpass, Barnett, Clarke, and Cloke, "Problematizing Choice," 236.
13. Rose, *Powers of Freedom*, 28.
14. Gramsci, *Selections from the Prison Notebooks*, 80.
15. Edward Bernays, "The Engineering of Consent," *ANNALS of the American Academy of Political and Social Science* 250 (1947): 113–120.
16. Wipperfurth, *Brand Hijack*, 119, 237.
17. Carey, *Communication as Culture*.
18. Atkin, *The Culting of Brands*, 4.
19. Carey, *Communication as Culture*, 18.
20. Kevin Spacey as "Kint" in *The Usual Suspects* (1995).

## NOTES TO APPENDIX

1. Thomas R. Lindlof, *Qualitative Communication Research Methods* (Thousand Oaks, CA: Sage Publications, 1995); Pertti Alasuutari, *Researching Culture: Qualitative Method and Cultural Studies* (London: Sage, 1995); Martyn Hammersley and Paul Atkinson. *Ethnography: Principles in Practice*, 3rd ed. (London: Routledge, 2007).
2. Holt, *How Brands Become Icons*, 223.

# BIBLIOGRAPHY

"Advertising by Medium." *Advertising Age*, December 19, 2011, 8.

"Agencies of the Decade." *Advertising Age*, December 14, 2009. http://adage.com/article/print-edition/book-tens-agencies-decade/141055/

Aitken, Lucy. "Why Clients Are Waking Up to the Global Reach of Viral Work." *Campaign*, May 14, 2004. http://www.brandrepublic.com/news/210976/

Alasuutari, Pertti. *Researching Culture: Qualitative Method and Cultural Studies*. London: Sage, 1995.

*Alternative media spending growth accelerates in 2007, hastening transition from traditional to alternative advertising & marketing strategies*. PQ Media, March 26, 2008. http://www.pqmedia.com/about-press-20080326-amf2008.html

Anderson, Chris. *The Long Tail: Why the Future of Business Is Selling Less of More*. New York: Hyperion, 2006.

Anderson, Mae. "Tall Tales: Advertising Steps into Interactive Fiction, Where the Buzz is Real—Even When the Stories Aren't." *Adweek*, October 11, 2004. http://adage.com/article/viewpoint/cannes-fest-recognize-mad-vine-a-fad/48792/

Andrejevic, Mark. *iSpy: Surveillance and Power in the Interactive Era*. Lawrence: University Press of Kansas, 2007.

———. "Watching Television without Pity: The Productivity of Online Fans." *Television and New Media* 9, no. 1 (2008): 24–46.

Anthony, Joseph. "Hip-Hop Culture Crosses into Brand Strategy." *Brand Channel*, September 12, 2005, http://www.brandchannel.com/brand_speak.asp?bs_id=120

Arvidsson, Adam. "Brands: A Critical Perspective." *Journal of Consumer Culture* 5, no. 2 (2005): 235–258.

———. *Brands: Meaning and Value in Media Culture*. London: Routledge, 2006.

Atkin, Douglas. *The Culting of Brands: When Customers Become True Believers*. New York: Portfolio Trade, 2005.

Balasubramanian, Siva K. "Beyond Advertising and Publicity: Hybrid Messages and Public Policy Issues." *Journal of Advertising* 23, no. 4 (1994): 29–46.

Balter, Dave, and John Butman. *Grapevine: The New Art of Word-of-Mouth Marketing*. New York: Portfolio Hardcover, 2005.

Banet-Weiser, Sarah, and Charlotte Lapsansky. "RED is the New Black: Brand Culture, Consumer Citizenship and Political Possibility." *International Journal of Communication* 2 (2008): 1248–1268.

Barber, Benjamin R. *Consumed: How Markets Corrupt Children, Infantilize Adults, and Swallow Citizens Whole*. New York: W. W. Norton & Co, 2007.

Barnes, Brooks. "It Seemed Like a Good Idea . . . " *Wall Street Journal*, April 30, 2007.

"BBDO/Proximity Malaysia Wins Echo Silver!" *Adoi Magazine*, October 21, 2008, http://www.adoimagazine.com/index.php/news/130-breaking-news-2008/3354-bbdoproximity-malaysia-wins-echo-silver

Benjamin, Walter. "The Work of Art in the Age of Mechanical Reproduction." In *Media and Cultural Studies: Keyworks*, edited by Meenakshi Gigi Durham and Douglas Kellner, 48–70. Malden, MA: Blackwell Publishers, 2001.

Benkler, Yochai. *The Wealth of Networks: How Social Production Transforms Markets and Freedom*. New Haven: Yale University Press, 2006.

Bennett, Drake. "Is This the Future of Advertising?" *Boston Globe*, September 24, 2006. http://www.boston.com/news/globe/ideas/articles/2006/09/24/is_this_the_future_of_advertising/

Bennett, Tony. "Introduction: Popular Culture and the 'Turn to Gramsci." In *Popular Culture and Social Relations*, edited by Tony Bennett, Colin Mercer, and Janet Woollacott, xi–xix. Milton Keynes, UK: Open University Press, 1986.

Bernard-Levy, Harriet. *Virus: The Outrageous History of Gyro Worldwide*. Regina, Saskatchewan: Gold Crown Press, 2008.

Bernard, Tara Siegel. "Small Firms Turn to Marketing Buzz Agents." *Wall Street Journal*, December 27, 2005. http://online.wsj.com/article/SB113563963024831678.html

Bernays, Edward L. "The Engineering of Consent." *ANNALS of the American Academy of Political and Social Science* 250 (1947): 113–120.

———. *Propaganda*. New York: Horace Liveright, 1928.

Berner, Robert. "I Sold It Through the Grapevine." *BusinessWeek*, May 29, 2006. http://www.businessweek.com/magazine/content/06_22/b3986060.htm

Bevir, Mark. "The Construction of Governance." In *Governance, Consumers and Citizens: Agency and Resistance in Contemporary Politics*, edited by Mark Bevir and Frank Trentmann, 25–48. New York: Palgrave Macmillan, 2007.

Bevir, Mark, and Frank Trentmann. "Introduction: Consumption and Citizenship in the New Governance." In *Governance, Consumers and Citizens: Agency and Resistance in Contemporary Politics*, edited by Mark Bevir and Frank Trentmann, 1–22. New York: Palgrave Macmillan, 2007.

Bond, Jonathan, and Richard Kirshenbaum. *Under the Radar: Talking to Today's Cynical Consumer*. New York: John Wiley & Sons, 1998.

Bourdieu, Pierre. "The Forms of Capital." In *The Sociology of Economic Life*, edited by Mark Granovetter and Richard Swedberg, 96–111. Boulder, CO: Westview Press, 2001.

Brabham, Daren C. "Crowdsourced Advertising: How We Outperform Madison Avenue." *FlowTV* 9, no. 10 (2009). http://flowtv.org/?p=3221

Brooker, Will, and Deborah Jermyn, eds. *The Audience Studies Reader*. London: Routledge, 2003.

Bruns, Axel. *Blogs, Wikipedia, Second Life, and Beyond: From Production to Produsage*. New York: Peter Lang, 2008.

Bulkeley, William M. "Pass it On: Advertisers Discover They Have a Friend in 'Viral' Marketing." *Wall Street Journal*, January 14, 2002.

Burgess, Jean, and Joshua Green. *YouTube: Online Video and Participatory Culture*. Cambridge: Polity, 2009.

Bush, Michael. "Text Mining Provides Marketers With the 'Why' Behind Demand." *Advertising Age*, July 27, 2009. http://adage.com/article/digital/marketing-text-mining-demand/138110/

Capps, Brooke. "The Reserved Ruler of In-Your-Face Marketing." *Advertising Age*, March 5, 2007. http://adage.com/article/print-edition/reserved-ruler-face-marketing/115372/

Carducci, Vince. "Culture Jamming: A Sociological Perspective."*Journal of Consumer Culture* 6, no. 1 (2006): 116–138.

Carey, James W. *Communication as Culture: Essays on Media and Society*. New York: Routledge, 1992.

Carl, Walter J. "What's All the Buzz About?: Everyday Communication and the Relational Basis of Word-of-Mouth and Buzz Marketing Practices." *Management Communication Quarterly* 19, no. 4 (2006): 601–634.

Carvajal, Doreen. "Dancers in the Crowd Bring Back 'Thriller.'" *New York Times*, March 10, 2008, http://www.nytimes.com/2008/03/10/business/media/10adco.html

Castells, Manuel. *Communication Power*. Oxford: Oxford University Press, 2009.

———. "Communication, Power and Counter-power in the Network Society." *International Journal of Communication* no. 1 (2007): 238–266.

———. *The Rise of the Network Society*. 2nd ed. Oxford: Blackwell Publishers, 2000.

Chuang, Tamara. "Ouch! Belkin Admits Employee Paid for Fake Reviews on Amazon." *Orange County Register*, January 21, 2009. http://gadgetress.freedomblogging.com/2009/01/20/ouch-belkin-admits-employee-posted-fake-reviews/8876/

Clarke, Alison J. "Tupperware: Suburbia, Sociality and Mass Consumption." In *Visions of Suburbia*, edited by Roger Silverstone, 132–160. London: Routledge, 1997.

———. *Tupperware: The Promise of Plastic in 1950s America*. Washington, DC: Smithsonian Institution Press, 1999.

Cohen, Lizabeth. *A Consumer's Republic: The Politics of Mass Consumption in Postwar America*. New York: Vintage, 2003.

Contreras, Esteban. "Interview: Alex Bogusky Talks Ads, CP+B Culture, Fun, and Focus." *Social Nerdia*, May 27, 2009. http://socialnerdia.com/index.php/2009/05/interview-alex-bogusky-cpb

Cova, Bernard, and Veronique Cova. "Tribal Marketing: The Tribalization of Society and its Impact on the Conduct of Marketing." *European Journal of Marketing* 36, no. 5 (2002): 595–620.

Cox, Lauren. "Top 7 Celebrity Drug Endorsements: Commercial or a Cause?" *ABC News*, April 1, 2009. http://abcnews.go.com/Health/CelebrityCafe/story?id=7209401&page=1

Creamer, Matthew. "Foul Mouth: Stealth Marketers Flirt With the Law."*Advertising Age*, October 3, 2005. http://adage.com/article/news/foul-mouth-stealth-marketers-flirt-law/104763/

Croteau, David, William Hoynes, and Stefania Milan. *Media/Society: Industries, Images, and Audiences*. 4th ed. Los Angeles: Sage, 2012.

Curtis, James. "Speed Branding." *Marketing*, November 20, 2003. http://www.marketing-magazine.co.uk/news/196087/

Cutlip, Scott M. *The Unseen Power: Public Relations, a History*. Hillsdale, NJ: Lawrence Erlbaum Associates, 1994.

Dahlén, Micael. "The Medium as a Contextual Cue: Effects of Creative Media Choice."*Journal of Advertising* 34, no. 3 (2005): 89–98.

Dahlén, Micael, and Mats Edenius. "When Is Advertising Advertising? Comparing Responses to Non-Traditional and Traditional Advertising Media." *Journal of Current Issues & Research in Advertising* 29, no. 1 (2007): 33–42.

Dahlgren, Peter. "Media Logic in Cyberspace: Repositioning Journalism and its Publics."*Javnost/The Public* 3, no. 3 (1996): 59–72.

Dávila, Arlene M. *Latinos, Inc.: The Marketing and Making of a People*. Berkeley: University of California Press, 2001.

Dean, Mitchell. *Governmentality: Power and Rule in Modern Society*. 2nd ed. Los Angeles: Sage Publications, 2010.

Dena, Christy. "Emerging Participatory Culture Practices: Player-Created Tiers in Alternate Reality Games." *Convergence* 14, no. 1 (2008): 41–57.

Deuze, Mark. "Convergence Culture in the Creative Industries." *International Journal of Cultural Studies* 10, no. 2 (2007): 243–263.

———. *Media Work*. Cambridge: Polity, 2007.

Diaz, Ann-Christine. "Best non-TV Campaigns." *Advertising Age*, December 14, 2009. http://adage.com/article/print-edition/book-tens-tv-campaigns-decade/141011/

Dolan, Matthew. "Ford Takes Online Gamble with New Fiesta." *Wall Street Journal*, April 8, 2009. http://online.wsj.com/article/SB123915162156099499.html

Dolbow, Sandra. "Landscape of the Giants."*Brandweek*, November 12, 2001.

Donaton, Scott. "Cannes Fest Can Recognize Mad + Vine is Not Just a Fad." *Advertising Age*, June 16, 2003. http://adage.com/article/viewpoint/cannes-fest-recognize-mad-vine-a-fad/48792/

———. *Madison & Vine: Why the Entertainment and Advertising Industries Must Converge to Survive*. New York: McGraw-Hill, 2004.

Donohue, Alex. "Use of Buzz Marketing on the Increase." *Brand Republic*, July 3, 2006. http://www.brandrepublic.com/news/566537/Use-buzz-marketing-increase/

Douglas, Susan J. "Personal Influence and the Bracketing of Women's History."*ANNALS of the American Academy of Political and Social Science* 608 (2006): 41–50.

Duffy, Brooke Erin. "Empowerment Through Endorsement? Polysemic Meaning in Dove's User-Generated Advertising." *Communication, Culture & Critique* 3, no. 1 (2010): 26–43.

Ebenkamp, Betsy. "Guerrilla Marketer Sam Ewen Finally Speaks about What Happened in Boston."*Brandweek*, February 19, 2007.

———. "Guerrilla Marketing '06: A Brandweek Staff Report" *Brandweek*, November 20, 2006. http://business.highbeam.com/137330/article-1G1-155028857/guerrilla-marketing-06-brandweek-staff-report

Eisenberg, Daniel. "It's an Ad, Ad, Ad, Ad World." *Time*, September 2, 2002. http://www.time.com/time/magazine/article/0,9171,1003158,00.html

Ewen, Sam. "Lose Control: It's Good for Your Brand."*Brandweek*, November 26, 2007. http://www.brandweek.com/bw/magazine/features/article_display.jsp?vnu_content_id=1003676853

Ewen, Stuart. *Captains of Consciousness: Advertising and the Social roots of the Consumer Culture*. 2nd ed. New York: Basic Books, 2001.

———. *PR! A Social History of Spin*. New York: Basic Books, 1996.

Fine, Jon. "What Makes Citizen Ads' Work." *BusinessWeek*, February 19, 2007. http://www.businessweek.com/magazine/content/07_08/b4022025.htm

Fitzgerald, Toni. "Big Driver Behind Out-of-Home: Digital." *Media Life*, August 14, 2009. http://www.medialifemagazine.com/artman2/publish/Alternative_media_43/Big_driver_behind_out-of-home_Digital.asp

Forgacs, David, ed. *The Antonio Gramsci Reader: Selected Writings, 1916–1935*. New York: New York University Press, 2000.

Foucault, Michel. *Discipline and Punish: The Birth of the Prison*. Translated by Alan Sheridan. New York: Vintage, 1977.

——. "The Ethics of the Concern of the Self as a Practice of Freedom." In *The Essential Works of Foucault, 1954–1984: Ethics Subjectivity and Truth*, edited by Paul Rabinow, translated by Robert Hurley, 281–302. New York: New Press, 1997.

——. "Governmentality." In *The Essential Works of Foucault, 1954–1984: Power*, edited by James D. Faubion, translated by Robert Hurley, 201–222. New York: New Press, 2000.

——. "Preface to *The History of Sexuality*, Volume Two." In *The Essential Works of Foucault, 1954–1984: Ethics Subjectivity and Truth*, edited by Paul Rabinow, translated by Robert Hurley, 199–205. New York: New Press, 1997.

——. "Security, Territory, and Population." In *The Essential Works of Foucault, 1954–1984: Ethics Subjectivity and Truth*, edited by Paul Rabinow, translated by Robert Hurley, 67–71. New York: New Press, 1997.

——. *Security, Territory, Population: Lectures at the Collège De France, 1977–78*. Edited by Michel Senellart. Basingstoke, Hampshire: Palgrave Macmillan, 2007.

——. "The Subject and Power." In *The Essential Works of Foucault, 1954–1984: Power*, edited by James D. Faubion, translated by Robert Hurley, 326–348. New York: New Press, 2000.

Frank, Thomas. *The Conquest of Cool: Business Culture, Counterculture, and the Rise of Hip Consumerism*. Chicago: University of Chicago Press, 1997.

Friel, Alan. "Navigating FTC's Guidance on Social Media Marketing." *Adweek*, November 30, 2009. http://www.adweek.com/news/advertising-branding/navigating-ftcs-guidance-social-media-marketing-100969

Gamerman, Ellen. "The New Pranksters." *Wall Street Journal*, September 12, 2008. http://online.wsj.com/article/SB122119092302626987.html

Gardyn, Rebecca. "Internet Trustbusters." *Creativity*, November 1, 2009.

Garfield, Bob. *The Chaos Scenario*. New York: Stielstra Publishing, 2009.

Geertz, Clifford. *The Interpretation of Cultures: Selected Essays*. New York: Basic Books, 1973.

Gitlin, Todd. *Inside Prime Time*. 2nd ed. Berkeley: University of California Press, 2000.

Gladwell, Malcolm. "The Coolhunt." *New Yorker*, March 17, 1997. http://www.gladwell.com/1997/1997_03_17_a_cool.htm

Gogoi, Pallavi. "Wal-Mart's Jim and Laura: The Real Story." *BusinessWeek Online*, October 9, 2006. http://www.businessweek.com/bwdaily/dnflash/content/oct2006/db20061009_579137.htm

Goldman, Robert, and Stephen Papson. "Advertising in the Age of Hypersignification." *Theory Culture Society* 11, no. 3 (1994): 23–53.

——. *Sign Wars: The Cluttered Landscape of Advertising*. New York: Guilford Press, 1996.

Goodman, Barak. "The Merchants of Cool." *Frontline*. PBS, February 27, 2001. http://www.pbs.org/wgbh/pages/frontline/shows/cool/

Gordon, Colin. "Governmental Rationality: An Introduction." In *The Foucault Effect: Studies in Governmentality*, edited by Graham Burchell, Colin Gordon, and Peter Miller, 1–52. Chicago: University of Chicago Press, 1991.

Gramsci, Antonio. *Selections from the Prison Notebooks*. Translated by Quintin Hoare and Geoffrey Nowell Smith. New York: International Publishers, 1971.

Gray, Jonathan. *Show Sold Separately: Promos, Spoilers, and Other Media Paratexts*. New York: New York University Press, 2010.

Greenberg, Karl. "Marketers of the Next Generation: Nissan's John Cropper." *Brandweek*, April 12, 2004. http://www.allbusiness.com/marketing-advertising/branding-brand-development/4687815-1.html

Grindstaff, Laura, and Joseph Turow. "Video Cultures: Television Sociology in the 'New TV' Age." *Annual Review of Sociology* 32, no. 1 (2006): 103–125.

Guevara, Ernesto. *Guerrilla Warfare*. Melbourne: Ocean Press, 2006.

Hall, Emma. "Don't Look Now, But the Crowd Just Might Steal Your Ad Account." *Advertising Age*, September 14, 2009. http://adage.com/article/global-news/unilever-embraces-crowdsourcing-sacks-lowe-peperami-biz/138978/

Hall, Stuart. "Encoding/Decoding." In *Culture, Media, Language: Working Papers in Cultural Studies, 1972–1979*, edited by Stuart Hall, Dorothy Hobson, Andrew Lowe, and Paul Willis, 128–138. London: Hutchinson, 1980.

Halpern, Michelle. "Uncapping Consumer Generated Content." *Marketing News*, July 17, 2006. http://www.marketingmag.ca/news/marketer-news/uncapping-consumer-generated-content-19721

Hammersley, Martyn, and Paul Atkinson. *Ethnography: Principles in Practice*. 3rd ed. London: Routledge, 2007.

Hampp, Andrew. "Lite-Brites, Big City and a Whole Load of Trouble." *Advertising Age*, February 5, 2007. http://adage.com/article/mediaworks/lite-brites-big-city-a-load-trouble/114752/

———. "A Reprise for Jingles on Madison Avenue." *Advertising Age*, September 6, 2010. http://adage.com/article/madisonvine-news/a-reprise-jingles-madison-avenue/145744/

Hanover, Dan. "Guerrilla Your Dreams." *Promo* 14, no. 7 (June 1), 2001.

Hardy, Jonathan. *Cross-Media Promotion*. New York: Peter Lang, 2010.

Harold, Christine. "Pranking Rhetoric: "Culture Jamming" as Media Activism." *Critical Studies in Media Communication* 21, no. 3 (2004): 189–211.

Harvey, David. *A Brief History of Neoliberalism*. New York: Oxford University Press, 2005.

Havens, Timothy, Amanda D. Lotz, and Serra Tinic. "Critical Media Industry Studies: A Research Approach." *Communication, Culture & Critique* 2, no. 2 (2009): 234–253.

Health, Joseph, and Andrew Potter, *Nation of Rebels: Why Counterculture Became Consumer Culture*. New York: HarperBusiness, 2004.

Hebdige, Dick. *Subculture: The Meaning of Style*. London: Methuen, 1979.

Hesmondhalgh, David. *The Cultural Industries*. 2nd ed. London: Sage Publications, 2007.

Hill, Jamie. "We're Not Immune to Viral Advertising—Yet." *Marketing Week*, March 25, 2004.

Himpe, Tom. *Advertising is Dead: Long Live Advertising!* New York: Thames & Hudson, 2006.

Holt, Douglas B. *How Brands Become Icons: The Principles of Cultural Branding*. Boston: Harvard Business School Press, 2004.

———. "Why do brands cause trouble? A dialectical theory of consumer culture and branding." *Journal of Consumer Research* 29, no. 1 (2002): 70–90.

Howard, Theresa. "'Viral' Advertising Spreads through Marketing Plans." *USA Today*, June 23, 2005. http://www.usatoday.com/money/advertising/2005-06-22-viral-usat_x.htm

Hynes, Maria, Scott Sharpe, and Bob Fagan. "Laughing With the Yes Men: The Politics of Affirmation." *Continuum: Journal of Media & Cultural Studies* 21, no. 1 (2007): 107–121.

Iezzi, Teressa. "Marketers Tapping into the Magic of an Alternate Reality." *Advertising Age*, November 21, 2005. http://adage.com/article/viewpoint/marketers-tapping-magic-alternate-reality/105343/

Innis, Harold Adams. *The Bias of Communication*. Toronto: University of Toronto Press, 1951.

Ives, Nat. "Guerrilla Campaigns are Going to Extremes, but Will the Message Stick" *New York Times*, June 24, 2004, http://www.nytimes.com/2004/06/24/business/

media-business-advertising-guerrilla-campaigns-are-going-extremes-but-will.
html?pagewanted=all&src=pm

Jaffe, Joseph. *Life After the 30-second Spot: Energize Your Brand with a Bold Mix of Alternatives to Traditional Advertising.* Hoboken, NJ: John Wiley & Sons, 2005.

Jenkins, Henry. *Convergence Culture: Where Old and New Media Collide.* New York: New York University Press, 2006.

———. *Textual Poachers: Television Fans and Participatory Culture.* New York: Routledge, 1992.

———. "The Cultural Logic of Media Convergence." *International Journal of Cultural Studies* 7, no. 1 (2004): 33–43.

Johnson, Bobbie. "Virgin Ends Ad Campaign with Anarchic Site over Images of Branson." *Guardian*, October 30, 2006. http://www.guardian.co.uk/technology/2006/oct/30/news. media

Jowett, Garth, and Victoria O'Donnell. *Propaganda and Persuasion.* 4th ed. Thousand Oaks, CA: Sage Publications, 2006.

Kaikati, Andrew M., and Jack G. Kaikati. "Stealth Marketing: How to Reach Consumers Surreptitiously." *California Management Review* 46, no. 4 (2004): 6–22.

Kang, Stephanie. "BMW Ran Risk with Role in Mockumentary." *Wall Street Journal*, June 20, 2008. http://online.wsj.com/article/SB121391470578790089.html

Katz, Elihu, and Paul Felix Lazarsfeld. *Personal Influence: The Part Played by People in the Flow of Mass Communications.* 2nd ed. New Brunswick, NJ: Transaction Publishers, 2006.

Keller, Ed. "In Search of True Marketplace Influencers: Influentials Inspire Buyer Confidence." *Advertising Age*, December 5, 2005. http://adage.com/article/viewpoint/search-true-marketplace-influencers-influentials-inspire-buyer-confidence/105452/

Keller, Ed, and Jon Berry. *The Influentials.* New York: Free Press, 2003.

———. "Word-of-Mouth: The Real Action is Offline." *Advertising Age*, December 4, 2006. http://adage.com/article/print-edition/word-mouth-real-action-offline/113584/

Kelly, Aidan, Katrina Lawlor, and Stephanie O'Donohoe. "Encoding Advertisements: The Creative Perspective." *Journal of Marketing Management* 21, no. 5 (2005): 505–528.

Khermouch, Gerry, and Jeff Green. "Buzz Marketing." *BusinessWeek*, July 30, 2001. http://www.businessweek.com/magazine/content/01_31/b3743001.htm

Kilby, Nathalie. "Viral: The Final Frontier." *Marketing Week*, August 30, 2007.

Kiley, David. "Advertising of, by and for the People." *BusinessWeek*, July 25, 2005. http://www.businessweek.com/magazine/content/05_30/b3944097.htm

Klein, Bethany. *As Heard on TV: Popular Music in Advertising.* Farnham, England: Ashgate, 2009.

Klein, Naomi. *No Logo.* New York: Picador USA, 2000.

Lasn, Kalle. *Culture Jam: The Uncooling of America.* New York: Eagle Brook, 1999.

Lawrence, Dallas. "Social Media and the FTC: What Businesses Need to Know." *Mashable*, December 16, 2009. http://mashable.com/2009/12/16/ftc-social-media/

Lazzarato, Maurizio. "Immaterial Labor." In *Radical Thought in Italy: A Potential Politics*, edited by Paolo Virno and Michael Hardt, 133–146. Minneapolis: University of Minnesota Press, 1996.

Lears, Jackson. *Fables of Abundance: A Cultural History of Advertising in America.* New York: Basic Books, 1994.

Leckenby, John D., and Hairong Li. "From the Editors: Why We Need the *Journal of Interactive Marketing*." *Journal of Interactive Advertising* 1, no. 1 (2000): 1–3.

Lehu, Jean-Marc. *Branded Entertainment: Product Placement & Brand Strategy in the Entertainment Business*. London: Kogan Page, 2007.

Leiss, William, Stephen Kline, and Sut Jhally. *Social Communication in Advertising: Persons, Products & Images of Well-Being*. 2nd ed. New York: Routledge, 1997.

Leiss, William, Stephen Kline, Sut Jhally, and Jacqueline Botterill. *Social Communication in Advertising: Consumption in the Mediated Marketplace*. 3rd ed. New York: Routledge, 2005.

Levin, Josh. "Bill Simmons, Brought to You by Miller Lite." *Brow Beat*, September 11, 2009. http://www.slate.com/blogs/blogs/browbeat/archive/2009/09/11/bill-simmons-brought-to-you-by-miller-lite.aspx

Levinson, Jay Conrad. *Guerrilla Marketing: Secrets for Making Big Profits from Your Small Business*. Boston: Houghton Mifflin, 1984.

Levinson, Paul. *Digital McLuhan: A Guide to the Information Millennium*. London: Routledge, 2001.

Lewis, Lisa A, ed. *The Adoring Audience: Fan Culture and Popular Media*. London: Routledge, 1992.

Lindlof, Thomas R. *Qualitative Communication Research Methods*. Thousand Oaks, CA: Sage Publications, 1995.

Lodziak, Conrad. *The Myth of Consumerism*. London: Pluto Press, 2002.

Lopiano-Misdom, Janine, and Joanne De Luca. *Street Trends: How Today's Alternative Youth Cultures are Creating Tomorrow's Mainstream Markets*. New York: HarperBusiness, 1997.

Lucas, Gavin, and Michael Dorian. *Guerrilla Advertising: Unconventional Brand Communication*. London: Lawrence King, 2006.

Lury, Celia. *Brands: The Logos of the Global Economy*. London: Routledge, 2004.

Maiese, Nicholas. "'Blair Witch' Casts its Spell." *Advertising Age*, March 20, 2000. http://adage.com/article/news/blair-witch-casts-spell/58984/

Mailer, Norman. "The White Negro." *Dissent*, Fall 1957, http://www.dissentmagazine.org/online.php?id=26

Malefyt, Timothy deWaal, and Brian Moeran, eds. *Advertising Cultures*. Oxford: Berg, 2003.

Malpass, Alice, Clive Barnett, Nick Clarke, and Paul Cloke. " Problematizing Choice: Consumers and Skeptical Citizens." In *Governance, Consumers and Citizens: Agency and Resistance in Contemporary Politics*, edited by Mark Bevir and Frank Trentmann, 231–256. New York: Palgrave Macmillan, 2007.

Manko, Katina. "'Now You are in Business for Yourself': The Independent Contractors of the California Perfume Company." *Business and Economic History* 26, no. 1 (1997): 5–26.

Marchand, Roland. *Advertising the American Dream: Making Way for Modernity, 1920–1940*. Berkeley: University of California Press, 1985.

———. *Creating the Corporate Soul: The Rise of Public Relations and Corporate Imagery in American Big Business*. Berkeley: University of California Press, 1998.

Maymann, Jimmy. *The Social Metropolis*. 2008. http://www.goviral.com/book_2008.html

McAllister, Matthew P. *The Commercialization of American Culture: New Advertising, Control and Democracy*. Thousand Oaks, CA: Sage Publications, 1996.

McClellan, Steve. "Word-of-Mouth Gains Volume." *Brandweek*, August 25, 2009. http://www.adweek.com/news/advertising-branding/word-mouth-gains-volume-106304

McFall, Elizabeth Rose. *Advertising: A Cultural Economy*. London: Sage, 2004.

McFall, Liz. "Advertising, Persuasion and the Culture/Economy Dualism." In *Cultural Economy: Cultural Analysis and Commercial Life*, edited by Paul Du Gay and Michael Pryke, 148–165. London: Sage Publications, 2002.

McGonigal, Jane Evelyn. "This Might Be a Game: Ubiquitous Play and Performance at the Turn of the Twenty-First Century." PhD diss., Berkeley: University of California, Berkeley, 2006. http://avantgame.com/McGonigal_THIS_MIGHT_BE_A_GAME_sm.pdf

McLuhan, Marshall. *Understanding Media: The Extensions of Man*. Cambridge, MA: MIT Press, 1994.

McQuail, Denis. (2000). *McQuail's mass communication theory*. 4th ed. New York: Sage.

McQuail, Denis, and Sven Windahl. *Communication Models: For the Study of Mass Communications*. 2nd ed. London: Longman Publishing Group, 1993.

Meltz, Barbara F. "Protecting Kids from Marketers' Clutches." *Boston Globe*, September 30, 2004. http://www.boston.com/yourlife/family/articles/2004/09/30/protecting_kids_from_marketers_clutches/?page=full

Moor, Liz. *The Rise of Brands*. Oxford: Berg, 2007.

Moore, Anne Elizabeth. *Unmarketable: Brandalism, Copyfighting, Mocketing, and the Erosion of Integrity*. New York: New Press, 2007.

Morrissey, Brian. "Clients Try to Manipulate 'Unpredictable' Viral Buzz." *Adweek*, March 19, 2007. http://www.adweek.com/news/advertising/clients-try-manipulate-unpredictable-viral-buzz-88325

———. "Izea: Trick or Tweet." *Adweek*, June 4, 2010. http://www.adweek.com/news/technology/get-ready-pay-tweet-99491

———. "Skittles Site Ends Extreme Social Makeover." *Adweek*, February 4, 2010. http://www.brandweek.com/bw/content_display/news-and-features/digital/e3i9f46c57380aa314fd4a92055eb8b7d88

Mosco, Vincent. *The Digital Sublime: Myth, Power, and Cyberspace*. Cambridge, MA: MIT Press, 2005.

"Most Influential Players in Marketing," *Advertising Age*, December 12, 2011, 8.

Mullman, Jeremy. "Anheuser-Busch Pulls the Plug on Bud.TV." *Advertising Age*, February 18, 2009, http://adage.com/article/madisonvine-news/anheuser-busch-pulls-plug-bud-tv/134701/

———. "What's in a Nickname? In Spirits World, An Implied Warm-and-Fuzzy relationship." *Advertising Age*, April 19, 2010.

Muniz, Albert M., and Thomas C. O'Guinn. "Brand Community." *Journal of Consumer Research* 27, no. 4 (2001): 412–432.

Murray, Iain. "Guerrilla Tactics to Get Your Word on the Street." *Marketing Week*, July 8, 2004.

Nelson, Richard Alan. "The Bulgari Connection: A Novel Form of Product Placement." *Journal of Promotion Management* 10, no. 1 (2004): 203–212.

*New PQ Media Report Finds U.S. Branded Entertainment Spending on Consumer Events & Product Placements Dipped Only 1.3% to $24.63 Billion in 2009 & on Pace to Grow 5.3% in 2010, Exceeding Most Advertising & Marketing Segments*. PQ Media, June 29, 2010. http://www.pqmedia.com/about-press-20100629-gbem2010.html

Newell, Jay, Charles T. Salmon, and Susan Chang, "The Hidden History of Product Placement," *Journal of Broadcasting & Electronic Media* 50, no. 4 (2006): 575–594.

Newman, Eric. "With The Wind In His Sails: Sailor Jerry Spiced Rum." *Brandweek*, February 25, 2008. http://business.highbeam.com/137330/article-1G1-175875867/ wind-his-sales-sailor-jerry-spiced-rum

Newmann, Janet. "Governance as Cultural Practice: Texts, Talk and the Struggle for Meaning." In *Governance, Consumers and Citizens: Agency and Resistance in Contemporary Politics*, edited by Mark Bevir and Frank Trentmann, 49–68. New York: Palgrave Macmillan, 2007.

Nicholson, Kate. "Are BMW's Audio Books a Gimmick?" *Campaign*, February 17, 2006. http://www.campaignlive.co.uk/news/541812/ Close-Up-Live-Issue—-BMWs-audio-books-gimmick/?DCMP=ILC-SEARCH

Nixon, Sean. *Advertising Cultures: Gender, Commerce, Creativity*. London: Sage Publications, 2003.

———. "The Pursuit of Newness: Advertising, Creativity and the 'Narcissism of Minor Differences.'" *Cultural Studies* 20, no. 1 (2006): 89-106.

Nolan, Hamilton. "Stop Calling Black People 'Urban.'" *Gawker*, March 21, 2012, http://gawker.com/5895216/stop-calling-black-people-urban

Nordfalt, Jens. "Track to the Future? A Study of Individual Selection Mechanisms Preceding Ad Recognition and their Consequences." *Journal of Current Issues & Research in Advertising* 27, no. 1 (2005): 19–29.

Nordyke, Kimberly. "Following 'Guerrilla' Incident, Adult Swim Makes Splash." *Brandweek*, February 28, 2007.

Nussbaum, Emily. "What Tina Fey Would Do For a Soy Joy." *New York Magazine*, October 5, 2008. http://nymag.com/news/features/51014/

O'Farrell, Claire. *Michel Foucault*. London: Sage, 2005.

O'Leary, Noreen. "Q & A: Robert Rasmussen." *Adweek*, June 30, 2008. http://www.adweek.com/news/technology/qa-robert-rasmussen-96247

Ornebring, Henrik. "Alternate Reality Gaming and Convergence Culture: The Case of Alias." *International Journal of Cultural Studies* 10, no. 4 (2007): 445–462.

"Out from the Irony Gap." *Boston Globe*, February 3, 2007. http://www.boston.com/news/globe/editorial_opinion/editorials/articles/2007/02/03/out_from_the_irony_gap/

Peterson, Richard A., and N. Anand. "The Production of Culture Perspective." *Annual Review of Sociology* 30 (2004): 311–334.

Petrecca, Laura. "Madison Avenue Wants You! (Or At Least Your Videos)." *USA Today*, June 21, 2007. http://www.usatoday.com/money/advertising/2007-06-20-cannes-cover-usat_N.htm

Pidd, Helen. "Radio 1 Pulls 'Promotional' Track for Brand of Hair Gel." *Guardian*, May 8, 2007. http://www.guardian.co.uk/media/2007/may/05/advertising.bbc

Pope, Daniel. *The Making of Modern Advertising*. New York: Basic Books, 1983.

Presbrey, Frank. *The History and Development of Advertising*. Garden City, NY: Doubleday, 1929.

Quart, Alissa. *Branded: The Buying and Selling of Teenagers*. Cambridge, MA: Perseus Publishing, 2003.

Quinn, Matt. "War (Video) Games." *Fast Company*, January 24, 2005. http://www.fastcompany.com/articles/2005/01/top-jobs-wardynski.html

Rabinow, Paul. "Introduction." In *The Foucault Reader*, edited by Paul Rabinow, 3–29. New York: Pantheon Books, 1984.

Radway, Janice A. *Reading the Romance: Women, Patriarchy, and Popular Literature*. Chapel Hill: University of North Carolina Press, 1984.

Richards, Jef I., and Catharine M. Curran. "Oracles on 'Advertising': Searching for a Definition." *Journal of Advertising* 31, no. 2 (2002): 63–77.

Ries, Al, and Laura Ries. *The Fall of Advertising and the Rise of PR.* New York: HarperBusiness, 2002.

Riewoldt, Otto, ed. *Brandscaping: Worlds of Experience in Retail Design.* Basel, Switzerland: Birkhäuser Basel, 2002.

Ritzer, George. *Modern Sociological Theory.* 7th ed. New York: McGraw-Hill, 2008.

Rose, Nikolas. *Powers of Freedom: Reframing Political Thought.* Cambridge: Cambridge University Press, 1999.

Rosen, Emanuel. *The Anatomy of Buzz: How to Create Word-of-Mouth Marketing.* New York: Doubleday/Currency, 2000.

Rosenwald, Michael S. "Reputations at Stake, Companies Try to Alter Word of Mouth Online." *The Washington Post,* March 29, 2010. http://www.washingtonpost.com/wp-dyn/content/article/2010/03/28/AR2010032802905.html?nav=emailpage

Rumbo, Joseph D. "Consumer Resistance in a World of Advertising Clutter: The Case of Adbusters." *Psychology and Marketing* 19, no. 2 (2002): 127–148.

Rust, Roland T., and Richard W. Oliver. "The Death of Advertising." *Journal of Advertising* 23, no. 4 (1994): 71–77.

Rust, Roland T., and Sajeev Varki. "Rising From the Ashes of Advertising." *Journal of Business Research* 37, no. 3 (1996): 173–181.

Sanders, Lisa. "Stories Around the Campfire." *Advertising Age,* November 21, 2005. http://adage.com/article/news/stories-campfire/105360/

Sass, Erik. "Red Ink: Newspaper Revs Tumble." *MediaDailyNews,* April 15, 2010. http://www.mediapost.com/publications/article/126257/red-ink-newspaper-revs-tumble.html

Schor, Juliet. *Born to Buy: The Commercialized Child and the New Consumer Culture.* New York: Scribner, 2004.

Schudson, Michael. *Advertising, the Uneasy Persuasion: Its Dubious Impact on American Society.* New York: Basic Books, 1986.

Segrave, Kerry. *Product Placement in Hollywood Films: A History.* Jefferson, NC: McFarland & Company, 2004.

Sender, Katherine. *Business, Not Politics: The Making of the Gay Market.* New York: Columbia University Press, 2004.

Serazio, Michael. "The Apolitical Irony of Generation Mash-Up: A Cultural Case Study in Popular Music." *Popular Music and Society* 31, no. 1 (2008): 79–94.

Shirky, Clay. *Here Comes Everybody: The Power of Organizing Without Organizations.* New York: Penguin Press, 2008.

Simon, Herbert. *Organizations.* New York: McGraw, 1957.

Simon, Herbert. "Designing Organizations for an Information-Rich World." In *Computers, Communications, and the Public Interest,* edited by Martin Greenberger, 40–41. Baltimore, MD: The Johns Hopkins Press, 1971.

Simon, Robert. *Gramsci's Political Thought: An Introduction.* London: Lawrence and Wishart, 1982.

Slater, Don. *Consumer Culture and Modernity.* Cambridge: Polity, 1997.

———. "Corridors of Power." In *The Politics of Field Research: Sociology Beyond Enlightenment,* edited by Jaber F Gubrium and David Silverman, 113–131. London: Sage Publications, 1989.

Smith, Ethan, and Julie Jargon. "Chew on This: Hit Song is a Gum Jingle." *Wall Street Journal,* July 28, 2008, http://online.wsj.com/article/SB121721123435289073.html

Soar, Matthew. "Encoding Advertisements: Ideology and Meaning in Advertising Production." *Mass Communication and Society* 3, no. 4 (2000): 415–437.

Spethmann, Betsy. "Bracing for Backlash." *Promo*, November 1, 2006. http://preview.promo-magazine.com/mag/marketing_bracing_backlash/

———. "Brand Illusions." *Promo*, February 1, 2002. http://promomagazine.com/mag/marketing_brand_illusions/

Spurgeon, Christina. *Advertising and New Media*. London: Routledge, 2008.

Stanley, T. L. "That's Advertainment!." *Brandweek*, February 28, 2010. http://nyi-www.brandweek.com/bw/content_display/news-and-features/direct/e3i7f27204a864d83e7dd4 4fb9ff07414c1

Stauber, John C., and Sheldon Rampton. *Toxic Sludge is Good for You: Lies, Damn Lies, and the Public Relations Industry*. Monroe, ME: Common Courage Press, 1995.

Stelter, Brian. "Product Plaements, Deftly Woven Into the Storyline," *New York Times*, March 1, 2009. http://www.nytimes.com/2009/03/02/business/media/02adco. html?_r=3&adxnnl=1&adxnnlx=1250100154-kMheUMUWrzpAssoFRn+4wQ

Stern, Barbara B. "A Revised Communication Model for Advertising: Multiple Dimensions of the Source, the Message, and the Recipient." *Journal of Advertising* 23, no. 2 (1994): 5–15.

Stewart, David W., and Paul A. Pavlou. "The Effects of Media on Marketing Communications." In *Media Effects: Advances in Theory and Research*, edited by Jennings Bryant and Mary Beth Oliver, 362–401. 3rd ed. New York: Routledge, 2009.

Storey, John. *Cultural Theory and Popular Culture: An Introduction*. 4th ed. Athens: University of Georgia Press, 2006.

Story, Louise. "A Boston Marketing Stunt that Bombed, or Did It?" *New York Times*, February 2, 2007. http://www.nytimes.com/2007/02/02/business/media/02guerilla.html

Tannen, Deborah. *You Just Don't Understand: Women and Men in Conversation*. New York: Ballantine, 1990.

Terranova, Tiziana. "Producing Culture for the Digital Economy." *Social Text* 63, no. 18 (2000): 33–58.

Thomas, Greg Metz. "Building the Buzz in the Hive Mind." *Journal of Consumer Behaviour* 4, no. 1 (2004): 64–72.

Thornton, Sarah. *Club Cultures: Music, Media, and Subcultural Capital*. Hanover, NH: University Press of New England, 1996.

Turner, Kathleen J. "Insinuating the Product Into the Message: An Historical Context for Product Placement." *Journal of Promotion Management* 10, no. 1 (2004): 9–14.

Turow, Joseph. *Niche Envy: Marketing Discrimination in the Digital Age*. Cambridge, MA: MIT Press, 2006.

Twitchell, James B. *Adcult USA: The Triumph of Advertising in American Culture*. New York: Columbia University Press, 1997.

"U.N. humanitarian game is a hit," *MSNBC*, June 10, 2005, http://www.msnbc.msn.com/id/8173381/

Verklin, David, and Bernice Kanner. *Watch This, Listen Up, Click Here: Inside the 300 Billion Dollar Business Behind the Media You Constantly Consume*. Hoboken, NJ: John Wiley & Sons, 2007.

Vranica, Suzanne. "Buzz Marketers Score Venture Dollars." *Wall Street Journal*, January 13, 2006.

———. "Getting Buzz Marketers to Fess Up." *Wall Street Journal*, February 9, 2005.

———. "Hellman's Targets Yahoo for Its Spread." *Wall Street Journal*, June 27, 2007, B4.

———. "Marketing Business Rebrands as an Entertainment Provider." *Wall Street Journal*, July 12, 2006.

———. "That Guy Showing Off His Hot New Phone May Be a Shill." *Wall Street Journal*, July 31, 2002.

Walker, Rob. *Buying In: The Secret Dialogue Between What We Buy and Who We Are*. New York: Random House, 2008.

Ward, Sandra. "Glad Men." *Barron's*, September 14, 2009.

Wasik, Bill. *And Then There's This: How Stories Live and Die in Viral Culture*. New York: Viking, 2009.

Wasserman, Todd. "What's the Buzz? One Organization Says 'Fraud.'" *Brandweek*, October 18, 2005. http://www.billboard.com/news/ask-billboard-1001307628.story#/news/ask-billboard-1001307628.story

———. "Word Games." *Brandweek*, April 24, 2006.

Webb, Rick. "Happy 5th birthday, Subservient Chicken." *Barbarian Blog*, April 6, 2009. http://www.barbariangroup.com/posts/1938-happy_5th_birthday_subservient_chicken

Wenner, Lawrence A. "On the Ethics of Product Placement in Media Entertainment." *Journal of Promotion Management* 10, no. 1 (2004): 101–132.

Wentz, Laurel, "Fines, Arrests, Beer: Here's One Guerrilla Effort That Has It All," *Advertising Age*, May 21, 2007, http://adage.com/article/print-edition/fines-arrests-beer-guerrilla-effort/116739/

Wernick, Andrew. *Promotional Culture: Advertising, Ideology, and Symbolic Expression*. London: Sage Publications, 1991.

Williams, Raymond. *Marxism and Literature*. Oxford: Oxford University Press, 1977.

Williamson, Judith. *Decoding Advertisements: Ideology and Meaning in Advertising*. London: Marion Boyars, 1978.

Wipperfurth, Alex. *Brand Hijack: Marketing Without Marketing*. New York: Portfolio Trade, 2005.

Wong, Elaine. "Pssst . . . CPG Cos. Love W-O-M." *Brandweek*, October 6, 2008.

Yudice, George. *The Expediency of Culture: Uses of Culture in the Global Era*. Durham: Duke University Press, 2003.

Zammit, Deanna. "Steven Grasse on the Spot." *Adweek*, October 20, 2004. http://www.adweek.com/news/advertising/steven-grasse-spot-74876

Zmuda, Natalie. "Ann Taylor Probe Shows FTC Keeping a Close Eye on Blogging." *Advertising Age*, May 3, 2010. http://adage.com/article/news/ann-taylor-case-shows-ftc-keeping-close-eye-blogging/143567/

Zwick, Detlev, Samuel K. Bonsu, and Aron Darmody. "Putting Consumers to Work: 'Co-Creation' and New Marketing Govern-Mentality." *Journal of Consumer Culture* 8, no. 2 (2008): 163–196.

## ABOUT THE AUTHOR

Michael Serazio is Assistant Professor in the Department of Communication at Fairfield University who writes about popular culture, advertising, and new media. An award-winning former journalist, he holds a PhD from the University of Pennsylvania, and his scholarly work has appeared in books and journals.